THE **BIG** BOOK OF
CHOCOLATE

JENNIFER DONOVAN

THE BIG BOOK OF CHOCOLATE

365 DECADENT & IRRESISTIBLE TREATS

DUNCAN BAIRD PUBLISHERS
LONDON

For my family: Kevin, Chris, and James
The Big Book of Chocolate
Jennifer Donovan

Distributed in the USA and Canada by
Sterling Publishing Co., Inc.
387 Park Avenue South
New York, NY 10016-8810

This edition first published in the UK and USA in 2008 by
Duncan Baird Publishers Ltd
Sixth Floor, Castle House
75–76 Wells Street
London W1T 3QH

Managing Editor: Grace Cheetham
Editors: Alison Bolus, Judith More
Managing Designer: Manisha Patel
Design: Sharon Spencer
Studio Photography: William Lingwood
Photography Assistants: Jamie Bowering, Kate Malone, Rob Warren
Food Stylist: Bridget Sargeson
Assistant Food Stylists: Stella Sargeson, Jack Sargeson
Prop Stylist: Helen Trent

Library of Congress Cataloging-in-Publication Data available
ISBN-13: 978-1-84483-620-8 ISBN-10: 1-84483-620-7
10 9 8 7 6 5 4 3 2 1

Typeset in DIN
Color reproduction by Scanhouse, Malaysia
Printed in China by Imago

For information about custom editions, special sales, premium and corporate
purchases, please contact Sterling Special Sales Department at 800-805-5489
or specialsales@sterlingpub.com.

Publisher's note: While every care has been taken in compiling the recipes
for this book, Duncan Baird Publishers, or any other persons who have been
involved in working on this publication, cannot accept responsibility for any
errors or omissions, inadvertent or not, that may be found in the recipes
or text, nor for any problems that may arise as a result of preparing one of
these recipes. If you are pregnant or breastfeeding or have any special dietary
requirements or medical conditions, it is advisable to consult a medical
professional before following any of the recipes contained in this book.

UNLESS OTHERWISE STATED:
• All recipes serve 4
• Use extra-large eggs
• 1 tsp. = 5ml • 1 tbsp. = 15ml • 1 cup = 240ml

CONTENTS

INTRODUCTION

There are few things in the world that evoke such intense emotions as chocolate. Silky, smooth, and sensuous, chocolate has been around for centuries. It is thought to have been discovered in Mexico by the Aztec Indians and then brought to Spain in the 16th century. It is believed that the Aztec Indians first used beans from the cacao tree to make a drink for royal occasions, and that the Spaniards made this bitter drink more palatable by adding cane sugar and spices such as cinnamon and vanilla. By the 17th century, drinking chocolate was fashionable throughout Europe; and by the 19th century, chocolate to eat had been developed, and traditional hand-manufacturing methods for making chocolates gave way to mass production.

Today, chocolate has become more popular than ever. Gourmet chocolate boutiques cater for the growing passion for top-quality chocolate. Around the world, consumers are demanding better-sourced and higher-quality ingredients, so fair trade chocolate (where the cocoa beans have been sourced directly from farmers at prices that allow the farming communities to thrive and expand) and organic chocolate are both reaching a wider market.

This comprehensive book explains all you need to know about chocolate. It guides the home cook through a range of delicous chocolate recipes, from fabulous homemade cakes, brownies, ice creams, puddings, and muffins to spectacular desserts and handmade chocolates. Some of them will be familiar favorites, while others will provide some new and exciting ways to use chocolate.

As well as providing a wealth of simple-to-follow recipes and briefly outlining the origins of chocolate, this book explains in simple terms the most common ingredients and methods used when cooking with chocolate—all designed to make the recipes even easier for you to reproduce at home.

WHAT IS CHOCOLATE?

Cocoa beans, from which chocolate is derived, are a product of the cacao tree. This is believed to have originated in the tropical areas of South America, although the exact location is a source of some dispute. A relatively delicate plant, the cacao tree needs protection from wind and a good amount of shade; it usually bears fruit in the fifth year of cultivation in natural conditions. Although there are about 20 different varieties of cacao plant, only three are widely used in the making of chocolate—Forastero, Crillo, and Trinitero.

The fruit of the cacao plant, known as "pods," contain between 20 and 50 cream-colored beans, and it takes about 400 beans to make just one pound of chocolate. The beans are fermented, dried, cleaned, and roasted. Then the roasted beans are ground to produce a thick cacao liquor, or cacao mass, and finally pressed to extract the fat, known as cocoa butter.

Cacao liquor and cocoa butter are the essential ingredients in any chocolate product, and the amount included varies from around 25 percent of the product's weight up to approximately 80 percent, occasionally more. Other ingredients, including sugar, vanilla, and milk, are added to the chocolate before it goes through the final processing stages. Generally, the sweeter the chocolate, the more sugar has been added and the less cacao liquor and cocoa butter it contains. The darker and more bitter the chocolate, the higher the cacao liquor and cocoa butter content; this is widely considered to be a superior chocolate. However, chocolate preferences vary between individuals, so it is best to experiment with what you have available to see which you prefer.

TYPES OF CHOCOLATE

There are a number of basic categories of chocolate. The first is dark chocolate, sometimes referred to as bittersweet or semi-sweet chocolate, or couverture. This is designed for both eating and cooking. Look for chocolate with a high cocoa content (usually marked as a percentage on the label). Ideally, the percentage should be somewhere between 70 and 85 percent, although it is important to remember what you are ultimately using it for.

The most readily available chocolate tends to range between 60 and 70 percent, which renders good results, though higher percentages do exist.

The recipes in this book have all been made with dark chocolate (where specified) with a cocoa butter content of 70 percent. However, if you want to enjoy the best-quality chocolate straight from the packet, be aware that many people prefer the highest cocoa butter content they can find, which can be up to about 85 percent. I prefer not to use a chocolate of that percentage for cooking because the result can often be too bitter for a chocolate sauce or cake, which requires a slightly sweeter finish.

Milk chocolate, also commonly available, generally contains less than 3 percent cocoa butter and has sugar, milk powder, and vanilla added. It is not as successful in baking and cooking as dark chocolate, but you can use it as a substitute in mousses, fillings, drinks, and cookies, particularly if they are destined for children, who prefer the less bitter flavor. Again, for the tastiest results, look for good-quality milk chocolate—many manufacturers use vegetable oils, artificial flavors, fillers, and milk solids in their products. Organic varieties of chocolate are a good choice here.

White chocolate, another widely available product, is technically not chocolate at all because it does not contain cacao liquor—it is made from cocoa butter, sugar, milk, and vanilla. Although not a pure chocolate, white chocolate is still very popular and gives good results in cooking.

Cocoa powder and chocolate drink mixes are also derived from chocolate. 'Dutch-processed' cocoa, where the cocoa is treated with an alkali to give a slightly different flavor and a darker appearance, is considered to have the best taste. Cocoa powder is derived from the pressed cake that remains after most of the cocoa butter has been removed. It may have 10 percent or more cocoa butter content. Most commercial chocolate drink mixes (which are designed to be made into hot or cold drinks) are usually made from a mixture of cocoa powder and sugar. Both cocoa powder and chocolate drink mixes have their uses in cooking, but, as with chocolate, the quality does vary, so experiment with the different brands and buy the best you can afford.

STORING CHOCOLATE

As a rough guide, chocolate will keep for a year if stored in the correct conditions. Store in a cool place—around 70°F—and don't refrigerate it unless the temperature is very hot because the moist environment of the refrigerator will shorten the life of the chocolate. Chocolate also absorbs the odors of foods stored around it, so be sure to keep it wrapped tightly in plastic wrap or in a container with a tight-fitting lid.

The white film sometimes found on chocolate that has been stored incorrectly is called a "bloom." This is caused by condensation that has melted the surface sugar on the chocolate, and, although it will not taste or look as nice as chocolate in good condition, it can still be used for melting or baking.

COOK'S INGREDIENTS

Most of the ingredients used in this book are widely available and are often very standard, but it is worth noting a few specific points.

Butter—all recipes, unless otherwise stated, use salted butter.

Eggs—extra-large eggs are used in all the recipes. Some recipes contain raw eggs, which carry a slight risk of salmonella, and should therefore be served with care and not be given to small children, pregnant women, or the elderly.

Flour—all-purpose flour and self-rising flour are used throughout this book. If you do not have any self-rising flour and need to make some, simply add 1 1/2 tsp. baking powder and 1/2 tsp. salt to every 1 cup all-purpose flour.

Gold leaf—this is an edible product and is most commonly available from specialist cake-decorating suppliers.

Gelatin—Leaf gelatin comes in solid sheets that you soak in cold water until they soften. They then dissolve easily in very warm liquid. You can buy powdered gelatin, which is usually sold in 1/4oz. envelopes; one envelope will set about 2 cups liquid.

Sugar—superfine sugar is used predominantly in the Baking chapter because its fine-grained quality gives the best results. However, you can substitute regular granulated sugar for superfine cup for cup.

COOK'S TOOLS

You will not need much specialist equipment when working with chocolate. The recipes in this book use a standard range of kitchen utensils, including loose-bottomed springform cake pans and fluted tart pans in a variety of shapes and sizes. However, some items you may not already have do make the process that much easier.

Baking beans—these are ceramic beads used to weigh down a pastry shell when baked 'blind', that is, without a filling.

Baking paper (sometimes called baking parchment)—this is used for lining pans and baking sheets.

Double boiler—this consists of a saucepan fitted with a smaller pan on top. The bottom pan holds water, which is heated, while the ingredients sit in the top, away from direct contact with the heat. It is useful for heating and melting delicate ingredients, such as chocolate and egg custards.

Electric hand mixer—this will enable you to beat and whisk ingredients with the minimum of effort. Alternatively, use a hand whisk or electric stand mixer (where applicable).

Food processor—use this to crush biscuits for crumb crusts and to bind cookie dough, among other culinary jobs.

Baking sheets and pans—use nonstick bakeware when possible, ideally silicone, which is durable and flexible. Note that cake and flan pans come in various depths, and it is important to use the recommended depth to avoid having too much or too little filling. Choose pans with loose bottoms for ease.

COOKING TECHNIQUES

Using a bain marie—this French cookery term refers to a "water bath." You use this method to cook food in the oven very gently (often fragile dishes such as baked custards) and to prevent overcooking. You place the dish in which the food is cooked inside a larger vessel (sometimes with a cloth underneath to protect the base), which you then fill with water to come half way up the dish.

Melting chocolate—chocolate is a delicate product and can burn easily. It melts best at temperatures between 104°F and 113°F.

A double boiler is effective (see above) and prevents the chocolate from overheating, but you can also melt chocolate in a single saucepan directly on the stove over a very low heat, as long as you watch it closely and stir it gently. Alternatively, you can use a microwave oven. The time needed will vary depending on the amount of chocolate being melted and the power of the microwave, so it's best to experiment to find out what works best for you. As a guide, use 30-second bursts until the chocolate is melted, stirring gently in between.

Tempering—this process involves heating and cooling chocolate at specific temperatures. It stabilizes the chocolate and gives it a shiny appearance and a hard texture. Tempering is mainly used by professional chocolate makers and can be done by hand or by machine. This process is not necessary for the recipes in this book.

FINISHING TOUCHES

Chocolate curls, leaves, and piped shapes are simple to make and add a special touch to the final product.

Making chocolate curls—a simple way is to sweep a wide-bladed vegetable peeler over a block of chocolate. Keep the chocolate cool, or the curls will lo0se their shape. A slightly more complicated way is to spread melted chocolate over a marble slab, if you have one, or the back of a large metal baking sheet. Leave to cool and then slide a long-bladed knife along the surface of the chocolate to create a curl. This can take a little practice but is very rewarding. You can use this technique with dark, milk, or white chocolate, or a combination of two or more, which can look quite impressive.

Making chocolate leaves—simply brush melted chocolate on the back of a clean, well-defined leaf and chill. When cold, simply peel off the leaf, leaving a delicate imprint of veins on the chocolate.

Piping chocolate shapes and lines—you can pipe chocolate shapes with a fine nozzle onto baking paper—but don't make them too delicate or they will fall apart. Chill, then lift off as required. You can also randomly pipe lines of dark and white chocolate quite densely over baking paper, then set aside to chill and break off pieces as required. This is a simple and effective method of decorating ice creams, mousses, and meringues.

BASIC RECIPES

Chocolate pastry cream

PREPARATION TIME 10 minutes   **COOKING TIME** 10 minutes   **MAKES** 2 cups

1¼ cups plus 1 tbsp. milk
3½ oz. bittersweet chocolate,
  broken into pieces
1 tsp. vanilla extract

2 egg yolks
3 tbsp. sugar
2 tbsp. all-purpose flour

1   In a medium-sized saucepan, heat the milk and chocolate together over low heat until the chocolate has just melted. Remove the saucepan from the heat and stir the mixture until smooth, then add the vanilla extract.
2   In a large bowl, whisk the egg yolks, sugar, and flour, using a hand whisk, then whisk in the warm chocolate milk. Return the mixture to the saucepan and cook over low heat until it thickens, stirring constantly with a wooden spoon. Continue cooking 1 minute.
3   Pour the pastry cream into a clean bowl and cover with a circle of baking paper to prevent a skin forming while it cools.

Creamy thick chocolate custard

PREPARATION TIME 10 minutes   **COOKING TIME** 10 minutes   **MAKES** 3¼ cups

1¾ cups milk
1¾ cups heavy cream
8 egg yolks

⅔ cup sugar
2 tbsp. unsweetened cocoa powder
1 tsp. vanilla extract

1   In a small saucepan, heat the milk and cream over low heat, until just warm. In a large bowl, whisk the egg yolks, sugar, and cocoa together, using a hand whisk, then whisk in the warm milk mixture. Return the mixture to the pan with the vanilla extract and stir constantly with a wooden spoon until the mixture begins to thicken and coats the back of the spoon. Do not boil.
2   Transfer to a clean bowl and let cool completely.

Fresh caramel sauce

PREPARATION TIME 5 minutes   **COOKING TIME** 5 minutes   **MAKES** 2 cups

½ cup plus 2 tsp. sugar
½ stick plus 1½ tsp. butter, chopped

1 cup plus 2 tbsp. heavy cream

1   In a medium-sized saucepan, stir together the sugar and butter over low heat until they melt, using a wooden spoon. Continue stirring gently until the mixture turns a light caramel color.
2   Remove the pan from the heat and add the cream (the sugar mixture will spatter, so be careful not to burn your hand), then return the pan to the heat and stir until well combined.
3   Pour the sauce into an airtight jar and set aside to cool completely before placing in the refrigerator. It will keep 2 to 3 days.

Chocolate crumb crust

PREPARATION TIME 10 minutes   **COOKING TIME** 10 minutes   **MAKES** 1 x 9in. crumb crust

9oz. graham crackers
2 tbsp. unsweetened cocoa powder

6 tbsp. butter, melted

1   Preheat the oven to 400°F.
2   Break up the crackers roughly with your hands and then pulse them in a food
    processor (or place them in a plastic bag and crush with a rolling pin) until they
    are fine crumbs. Add the cocoa and melted butter and pulse until the mixture is
    well combined.
3   Empty the mixture into a greased 9in. springform pan, press it over the bottom
    and up the sides of the pan (according to the recipe), and bake in the hot oven
    10 minutes. Remove from the oven and let the crust cool completely before
    removing it from the pan.

Choux pastry

PREPARATION TIME 10 minutes   **COOKING TIME** 5 minutes
MAKES 6 large éclairs or 12 profiteroles

2 tsp. sugar
5 tbsp. chilled butter, chopped

¾ cup all-purpose flour, sifted
2 eggs, lightly beaten

1   In a medium-sized saucepan, combine the sugar, butter, and ¾ cup water over
    low heat and stir constantly until the butter has just melted. Remove from the
    heat and add the flour all at once to the butter mixture, stirring well with a
    wooden spoon. (The mixture will form a thick dough.)
2   Return the saucepan to the heat and continue stirring 1 minute, or until the
    dough comes away from the sides of the saucepan.
3   Remove the saucepan from the heat and beat in the eggs, using an electric
    hand mixer. For best results, use the dough while still warm.

Sweet shortcrust pastry

PREPARATION TIME 10 minutes, plus chilling   **COOKING TIME** 30 to 35 minutes
MAKES 1 x 9in. pastry shell or 4 to 6 individual pastry shells

2 cups all-purpose flour,
    plus extra for rolling out
3 tbsp. powdered sugar

1 stick plus 3 tbsp. chilled butter,
    chopped
2 egg yolks

1   In a large bowl, combine the flour and powdered sugar. Add the butter and rub it
    in with your fingertips until it forms small crumbs. (Alternatively, do this in a food
    processor, but work quickly or the crust will be tough.) Work in the egg yolks
    and just enough of 2 tbsp. iced water to form a dough, using a flat-bladed knife
    or spatula. Note that the less water you use, the more tender the crust will be.
    Wrap the dough in plastic wrap and refrigerate 15 minutes.
2   Preheat the oven to 350°F. Roll out the dough on a lightly floured surface
    to about ¼in. thick, to fit a 9in. fluted loose-bottomed tart pan, 1½in. deep.
    Place the dough in the pan to form a pastry shell, taking care not to stretch
    it, and trim around the edge.
3   Line the pastry shell with baking paper and fill with baking beans. Bake in the
    hot oven 20 to 25 minutes, then remove from the oven and gently lift out the
    paper and beans. Return the pan to the oven a further 8 to 10 minutes, or
    until the pastry is dry and golden brown. (Alternatively, divide the pastry into
    4 or 6 pieces and roll each one out to fit a 4in. fluted loose-bottomed tart pan,
    1½in. deep, and bake 10 to 12 minutes, then a further 5 to 7 minutes.)

VARIATION To make Chocolate Shortcrust Pastry, add 1 tbsp. unsweetened cocoa powder with
the flour and bake the dough until it is dry and dark brown.

CHAPTER 1

Chocolate Heaven

While chocolate cakes, pastries, and desserts are, by their very nature, simply heavenly, sometimes the occasion calls for something just a little extra-special. The recipes in this chapter take chocolate that one step further. Perfect for a special celebration or when you just feel like being indulgent, this chapter's delicious desserts and sweet treats are the ultimate in chocolate bliss. From creamy cheesecakes such as Raspberry Ripple White Chocolate Cheesecake to whipped delights such as Chocolate Mousse Cake, Chocolate Roulade with Cinnamon Cream, and Chocolate Pavlova, there is a recipe here to suit every taste. Most of the recipes included in this chapter can be prepared in advance, making cooking even more relaxing. For that very special celebration, you will also find a range of hot and cold soufflés. Despite their reputation, these are really simple to master and require only a speedy transfer from the oven to the table and a group of hungry friends or family! So, whatever the celebration (or your craving), there is sure to be a recipe here that will fit the bill perfectly.

001 Mocha marble cheesecake

PREPARATION TIME 25 minutes, plus chilling   **COOKING TIME** 40 to 45 minutes
MAKES 1 x 9in. cheesecake

butter, for greasing
1 recipe quantity Chocolate Crumb
   Crust (see page 13)
10½oz. cream cheese, softened
7oz. ricotta cheese
¾ cup plus 2 tbsp. sugar
3 tsp. cornstarch
3 eggs, lightly beaten

2 tsp. vanilla extract
2 cups plus 1 tbsp. crème fraîche
1 cup plus 1 tbsp. heavy cream
2 tsp. instant coffee powder
2 tbsp. coffee liqueur
3½oz. bittersweet chocolate,
   melted and left to cool

1   Preheat the oven to 325°F. Grease a 9in. springform pan with butter and press the prepared chocolate crumb crust into the bottom.
2   In a large bowl, beat the cream cheese, ricotta, and sugar together, using an electric hand mixer, until smooth. Add the cornstarch, eggs, and vanilla extract and beat until just combined, then stir in the crème fraîche and cream. Divide the mixture evenly between 2 bowls. Blend the coffee, liqueur, and melted chocolate into one half of the mixture, using the electric hand mixer, and leave the other half plain.
3   Pour both of the mixtures over the crumb crust (use two hands and do this at the same time, if possible). Using a fork, swirl the mixtures together to create a marbled effect.
4   Bake in the hot oven 40 to 45 minutes, or until the cheesecake is firm around the edges but still slightly wobbly in the middle. Remove from the oven and let cool in the pan completely.
5   Refrigerate the cheesecake 2 hours or overnight, then remove from the pan.

002 Chilled chocolate cheesecake

PREPARATION TIME 25 minutes, plus chilling   **MAKES** 1 x 9in. cheesecake

½ stick butter, softened, plus extra
   for greasing
1 recipe quantity Chocolate Crumb
   Crust (see page 13)
14oz. cream cheese, softened

2 eggs, lightly beaten
5 tbsp. sugar
5½oz. bittersweet chocolate,
   melted and left to cool
chocolate shavings, to scatter

1   Grease a 9in. springform pan with butter and press the prepared chocolate crumb crust into the bottom.
2   In a large bowl, beat the cream cheese, eggs, sugar, butter, and melted chocolate together until the mixture is smooth and thick, using an electric hand mixer. Spoon the cheese mixture over the bottom of the crumb crust and smooth the surface with a palette knife. Refrigerate the cheesecake 2 hours or overnight.
3   Remove the cheesecake from the pan and scatter with chocolate shavings just before serving.

003 Chocolate sour cream cheesecake

PREPARATION TIME 20 minutes, plus chilling **COOKING TIME** 45 to 50 minutes
MAKES 1 x 9in. cheesecake

butter, for greasing
1 recipe quantity Chocolate Crumb
  Crust (see page 13)
14oz. cream cheese, softened
¾ cup plus 1 tbsp. sweetened,
  condensed milk

3 eggs, lightly beaten
1 cup plus 2 tbsp. sour cream
7oz. bittersweet or milk chocolate,
  melted and left to cool
1 tsp. vanilla extract

1 Preheat the oven to 350°F. Grease a 9in. springform pan with butter and press the prepared chocolate crumb crust into the bottom.
2 In a large bowl, beat the cream cheese until light, using an electric hand mixer. Add the sweetened condensed milk, eggs, sour cream, melted chocolate, and vanilla extract and continue beating until well combined. Pour the mixture over the crumb crust.
3 Bake in the hot oven 45 to 50 minutes, or until the cheesecake is firm around the edges but still slightly wobbly in the middle. Remove from the oven and let cool in the pan completely.
4 Refrigerate the cheesecake 2 hours or overnight, then remove from the pan.

004 Chocolate hazelnut cheesecake

PREPARATION TIME 20 minutes, plus chilling **COOKING TIME** 40 to 45 minutes
MAKES 1 x 9in. cheesecake

butter, for greasing
1 recipe quantity Chocolate Crumb
  Crust (see page 13)
7oz. cream cheese, softened
8oz. ricotta cheese
⅓ cup plus 4 tsp. sugar
2 egg yolks

2 tbsp. chocolate hazelnut paste
7oz. bittersweet or milk chocolate,
  melted and cooled
1 cup plus 2 tbsp. heavy cream,
  whipped to soft peaks

1 Preheat the oven to 350°F. Grease a 9in. springform pan with butter and press the prepared chocolate crumb crust into the bottom.
2 In a large bowl, beat the cream cheese, ricotta, and sugar together until smooth, using an electric hand mixer. Beat in the egg yolks and chocolate hazelnut paste until smooth, then stir in the melted chocolate and cream. Pour the mixture over the crumb crust.
3 Bake in the hot oven 40 to 45 minutes, or until the cheesecake is firm around the edges but still slightly wobbly in the middle. Remove from the oven and let cool in the pan completely.
4 Refrigerate the cheesecake 2 hours or overnight, then remove from the pan.

005 Raspberry ripple white chocolate cheesecake

PREPARATION TIME 25 minutes, plus chilling **COOKING TIME** 45 to 50 minutes
MAKES 1 x 9in. cheesecake

butter, for greasing
1 recipe quantity Chocolate Crumb
   Crust (see page 13)
1lb. 2oz. cream cheese, softened
¾ cup plus 2 tbsp. sugar
2 tbsp. all-purpose flour

4 eggs, lightly beaten
9oz. white chocolate, melted
   and left to cool
2 tsp. vanilla extract
½ cup heavy cream
1 cup raspberries, puréed

1   Preheat the oven to 350°F. Grease a 9in. springform pan with butter and press
the prepared chocolate crumb crust into the bottom.
2   In a large bowl, beat the cream cheese and sugar together until light and
creamy, using an electric hand mixer. Add the flour, eggs, melted chocolate,
and vanilla extract and beat until just combined. Stir in the cream. Gently swirl
through the raspberry purée, using a wooden spoon and taking care not to over-
mix. Pour the filling mixture over the crumb crust.
3   Bake in the hot oven 45 to 50 minutes, or until the cheesecake is firm around
the edges but still slightly wobbly in the middle. Remove from the oven and let
cool in the pan completely.
4   Refrigerate the cheesecake 2 hours or overnight, then remove from the pan.

006 Chocolate & vanilla ripple cheesecake

PREPARATION TIME 20 minutes, plus chilling **COOKING TIME** 40 to 45 minutes
MAKES 1 x 9in. cheesecake

butter, for greasing
1 recipe quantity Chocolate Crumb
   Crust (see page 13)
1lb. 2oz. cream cheese, softened
¾ cup plus 2 tbsp. sugar

2 eggs, lightly beaten
¾ cup plus 1 tbsp. heavy cream
5½oz. bittersweet chocolate, melted
   and left to cool
1 tsp. vanilla extract

1   Preheat the oven to 325°F. Grease a 9in. springform pan with butter and press
the prepared chocolate crumb crust into the bottom.
2   In a large bowl, beat the cream cheese and sugar together until smooth, using
an electric hand mixer. Beat in the eggs, then gently stir in the cream. Divide the
mixture evenly between 2 bowls. Stir the melted chocolate into one portion and
the vanilla extract into the other. Pour the vanilla mixture over the crumb crust
and top with the chocolate one. Using a fork, swirl the two mixtures together
gently to create a rippled effect.
3   Bake in the hot oven 40 to 45 minutes, or until the cheesecake is firm around
the edges but still slightly wobbly in the middle. Remove from the oven and let
cool in the pan completely.
4   Refrigerate the cheesecake 2 hours or overnight, then remove from the pan.

007 Mini white chocolate cheesecakes

PREPARATION TIME 30 minutes, plus chilling   **COOKING TIME** 20 to 25 minutes
MAKES 6 mini cheesecakes

butter, for greasing
½ recipe quantity Chocolate Crumb
  Crust (see page 13)
7oz. cream cheese, softened
5 tbsp. sugar

1 egg, lightly beaten
4½oz. white chocolate, melted
  and left to cool
scant ½ cup heavy cream

1. Preheat the oven to 350°F. Grease 6 holes of a large muffin pan with butter and line each with a strip of baking paper, extending it up the sides. Divide the crumb crust mixture evenly between the holes and press down firmly to form the bottoms of the cheesecakes.
2. In a large bowl, beat the cream cheese and sugar together until light and fluffy, using an electric hand mixer, then beat in the egg. Stir in the melted chocolate and cream, using a wooden spoon, then divide the mixture between the holes.
3. Bake in the hot oven 20 to 25 minutes, or until the cheesecakes are just set and beginning to brown. Remove from the oven and let cool in the pan 15 minutes.
4. Remove the cheesecakes from the pan, using the strips of baking paper to help you, transfer to individual plates, and let cool completely. Chill 1 hour before serving.

008 Chocolate mascarpone cheesecake

PREPARATION TIME 20 minutes, plus chilling **COOKING TIME** 50 to 55 minutes
MAKES 1 x 9in. cheesecake

butter, for greasing
1 recipe quantity Chocolate Crumb
  Crust (see page 13)
9oz. mascarpone cheese, softened
5^1/₂oz. bittersweet chocolate, melted
  and left to cool

^{1}/₂ cup plus 1 tbsp. ground almonds
3 eggs, separated
^{1}/₂ cup heavy cream, whipped
  to soft peaks
^{1}/₃ cup plus 4 tsp. sugar

1 Preheat the oven to 325°F. Grease a 9in. springform pan with butter and press the prepared chocolate crumb crust into the bottom.
2 In a large bowl, beat the mascarpone until light and creamy, using an electric hand mixer. Stir in the melted chocolate, ground almonds, and egg yolks until just combined, using a wooden spoon, then gently fold in the cream. In a clean bowl, whisk the egg whites until soft peaks form, using an electric hand mixer. Gradually add the sugar, whisking until the mixture is stiff and glossy. Fold the whisked whites into the chocolate mixture, using a metal spoon, then pour the mixture over the crumb crust.
3 Bake in the hot oven 50 to 55 minutes, or until the cheesecake is firm around the edges but still slightly wobbly in the middle. Remove from the oven and let cool in the pan completely.
4 Refrigerate the cheesecake 2 hours or overnight, then remove from the pan.

009 Chocolate-banana mascarpone cheesecake

PREPARATION TIME 20 minutes, plus chilling **COOKING TIME** 45 to 50 minutes
MAKES 1 x 9in. cheesecake

butter, for greasing
1 recipe quantity Chocolate Crumb
  Crust (see page 13)
9oz. mascarpone cheese, softened
^{1}/₂ cup plus 2 tsp. packed light
  brown sugar
3 eggs, lightly beaten

3^1/₂oz. bittersweet or milk chocolate,
  melted and left to cool
2 large ripe bananas, mashed
2 tbsp. cornstarch
^{1}/₂ cup heavy cream
1 tbsp. rum
1 tsp. vanilla extract

1 Preheat the oven to 325°F. Grease a 9in. springform pan with butter and press the prepared chocolate crumb crust into the bottom.
2 In a large bowl, beat the mascarpone and brown sugar together until creamy, using an electric hand mixer. Add the eggs, and beat until combined. Stir in the melted chocolate, bananas, cornstarch, cream, rum, and vanilla extract, using a wooden spoon, then pour the mixture over the crumb crust.
3 Bake in the hot oven 45 to 50 minutes, or until the cheesecake is firm around the edges but still slightly wobbly in the middle. Remove from the oven and let cool in the pan completely.
4 Refrigerate the cheesecake 2 hours or overnight, then remove from the pan.

010 White chocolate cheesecake

PREPARATION TIME 20 minutes, plus chilling   **COOKING TIME** 40 to 45 minutes
MAKES 1 x 9in. cheesecake

butter, for greasing
1 recipe quantity Chocolate Crumb
   Crust (see page 13)
7oz. cream cheese, softened
$^1/_3$ cup plus 4 tsp. sugar

2 eggs, lightly beaten
$^3/_4$ cup plus 1 tbsp. heavy cream
7oz. white chocolate, melted
   and left to cool

1   Preheat the oven to 325°F. Grease a 9in. springform pan with butter and press
    the prepared chocolate crumb crust into the bottom.
2   In a large bowl, beat the cream cheese and sugar together until light and
    smooth, using an electric hand mixer. Add the eggs a little at a time. Stir in the
    cream and melted chocolate, then pour the mixture over the crumb crust.
3   Bake in the hot oven 40 to 45 minutes, or until the cheesecake is firm around
    the edges but still slightly wobbly in the middle. Remove from the oven and let
    cool in the pan completely.
4   Refrigerate the cheesecake 2 hours or overnight, then remove from the pan.

011 White chocolate & blueberry cheesecake

PREPARATION TIME 25 minutes, plus chilling   **COOKING TIME** 45 to 50 minutes
MAKES 1 x 9in. cheesecake

butter, for greasing
1 recipe quantity Chocolate Crumb
   Crust (see page 13)
14oz. cream cheese, softened
$^1/_3$ cup plus 4 tsp. sugar
3 eggs, lightly beaten
2 egg yolks

1 tbsp. all-purpose flour
1 tsp. vanilla extract
$^1/_2$ cup heavy cream
10$^1/_2$oz. white chocolate, melted
   and left to cool
1$^1/_2$ cups blueberries

1   Preheat the oven to 325°F. Grease a 9in. springform pan with butter and press
    the prepared chocolate crumb crust into the base.
2   In a large bowl, beat the cream cheese and sugar together until smooth, using an
    electric hand mixer. Add the eggs and yolks, flour, and vanilla extract and whisk
    until just combined. Stir in the cream and melted chocolate, using a wooden
    spoon, then fold in the blueberries. Pour the mixture over the crumb crust.
3   Bake in the hot oven 45 to 50 minutes, or until the cheesecake is firm around
    the edges but still slightly wobbly in the middle. Remove from the oven and let
    cool in the pan completely.
4   Refrigerate the cheesecake 2 hours or overnight, then remove from the pan.

012   Strawberry, hazelnut & chocolate shortcakes

PREPARATION TIME 35 minutes, plus chilling   **COOKING TIME** 10 to 12 minutes

7 tbsp. butter, softened, plus
  extra for greasing
¼ cup all-purpose flour
2 tbsp. rice flour
2 tbsp. powdered sugar, plus
  extra, sifted, for dusting
1 tbsp. unsweetened cocoa powder

2 tbsp. roasted hazelnuts,
  finely chopped
1 recipe quantity Chocolate Pastry
  Cream (see page 12)
1 cup strawberries, hulled and sliced
2³/₄oz. bittersweet chocolate, melted
  and left to cool

1   Preheat the oven to 350°F. Grease a large baking sheet with butter. In a large
bowl, whisk the butter until light and creamy, using an electric hand mixer.
Gently stir in the all-purpose flour, rice flour, powdered sugar, cocoa, and
hazelnuts until the mixture forms a dough.

2   Cover the dough with plastic wrap and refrigerate 20 minutes. Roll it out on
a floured surface to about ¼in. thick. Cut out 8 circles, using a large cookie
cutter, and prick each circle 3 or 4 times with a fork.

3   Place on the prepared baking sheet and bake in the hot oven 10 to 12 minutes,
or until the shortcakes are golden brown. Remove from the oven and let cool on
the tray for a few minutes. Transfer to a wire rack to cool completely.

4   When ready to serve, assemble the shortcakes. Place a shortcake round on
each plate and spoon over a large dollop of Chocolate Pastry Cream, plus some
of the sliced strawberries. Drizzle over the melted chocolate, then cover with
a second shortcake. Dust with powdered sugar before serving.

013   Chocolate éclairs

PREPARATION TIME 40 minutes, plus chilling   **COOKING TIME** 20 to 25 minutes
MAKES 6 large éclairs

1 recipe quantity Choux Pastry
  (see page 13)
1 cup plus 2 tbsp. heavy cream,
  whipped to soft peaks

1 recipe quantity Dark Chocolate
  Ganache (see page 209)

1   Preheat the oven to 425°F. Line a large baking sheet with baking paper. Spoon
the choux pastry into a piping bag with a plain ½in. nozzle and pipe 6 x 5in. pastry
lengths on the baking sheet. Sprinkle lightly with water.

2   Bake in the hot oven 20 to 25 minutes, or until the éclairs are a deep golden
brown. It is important to make sure that the middles are as dry as possible to
achieve the best result.

3   Remove the éclairs from the oven and transfer to a wire rack. Pierce the base
of each éclair with a small, sharp knife to make a tiny hole through which the
steam can escape. Let cool completely, then split lengthwise and scrape out
any wet dough that remains.

4   Using a piping bag with a ½in. star or round nozzle, pipe the whipped cream
into the middle of each éclair. Using a palette knife, smooth a layer of dark
chocolate ganache along the top of each éclair. Refrigerate the éclairs
30 minutes before serving.

014 Profiteroles with coffee cream & chocolate sauce

PREPARATION TIME 40 minutes **COOKING TIME** 20 to 25 minutes **MAKES** 12 profiteroles

1 recipe quantity Choux Pastry
  (see page 13)
1 cup plus 2 tbsp. heavy cream
2 tsp. instant coffee powder

1 tbsp. coffee liqueur
2 tbsp. sugar
1 recipe quantity Rich Chocolate
  Sauce (see page 204)

1 Preheat the oven to 425°F. Line a large baking sheet with baking paper. Spoon 12 tablespoonfuls of the choux pastry onto the baking sheet and sprinkle lightly with water.

2 Bake in the hot oven 20 to 25 minutes, or until the profiteroles are a deep golden brown. It is important to make sure that the middles are as dry as possible to achieve the best result.

3 Remove the profiteroles from the oven and transfer to a wire rack. Pierce each profiterole with a small, sharp knife to make a tiny hole through which the steam can escape. Let cool completely, then split horizontally and scrape out any wet dough that remains.

4 For the filling, put the cream, coffee, liqueur, and sugar in a bowl and whip to soft peaks, using an electric hand mixer. Spoon the creamy filling into the profiteroles. Place 3 profiteroles on each plate and pour the rich chocolate sauce over.

015   Strawberry profiteroles with chocolate sauce

PREPARATION TIME 25 minutes   **COOKING TIME** 20 to 25 minutes   **MAKES** 12 profiteroles

1 recipe quantity Choux Pastry
(see page 13)
1 recipe quantity Chocolate Pastry
Cream (see page 12)
1 tbsp. strawberry liqueur

1 to 2 tbsp. heavy cream (optional)
1 cup strawberries, sliced
1 recipe quantity Rich Chocolate
Sauce (see page 204)

1   Preheat the oven to 425°F. Line a large baking sheet with baking paper. Spoon
12 tablespoonfuls of the choux pastry on to the baking sheet. Sprinkle lightly
with water.

2   Bake in the very hot oven 20 to 25 minutes, or until the profiteroles are a deep
golden brown. It is important to make sure that the middles are as dry as
possible to achieve the best result.

3   Remove the profiteroles from the oven and transfer to a wire rack. Pierce each
profiterole with a small, sharp knife to make a tiny hole through which the
steam can escape. Let cool completely, then split lengthwise and scrape out
any wet dough that remains.

4   For the filling, place the chocolate pastry cream and the liqueur in a bowl and
gently stir together, using a wooden spoon, adding a little heavy cream if it
is too thick. Fold in the strawberries, then spoon the filling into the profiteroles.
Place 3 profiteroles on each plate and pour the rich chocolate sauce over.

016   Passionfruit profiteroles with white chocolate sauce

PREPARATION TIME 20 minutes   **COOKING TIME** 20 to 25 minutes   **MAKES** 12 profiteroles

1 recipe quantity Choux Pastry
(see page 13)
4 passionfruit
3 tbsp. powdered sugar, plus extra,
sifted, for dusting

1 cup plus 2 tbsp. heavy cream,
whipped to soft peaks
1 recipe quantity White Chocolate
Sauce (see page 206)

1   Preheat the oven to 425°F. Line a large baking sheet with baking paper.
Spoon 12 tablespoonfuls of the choux pastry on the baking sheet.
Sprinkle lightly with water.

2   Bake in the very hot oven 20 to 25 minutes, or until the profiteroles are a deep
golden brown. It is important to make sure that the middles are as dry as
possible to achieve the best result.

3   Remove the profiteroles from the oven and transfer to a wire rack. Pierce each
profiterole with a small, sharp knife to make a tiny hole through which the
steam can escape. Let cool completely, then split lengthwise and scrape out
any wet dough that remains.

4   Remove the fruity pulp from the passionfruit and place in a bowl. Mix in the
powdered sugar, using a wooden spoon, and fold it into the whipped cream.
Spoon the passionfruit cream into the profiteroles. Place 3 profiteroles on each
plate and dust with powdered sugar. Serve the white chocolate sauce separately.

017 Chocolate macadamia nut tart

PREPARATION TIME 40 minutes **COOKING TIME** 1 hour **MAKES** 1 x 9in. tart

1 recipe quantity Chocolate
  Shortcrust Pastry (see page 13)
2 tbsp. butter, chopped
1oz. bittersweet chocolate,
  broken into pieces
2 eggs
5 tbsp. sugar

¾ cup plus 1 tbsp. honey
1 tsp. vanilla extract
1¼ cups macadamia nuts,
  roughly chopped
powdered sugar, sifted,
  for dusting (optional)

1 Preheat the oven to 350°F. Roll the pastry out on a lightly floured surface to about ¼in. thick and ease into a 9in. fluted, loose-bottomed flan pan, 1½in. deep. Line the pastry case with baking paper and fill with baking beans. Bake in the hot oven 20 minutes. Remove the paper and beans from the pastry shell and bake in the hot oven a further 5 to 10 minutes, or until the pastry is dark brown.

2 For the filling, in a small saucepan, heat the butter and chocolate together over low heat until just melted. Remove from the heat and set aside to cool. In a large bowl, beat the eggs and sugar together until light and creamy, using an electric hand mixer, then beat in the honey, chocolate mixture, and the vanilla extract. Stir in the nuts, then pour the filling into the prepared pastry shell, being careful not to overfill.

3 Bake in the hot oven 30 to 35 minutes, or until the filling is just firm. Remove from the oven and let the tart cool completely in the pan, then dust with powdered sugar, if desired.

018 Grasshopper pie

PREPARATION TIME 20 minutes, plus chilling **COOKING TIME** 5 minutes **MAKES** 1 x 9in. pie

4 sheets leaf gelatin
2 tbsp. crème de menthe liqueur
2 egg whites
3 tbsp. plus 1 tsp. sugar
1 cup plus 2 tbsp. heavy cream,
  whipped to soft peaks

3½oz. bittersweet chocolate,
  melted and left to cool
3 tbsp. mint leaves,
  finely chopped
1 Chocolate Crumb Crust, baked
  (see page 13)
3 tbsp. bittersweet chocolate, grated

1 In a large bowl, soak the gelatin sheets in cold water 5 to 10 minutes until soft, then remove them and wring out any excess water.

2 In a small saucepan, heat the crème de menthe liqueur over low heat, then add the soaked gelatin. Remove the pan from the heat and stir with a metal spoon until the gelatin is completely dissolved. Set aside to cool slightly.

3 In a large bowl, whisk the egg whites to soft peaks, using an electric hand mixer, then add the sugar gradually, whisking until stiff. Using a metal spoon, fold the whipped cream into the egg whites with the gelatin mixture, melted chocolate, and mint leaves.

4 Pour the filling mixture into the chocolate crumb crust and smooth the top with a palette knife. Sprinkle over the grated chocolate. Refrigerate the pie 2 hours, or until set, before serving.

019   Strawberry & chocolate mille-feuilles

PREPARATION TIME 45 minutes, plus cooling   **COOKING TIME** 20 to 25 minutes

13oz. ready-rolled puff pastry
2 tbsp. milk
4 tsp. sugar
1 cup plus 2 tbsp. heavy cream,
  whipped to soft peaks

1 cup strawberries, hulled
  and thinly sliced
3½oz. bittersweet or milk chocolate,
  melted and left to cool
powdered sugar, sifted, for dusting

1   Preheat the oven to 375°F. Roll the pastry out on a lightly floured surface
to ½in. thick. Cut into 8 rectangles, each about 4 x 2¾in. Place the rectangles on
a large baking sheet and lightly brush the top of each one with milk. Using a
fork, prick the pastry in 5 or 6 places, then sprinkle with sugar.

2   Bake the rectangles in the hot oven 20 to 25 minutes, or until the pastry rises
and is golden brown. Remove from the oven and let the rectangles cool
completely on the baking sheet.

3   To assemble the mille-feuilles, place a rectangle on each plate and spread
a spoonful of whipped cream over. Top the cream with one-eighth of the
strawberries and drizzle over one-eighth of the melted chocolate. Repeat with
a second set of layers—pastry, cream, strawberries, and chocolate—then dust
the mille-feuilles with powdered sugar and serve immediately.

020   Chocolate custard mille-feuilles

PREPARATION TIME 45 minutes, plus cooling   **COOKING TIME** 20 to 25 minutes

13oz. ready-rolled puff pastry
2 tbsp. milk
4 tsp. sugar
1 recipe quantity Chocolate Pastry
  Cream (see page 12)

powdered sugar, sifted, for dusting
1 recipe quantity Chocolate Rum
  Sauce (see page 206)

1   Preheat the oven to 375°F. Roll the pastry out on a lightly floured surface
to ½in. thick. Cut into 8 rectangles, each about 4½ x 2in. Place the rectangles
on a large baking sheet and lightly brush the top of each one with milk. Using a
fork, prick the pastry in 5 or 6 places, then sprinkle with sugar.

2   Bake the rectangles in the hot oven 20 to 25 minutes, or until the pastry rises
and is golden brown. Remove from the oven and let the rectangles cool
completely on the baking sheet.

3   To assemble the mille-feuilles, place a rectangle on each plate and spread
a large spoonful of chocolate pastry cream over (some will be left over).
Place a second pastry layer on top of each mille-feuille and dust with powdered
sugar. Serve with the chocolate rum sauce.

021 Chocolate nut bavarois

PREPARATION TIME 25 minutes, plus cooling and chilling   **COOKING TIME** 5 minutes

¾ cup plus 1 tbsp. milk
2 tbsp. chocolate hazelnut paste
2 tbsp. hazelnut liqueur
3½oz. bittersweet or milk chocolate,
   broken into pieces
3 sheets leaf gelatin

4 egg yolks
3 tbsp. plus 1 tsp. sugar
1 cup plus 2 tbsp. heavy cream,
   whipped to soft peaks
chocolate curls, to sprinkle
   (optional)

1   In a medium-sized saucepan, heat the milk, chocolate hazelnut paste, liqueur,
    and chocolate over low heat until the chocolate has melted, stirring constantly
    with a wooden spoon. Remove from the heat and stir until smooth, then set
    aside to cool.
2   Meanwhile, soak the gelatin sheets in a bowl of cold water 5 to 10 minutes until
    soft, then remove them, wring out any excess water, and stir into the chocolate
    mixture until they dissolve. In a clean bowl, beat the egg yolks and sugar
    together, using a hand whisk, then gradually add to the cooled chocolate
    mixture. Pour into a clean bowl and set aside about 1½ hours until cool and
    beginning to thicken.
3   Gently fold in the cream, using a metal spoon, then pour the mixture into
    a 2-cup gelatin mold. Refrigerate 3 hours or overnight. Sprinkle with chocolate
    curls, if desired, before serving.

022 Mocha bavarois

PREPARATION TIME 20 minutes, plus cooling and chilling   COOKING TIME 5 minutes

¾ cup plus 1 tbsp. milk
2 tsp. instant coffee powder
4½oz. bittersweet or milk
  chocolate, broken into pieces
3 sheets leaf gelatin

1½ cups plus 2 tbsp. heavy cream,
  whipped to soft peaks
chocolate-coated coffee beans,
  to decorate

1   In a medium-sized saucepan, heat the milk, coffee, and chocolate together
    over low heat until the chocolate is just melted. Remove from the heat
    and stir until smooth, using a wooden spoon.
2   Meanwhile, soak the gelatin sheets in a bowl of cold water 5 to 10 minutes
    until soft, then remove them, wring out any excess water, and stir into the
    mocha mixture until they dissolve. Pour into a clean bowl and set aside about
    1 hour until cool and beginning to thicken. Fold in two-thirds of the whipped
    cream using a metal spoon and divide the mixture equally between 4 glasses.
    Refrigerate 3 hours or overnight.
3   Top each glass with a spoonful of the remaining whipped cream and a few
    chocolate-covered coffee beans just before serving.

023 Dark chocolate orange bavarois

PREPARATION TIME 25 minutes, plus cooling and chilling   COOKING TIME 5 minutes

¾ cup plus 1 tbsp. milk
4½oz. bittersweet chocolate,
  broken into pieces
2 tbsp. orange liqueur
3 sheets leaf gelatin

zest of 1 orange, finely grated
1½ cups plus 2 tbsp. heavy cream,
  whipped to soft peaks
orange slices, to decorate

1   In a medium-sized saucepan, heat the milk, chocolate, and orange liqueur
    together over low heat until the chocolate is just melted. Remove from the heat
    and stir until smooth, using a wooden spoon.
2   Meanwhile, soak the gelatin sheets in a bowl of cold water 5 to 10 minutes until
    soft, then remove them, wring out any excess water, and stir into the chocolate
    mixture until they dissolve. Pour into a clean bowl and set aside about 1 hour
    until cool and beginning to thicken.
3   Fold in the orange zest and two-thirds of the whipped cream, using a metal
    spoon, and divide the mixture equally between 4 dishes. Refrigerate 3 hours
    or overnight. Top each dish with a spoonful of the remaining whipped cream
    and decorate with orange slices just before serving.

024   Chocolate & coconut bavarois

PREPARATION TIME 35 minutes, plus cooling and chilling   **COOKING TIME** 5 minutes

1/3 cup plus 2 tbsp. milk
1/3 cup plus 2 tbsp. coconut cream
4½oz. bittersweet or milk chocolate,
  broken into pieces
2 tbsp. coconut liqueur

3 sheets leaf gelatin
1½ cups plus 2 tbsp. heavy cream,
  whipped to soft peaks
2 tbsp. toasted flaked coconut

1 In a medium-sized saucepan, heat the milk, coconut cream, chocolate, and liqueur together over low heat until the chocolate is just melted. Remove from the heat and stir until smooth, using a wooden spoon.

2 Meanwhile, soak the gelatin sheets in a bowl of cold water 5 to 10 minutes until soft, then remove them, wring out any excess water, and stir into the chocolate mixture until they dissolve. Pour into a clean bowl and set aside about 1 hour until cool and beginning to thicken. Fold in two-thirds of the whipped cream, using a metal spoon, and divide the mixture equally between 4 dishes. Refrigerate 3 hours or overnight.

3 Top each dish with a spoonful of whipped cream and sprinkle with toasted coconut before serving.

025   White chocolate bavarois with blueberries

PREPARATION TIME 20 minutes, plus cooling and chilling   **COOKING TIME** 5 minutes

¾ cup plus 1 tbsp. milk
4½oz. white chocolate,
  broken into pieces
3 sheets leaf gelatin

1 cup plus 2 tbsp. heavy cream,
  whipped to soft peaks
1 cup blueberries

1 In a small saucepan, heat the milk and chocolate together over low heat, until the chocolate is just melted. Remove from the heat and stir until smooth, using a wooden spoon.

2 Meanwhile, soak the gelatin sheets in a bowl of cold water 5 to 10 minutes until soft, then remove them, wring out any excess water, and stir into the chocolate mixture until they dissolve. Pour into a clean bowl and set aside about 1 hour until cool and beginning to thicken.

3 Fold in the whipped cream, using a metal spoon, and divide the mixture equally between 4 dishes. Refrigerate 3 hours or overnight. Top each dish with blueberries just before serving.

026 White chocolate panna cottas

PREPARATION TIME 15 minutes, plus cooling and chilling   **COOKING TIME** 5 minutes

3 sheets leaf gelatin
1 cup plus 2 tbsp. heavy cream
½ cup milk
3½oz. white chocolate,
  broken into pieces

2 tbsp. sugar
1 tsp. vanilla extract
1 cup raspberries
2 tbsp. powdered sugar, sifted

1 Soak the gelatin sheets in a bowl of cold water 5 to 10 minutes until soft.
2 In a small saucepan, heat the cream, milk, chocolate, sugar, and vanilla extract together over low heat until the chocolate is just melted. Remove from the heat and stir with a wooden spoon until smooth. Remove the gelatin from the water and wring out any excess. Drop the gelatin into the cream mixture and stir briefly until dissolved.
3 Divide the mixture evenly between 4 x ½-cup molds on a tray and set aside to cool about 30 minutes. Refrigerate the panna cottas 3 hours or overnight.
4 In a blender, pulse the raspberries to a purée with the powdered sugar to make a coulis. Dip the molds briefly into hot water and run a sharp knife around the sides. Turn the panna cottas out onto 4 plates and serve with the coulis.

027 Coconut & white chocolate panna cottas

PREPARATION TIME 15 minutes, plus cooling and chilling   **COOKING TIME** 5 minutes

2 sheets leaf gelatin
1¼ cups plus 1 tbsp. coconut cream
⅓ cup plus 2 tbsp. milk
3½oz. white chocolate, broken
   into pieces
2 tbsp. sugar

1 tbsp. white rum
pieces of pineapple,
   for serving (optional)

1   Soak the gelatin sheets in a bowl of cold water 5 to 10 minutes until soft.
2   In a large saucepan, mix the coconut cream, milk, chocolate, and sugar
   together over low heat until the chocolate is just melted. Remove from the heat.
   Remove the gelatin from the water and wring out any excess. Drop the gelatin
   into the cream mixture and stir briefly until dissolved. Stir in the rum.
3   Divide the mixture evenly between 4 x ½-cup molds on a tray and set aside
   to cool about 30 minutes. Refrigerate the panna cottas 3 hours or overnight.
4   Dip the molds briefly into hot water and run a sharp knife around the sides.
   Turn the panna cottas out onto 4 plates and serve with pieces of pineapple,
   if desired.

028 Mocha panna cottas

PREPARATION TIME 20 minutes, plus cooling and chilling   **COOKING TIME** 5 minutes

3 sheets leaf gelatin
1¼ cups plus 1 tbsp. heavy
   or light cream
¾ cup plus 1 tbsp. milk
3 tbsp. plus 1 tsp. sugar

3½oz. bittersweet chocolate,
   broken into pieces
1 tsp. instant coffee powder
1 tsp. vanilla extract
berries, for serving (optional)

1   Soak the gelatin sheets in a bowl of cold water 5 to 10 minutes until soft.
2   In a large saucepan, heat the cream, milk, and sugar until it is just boiling,
   then add the chocolate, coffee, and vanilla extract. Remove the gelatin from
   the water and wring out any excess. Drop the gelatin into the cream mixture
   and stir briefly until dissolved. Stir well until combined and the chocolate
   is just melted, using a wooden spoon.
3   Divide the mixture evenly between 4 x ½-cup molds on a tray and set aside to
   cool about 30 minutes. Refrigerate the cooled panna cottas 3 hours or overnight.
4   Dip the molds briefly into hot water and run a sharp knife around the sides.
   Turn the panna cottas out onto 4 plates, and serve with berries, if using.

029 Quickest-ever dark chocolate mousse

PREPARATION TIME 10 minutes, plus chilling

2 egg whites
5 tbsp. sugar
7oz. bittersweet chocolate,
   melted and left to cool

1 cup plus 2 tbsp. heavy cream,
   whipped to soft peaks

1   In a large bowl, whisk the egg whites until soft peaks form, using an electric
   hand mixer. Add the sugar gradually while continuing to whisk until the whites
   are thick and shiny. Using a metal spoon, fold in the melted chocolate and cream.
2   Using a large spoon, divide the mousse between 4 dishes and refrigerate
   30 minutes before serving.

030 White chocolate & passionfruit mousse

PREPARATION TIME 20 minutes, plus chilling   **COOKING TIME** 5 minutes

7oz. white chocolate,
   broken into pieces

1½ cups plus 2 tbsp. heavy cream
3 ripe passionfruit

1 In a small saucepan, heat the chocolate and ⅓ cup plus 2 tbsp. of the cream together over low heat until the chocolate is just melted. Remove from the heat and stir with a wooden spoon until smooth. Set aside to cool.
2 Using a sharp knife, remove the pulp from the passionfruit. Whip the remaining cream until it forms soft peaks, using an electric hand mixer. In a large bowl, fold the fruit pulp into the chocolate mixture, using a metal spoon, along with the whipped cream.
3 Using a large spoon, divide the mousse between 4 dishes and refrigerate 30 minutes before serving.

031 Chocolate nougat mousse

PREPARATION TIME 10 minutes, plus chilling

2 egg whites
3 tbsp. plus 1 tsp. sugar
7oz. bittersweet chocolate,
   melted and left to cool
1 tbsp. hazelnut liqueur

5½oz. torrone-style nougat pieces,
   finely chopped
1 cup plus 2 tbsp. heavy cream,
   whipped to soft peaks

1 In a large bowl, whisk the egg whites until soft peaks form, using an electric hand mixer. Add the sugar gradually, continuing to whisk until the whites are thick and shiny. Using a metal spoon, fold in the melted chocolate, liqueur, nougat, and whipped cream, just until combined.
2 Using a large spoon, divide the mousse between 4 dishes and refrigerate 30 minutes before serving.

032 Coffee, chocolate & praline mousse

PREPARATION TIME 20 minutes, plus chilling   **COOKING TIME** 5 minutes

7oz. bittersweet chocolate,
   broken into pieces
2 tsp. instant coffee powder
1 tbsp. hazelnut liqueur

¼ cup chocolate hazelnut spread
3 eggs, separated
chocolate-coated coffee beans,
   for serving (optional)

1 In a medium-sized saucepan, heat the chocolate, coffee, and liqueur together over low heat until the chocolate is just melted. Remove from the heat and stir with a wooden spoon until smooth. Stir in the hazelnut spread and let cool 10 minutes. Stir in the egg yolks.
2 In a large bowl, whisk the egg whites until stiff, using an electric hand mixer, then fold into the chocolate mixture, using a metal spoon.
3 Using a large spoon, divide the mousse between 4 dishes and refrigerate 30 minutes. Decorate with the chocolate coffee beans, if using, before serving.

033 Mocha rum mousse

PREPARATION TIME 20 minutes, plus chilling   **COOKING TIME** 5 minutes

9oz. bittersweet chocolate,
  broken into pieces
2 tsp. instant coffee powder

4 eggs, separated
3 tbsp. dark rum
chocolate, grated, for sprinkling

1   In a small saucepan, melt the chocolate over low heat, stir in the coffee with
    a metal spoon, then set aside to cool. When cool, stir in the egg yolks and rum.
    In a large bowl, whisk the egg whites until stiff, using an electric hand mixer,
    and mix into the chocolate mixture until well combined.
2   Using a large spoon, divide the mixture between 4 dishes and sprinkle with
    grated chocolate. Refrigerate 1 hour before serving.

034 Cappuccino mousse

PREPARATION TIME 20 minutes, plus chilling

7oz. bittersweet chocolate,
  melted and left to cool
3 eggs, separated
1 tbsp. coffee liqueur

½ cup heavy cream, whipped
  to soft peaks
2 tbsp. chocolate drink mix, sifted

1   In a large bowl, mix the melted chocolate and egg yolks together using a metal
    spoon, then stir in the liqueur. In a clean bowl, whisk the egg whites until stiff,
    using an electric hand mixer, and stir into the chocolate mixture until they are
    well combined.
2   Using a large spoon, divide the mixture evenly between 4 dishes and refrigerate
    1 hour. Just before serving, top each mousse with whipped cream and sprinkle
    the chocolate drink mix over.

035 Chocolate liqueur mousse with raisins

PREPARATION TIME 25 minutes, plus chilling   **COOKING TIME** 5 minutes

½ cup raisins
3 tbsp. orange liqueur
6oz. bittersweet chocolate,
  broken into pieces

2 tbsp. milk
2 egg whites
1½ cups plus 2 tbsp. heavy cream,
  whipped to soft peaks

1   Place the raisins in a small bowl and cover with the liqueur. Microwave the
    liqueur-soaked raisins for 1 minute, then set aside until cold.
2   In a small saucepan, heat the chocolate and milk together over low heat until
    the chocolate is just melted. Remove from the heat and stir until smooth, using
    a wooden spoon.
3   In a large bowl, whisk the egg whites until stiff, using an electric hand mixer.
    Using a metal spoon, fold the whisked whites into the chocolate mixture with
    two-thirds of the whipped cream and the marinated raisins.
4   Using a large spoon, divide the mixture evenly between 4 dishes and chill for
    1 hour before serving. Decorate each mousse with the remaining cream.

036 White chocolate mousse with raspberries

PREPARATION TIME 20 minutes, plus chilling **COOKING TIME** 5 minutes

1½ cups raspberries, plus extra
   for serving (optional)
⅔ cup milk
7oz. white chocolate, broken
   into pieces

1 tsp. vanilla extract
2 sheets leaf gelatin
¾ cup plus 1 tbsp. heavy cream,
   whipped to soft peaks
chocolate curls, for decorating

1 Divide the raspberries evenly between 4 small glasses. In a small saucepan, heat the milk, white chocolate, and vanilla extract over low heat until the chocolate is just melted, stirring frequently with a wooden spoon.

2 In a small bowl, soak the gelatin in cold water until soft. Remove the gelatin from the bowl and squeeze out any excess water, then stir the gelatin into the chocolate milk until dissolved. Pour into a clean bowl and set aside until cool and beginning to thicken. Fold the whipped cream into the chocolate mixture using a metal spoon, then spoon the resulting mousse over the raspberries in the glasses. Refrigerate 3 hours or overnight.

3 Use the chocolate curls and the extra raspberries, if using, to decorate the top of each mousse.

037 Dark chocolate marquise

PREPARATION TIME 30 minutes, plus chilling   **COOKING TIME** 5 minutes   **SERVES** 4 to 6

1lb. bittersweet chocolate,
  broken into pieces
7 tbsp. butter,
  chopped

1 cup plus 2 tbsp. heavy cream,
  whipped to soft peaks
berries, for serving (optional)

1   Line a 9in. loaf pan with plastic wrap.
2   In a medium-sized saucepan, heat the chocolate and butter together over
    low heat until the chocolate is just melted. Remove from the heat and stir
    until smooth, using a wooden spoon. Set aside to cool to room temperature.
    When cool, fold in the whipped cream using a metal spoon, then pour into the
    prepared loaf pan. Refrigerate the marquise 3 hours or overnight.
3   When ready to serve, unmold the marquise from the pan and remove the plastic
    wrap around it. Dip a sharp knife in hot water to heat it, then cut the marquise
    into ½in. slices and place on individual plates. Serve the marquise decorated
    with berries, if using.

038 Chocolate truffle dessert

PREPARATION TIME 15 minutes, plus chilling

4½oz. bittersweet chocolate,
  melted and left to cool
½ cup Creamy Thick Chocolate
  Custard (see page 12)

1 cup heavy cream, whipped
  to soft peaks
cocoa powder, sifted, for dusting

1   Line a baking sheet with baking paper and place 4 small pastry rings on top.
2   In a large bowl, using a metal spoon, fold together the chocolate, chocolate
    custard, and cream. Spoon the mixture evenly into the rings, cover with plastic
    wrap, and refrigerate 1 hour or overnight.
3   Remove the plastic wrap, then, using a spatula, slide the rings onto 4 plates.
    Loosen the rings with a sharp knife and lift them off the desserts. Dust each
    dessert with a little cocoa before serving.

039 White chocolate, blueberry & citrus creams

PREPARATION TIME 15 minutes, plus chilling

3 eggs, separated
4½ oz. white chocolate,
  melted and left to cool

½ cup heavy cream
zest of 1 lime, finely grated
1 cup blueberries

1   In a large bowl, beat the egg yolks into the melted chocolate, using an electric
    hand mixer. Using a wooden spoon, stir in the cream and lime zest.
2   In a clean bowl, whip the egg whites to soft peaks, using clean attachments for
    the electric hand mixer, then fold into the chocolate mixture with a metal spoon.
3   Divide the blueberries evenly between 4 glasses and pour the chocolate mixture
    over. Refrigerate 2 to 3 hours before serving.

040   Strawberries romanoff with white chocolate

PREPARATION TIME 40 minutes, plus chilling

2 cups strawberries, hulled
  and sliced
2 tbsp. orange liqueur
2 tbsp. powdered sugar

1 cup plus 2 tbsp. heavy cream
1 tbsp. sugar
3½oz. white chocolate, melted
  and cooled

1 In a large bowl, stir together the strawberries, liqueur, and powdered sugar. Refrigerate the mixture 30 minutes to allow the flavors to mingle.

2 In a clean bowl, whisk the heavy cream and sugar together to form soft peaks, using an electric hand mixer, then stir in the melted chocolate. Purée half of the strawberry mixture in a blender, then, using a metal spoon, gently fold it into the cream mixture with the remaining strawberries.

3 Divide the mixture evenly between 4 dishes.

041   Brandy snaps with chocolate cream

PREPARATION TIME 20 minutes   **COOKING TIME** 10 to 15 minutes
MAKES 8 filled brandy snaps

½ stick butter, chopped,
  plus extra for greasing
3 tbsp. plus 1 tsp. sugar
1½ tbsp. light corn syrup

¼ cup all-purpose flour
1 recipe quantity Chocolate Chantilly
  Cream (see page 208)

1 Preheat the oven to 375°F. Grease 2 large baking sheets with butter.

2 In a small saucepan, heat the butter, sugar, and light corn syrup over low heat until the butter melts, then remove from the heat and stir in the flour, using a wooden spoon. Place 4 heaped teaspoonfuls of the mixture on each baking sheet, leaving enough room around each spoonful for the cookies to spread.

3 Bake in the hot oven 6 to 8 minutes, or until the cookies have spread and are golden. Remove from the oven and let cool 1 to 2 minutes on the baking sheets. Gently remove a cookie from the sheet with a large spatula. Working quickly, roll it around the handle of a wooden spoon, leaving it on the handle for a few minutes to set. Gently remove the set cookie and place it on a wire rack to cool completely. Repeat the rolling process with the rest of the cookies.

4 When ready to serve, pipe some chocolate chantilly cream into the middle of each brandy snap.

042 Chocolate & chestnut mess

PREPARATION TIME 10 minutes

1¼ cups plus 1 tbsp. heavy cream
6 tbsp. canned, sweetened
   chestnut purée
4½oz. bittersweet chocolate, grated

2 tbsp. coffee liqueur
1 tbsp. sugar
8 crispy-style meringues

1   In a large bowl, whip the cream and chestnut purée until the mixture is just beginning to thicken, using an electric hand mixer. Add 3½oz. of the grated chocolate, the liqueur, and sugar and whip until the mixture is smooth and holds its shape lightly (taking care not to over-whip).
2   Put the meringues in a plastic bag, crush them lightly with a rolling pin, then empty them into the cream mixture and fold in, using a metal spoon.
3   Spoon the mixture into 4 dishes and sprinkle the remaining grated chocolate over the top.

043 White chocolate & raspberry Eton mess

PREPARATION TIME 10 minutes

1¼ cups heavy cream
1 tbsp. sugar
2 tbsp. raspberry liqueur
8 crispy-style meringues

3½oz. white chocolate, melted
   and left to cool
1 cup raspberries, lightly crushed

1   In a large bowl, whip the cream, sugar, and liqueur together until the mixture just forms soft peaks, using an electric hand mixer.
2   Put the meringues in a plastic bag, crush them lightly with a rolling pin, then empty them into the cream mixture and mix together, using a wooden spoon. Fold in the melted chocolate and raspberries.
3   Spoon the mixture into 4 dishes and serve immediately.

044 Chocolate zabaglione

PREPARATION TIME 10 minutes   **COOKING TIME** 7 to 8 minutes

8 egg yolks
¼ cup sugar
5 tbsp. Marsala wine

3½oz. bittersweet chocolate,
   melted and left to cool
4 Italian ladyfinger cookies

1   In a large, heatproof bowl, beat together the yolks, sugar, and Marsala wine,
    using an electric hand mixer. Place the bowl over a pan of gently simmering
    water (making sure that the bowl does not touch the water or the eggs will
    scramble). Whisk vigorously until the mixture is frothy and just starting to
    thicken (this will take about 7 to 8 minutes), using a hand whisk.
2   Remove the bowl from the heat and beat in the melted chocolate, using
    an electric hand mixer.
3   Using a large spoon, divide the mixture evenly between 4 dishes.
    Serve immediately, accompanied by the ladyfingers.

045 Chilled chocolate zabaglione

PREPARATION TIME 20 minutes, plus chilling   **COOKING TIME** 7 to 8 minutes

5 egg yolks
¼ cup sugar
5 tbsp. Marsala wine
3½oz. bittersweet chocolate,
   melted and left to cool

1 cup plus 2 tbsp. heavy cream,
   whipped to soft peaks
chocolate, grated, to decorate
   (optional)

1   In a large, heatproof bowl, beat together the yolks, sugar, and Marsala wine, using an electric hand mixer. Place the bowl over a pan of gently simmering water (making sure that the bowl does not touch the water or the eggs will scramble). Whisk vigorously until the mixture is frothy and just starting to thicken (this will take about 7 to 8 minutes), using a hand whisk.

2   Remove the bowl from the heat and pour the mixture into a large, clean bowl. Beat in the melted chocolate, using an electric hand mixer. Let cool and then refrigerate 30 minutes, stirring occasionally.

3   Remove from the refrigerator and fold in the whipped cream, using a metal spoon. Using a large spoon, divide the mixture evenly between 4 dishes or tall glasses and decorate each with a little grated chocolate, if using, before serving.

046 Zuccotto

PREPARATION TIME 25 minutes, plus chilling   **SERVES** 4 to 6

10½oz. plain butter or sponge cake
3 tbsp. cherry liqueur
3 tbsp. almond liqueur
2 cups plus 2 tbsp. heavy cream,
   whipped to soft peaks
¾ cup plus 1 tbsp. powdered sugar

5½oz. bittersweet chocolate,
   roughly chopped
⅓ cup roasted almonds, chopped
2 tbsp. roasted hazelnuts, chopped
½ cup chopped figs
cocoa powder and powdered sugar,
   sifted together, for dusting

1   Line a 1½-quart bowl with plastic wrap.

2   Cut the cake into ¼in. thin slices, then cut each slice in half to make triangles. Line the bowl with the cake, cutting smaller pieces to fit any gaps. Reserve the remaining cake for the top. In a small bowl, combine the cherry and almond liqueurs, then use a pastry brush to brush it evenly over the cake.

3   In a large bowl, fold together the whipped cream, powdered sugar, chocolate, almonds, hazelnuts, and figs. Spoon this mixture into the middle of the cake-lined bowl, then top with the remaining cake. Cover the bowl with plastic wrap, then refrigerate 3 hours or overnight.

4   When ready to serve, turn it out onto a serving plate. Dust the cocoa and powdered sugar over the zuccotto before serving.

047   Individual berry & white chocolate trifles

PREPARATION TIME 25 minutes, plus chilling

3½oz. ladyfinger cookies or
   plain sponge cake, sliced
2 cups mixed berries, such as
   strawberries, raspberries,
   and blackberries
juice and zest of 1 orange
1 tbsp. powdered sugar

6 tbsp. strawberry liqueur
1 recipe quantity Creamy Thick
   Chocolate Custard (see page 12)
3½oz. white chocolate, melted
   and left to cool
1 cup plus 2 tbsp. heavy cream,
   whipped to soft peaks

1   Break the ladyfingers or sliced cake into small pieces and divide evenly between
    4 tall glasses.
2   Slice the strawberries and combine them in a large bowl with the remaining
    berries. Add the orange juice, 1 tsp. of orange zest, and the powdered sugar
    and berries and set aside 15 minutes for the flavors to mingle.
3   Sprinkle the liqueur over the ladyfingers or sponge cake. Divide the berries
    and their juice between the glasses, reserving ¼ cup for decorating. Add a layer
    of creamy thick chocolate custard to each glass, then refrigerate the trifles
    2 hours or overnight.
4   Just before serving, fold the melted chocolate into the cream, using a metal
    spoon. Divide the chocolate cream between the glasses, spooning it over the
    berry layer. Decorate each glass with 1 tbsp. of the reserved berries.

048   Fig, chocolate & Marsala trifle

PREPARATION TIME 20 minutes, plus chilling   **SERVES** 4 to 6

7oz. ladyfinger cookies or
   plain sponge cake, sliced
6 tbsp. Marsala wine
8 ripe figs, sliced
¾ cup slivered almonds, roasted
5½oz. bittersweet chocolate,
   chopped roughly

1 recipe quantity Creamy Thick
   Chocolate Custard (see page 12)
1 cup plus 2 tbsp. heavy cream,
   whipped to soft peaks
chocolate curls, for decorating

1   Place the ladyfingers or sliced cake in the base of a large serving bowl
    and drizzle over the Marsala wine. Layer the sliced figs on top of the cake
    and sprinkle with the slivered almonds and chocolate. Spoon the creamy thick
    chocolate custard over the almonds in an even layer, then top with the cream.
2   Sprinkle the top of the custard with chocolate curls, then refrigerate the
    trifle 2 hours before serving.

049 Black cherry trifle

PREPARATION TIME 30 minutes, plus chilling   **SERVES** 4 to 6

7oz. ladyfinger cookies or
   plain sponge cake, sliced
¼ cup cherry brandy
2 cups canned cherries, drained,
   syrup reserved
1 recipe quantity Creamy Thick
   Chocolate Custard (see page 12)

1 cup plus 2 tbsp. heavy cream
2 tbsp. sugar
3½oz. bittersweet chocolate,
   melted and left to cool
6 ripe cherries

1   Place the ladyfingers or sliced cake into the bottom of a large serving bowl and
    sprinkle with the cherry brandy. Scatter the cherries over the ladyfingers or
    cake, along with ¼ cup of the reserved syrup, then top with the creamy thick
    chocolate custard.
2   In a large bowl, whip the cream with the sugar until thick but not too stiff, using
    an electric hand mixer, then spread it over the custard in the bowl. Drizzle over
    half of the melted chocolate. Refrigerate the trifle 2 hours or overnight.
3   Meanwhile, half-dip the cherries in the remaining melted chocolate, let
    them set on the baking paper, and then use to decorate the trifle.

050 Quick tiramisu with chocolate

PREPARATION TIME 10 minutes

7oz. mascarpone cheese, softened
2 egg yolks
¾ cup plus 1 tbsp. powdered
   sugar, sifted
¾ cup plus 2 tbsp. heavy cream

3½oz. bittersweet or semi-sweet
   chocolate, melted and left to cool
6 ladyfinger cookies
½ cup strong coffee
¼ cup Marsala wine
¼ cup chocolate shavings

1 In a large bowl, beat the mascarpone, egg yolks, and powdered sugar together, using an electric hand mixer. Blend in the cream and melted chocolate.
2 Break the ladyfingers up into small pieces and divide them evenly between 4 dishes.
3 In a small bowl, combine the coffee and Marsala wine and pour this over the ladyfingers, then spoon the mascarpone mixture over the cookies. Top with the chocolate shavings before serving.

051 White chocolate tiramisu with raspberries

PREPARATION TIME 20 minutes, plus chilling **SERVES** 4 to 6

2 eggs, separated, plus 3 yolks
⅓ cup plus 4 tsp. sugar
9oz. mascarpone cheese, softened
3½oz. white chocolate, melted
   and left to cool
1 cup plus 2 tbsp. strong coffee

¼ cup raspberry liqueur
10 ladyfinger cookies
2 cups raspberries
¼ cup grated white and
   bittersweet chocolate

1 In a large bowl, beat all the egg yolks and the sugar together until light and creamy, using an electric hand mixer. Blend in the mascarpone and melted chocolate until combined. In a clean bowl, whisk the egg whites until stiff but not dry, using clean attachments for the electric hand mixer, then, using a metal spoon, fold the whisked whites into the mascarpone mixture.
2 In a clean bowl, combine the coffee and liqueur and dip the ladyfingers into the mixture, allowing them to soak up some of the liquid.
3 Use the soaked ladyfingers to line the bottom of a serving dish about 11 x 7 x 2½in. Sprinkle the raspberries over the ladyfingers in a layer, then pour the mascarpone mixture over the fruit and sprinkle with the grated chocolate. Refrigerate 2 hours before serving.

052 Dark chocolate tiramisu

PREPARATION TIME 20 minutes, plus chilling   **SERVES** 4 to 6

2 eggs, separated, plus 3 yolks
1/3 cup plus 4 tsp. sugar
9oz. mascarpone cheese, softened
3½oz. bittersweet chocolate, melted
 and left to cool, plus ¼ cup grated

1½ cups strong coffee
¼ cup Marsala wine
20 ladyfinger cookies
2 tbsp. unsweetened cocoa powder,
 sifted

1   In a large bowl, beat all the egg yolks and the sugar together until light and
 creamy, using an electric hand mixer. Blend in the mascarpone and melted
 chocolate until combined. In a clean bowl, whisk the egg whites until stiff but
 not dry, using clean attachments for the electric hand mixer, then, using a
 metal spoon, fold the whisked whites into the mascarpone mixture.
2   In a clean bowl, combine the coffee and Marsala wine and dip the ladyfingers
 into the mixture, allowing them to soak up some of the liquid.
3   Use 10 of the soaked ladyfingers to line the bottom of a serving dish about
 11 x 7 x 2½in. Pour half the mascarpone mixture over the cookie layer, then
 cover with the remaining ladyfingers, followed by the remaining mascarpone.
 Dust the top with cocoa, sprinkle with the grated chocolate, and refrigerate
 2 hours before serving.

053 Chocolate meringue torte

PREPARATION TIME 30 minutes, plus cooling   **COOKING TIME** 50 to 60 minutes
MAKES 1 x 9in. torte

5 egg whites
1¼ cups plus 1 tbsp. sugar
2 tbsp. unsweetened cocoa powder,
   sifted
1 tsp. vanilla extract

1 recipe quantity Chocolate Chantilly
   Cream (see page 208)
chocolate shavings or grated
   chocolate, to decorate

1   Preheat the oven to 275°F. Draw a 9in. circle on 2 sheets of baking paper,
    turn them over, and use to line 2 baking sheets.
2   In a large bowl, whisk the egg whites to soft peaks, using an electric hand
    mixer, then gradually whisk in the sugar until thick and glossy. Whisk in the
    cocoa and vanilla extract. Spoon on to the prepared sheets and, using a palette
    knife, spread over the circles on the baking paper. Using a spatula, smooth
    the tops of the meringue rounds.
3   Bake in the warm oven 50 to 60 minutes, or until crisp. Turn off the oven and
    let the meringues cool completely in the oven on the baking sheets.
4   When the meringues are cold, remove them from the oven and carefully peel
    away the lining paper. Sandwich the two meringues together using two-thirds
    of the chocolate chantilly cream, place on a serving plate, and spread the
    remaining cream on top. Decorate with chocolate shavings or grated
    chocolate before serving.

054 Chocolate roulade with cinnamon cream

PREPARATION TIME 25 minutes, plus cooling   **COOKING TIME** 10 to 12 minutes
SERVES 4 to 6

butter, for greasing
⅓ cup plus 4 tsp. sugar
4 eggs, separated
7oz. bittersweet chocolate,
   melted and left to cool

1 cup plus 2 tbsp. heavy cream
2 tbsp. powdered sugar, plus extra,
   sifted, for dusting
2 tsp. cinnamon

1   Preheat the oven to 350°F. Grease a 9 x 13in. jelly roll pan with butter and line
    the bottom and sides with baking paper.
2   In a large bowl, beat the sugar and egg yolks together until thick and creamy,
    using an electric hand mixer, then stir in the melted chocolate, using a wooden
    spoon. In a clean bowl, whisk the egg whites until stiff but not dry, using clean
    attachments for the electric hand mixer, then gently fold into the chocolate
    mixture, using a metal spoon. Pour the mixture into the prepared pan and
    spread evenly, using a palette knife.
3   Bake in the hot oven 10 to 12 minutes until just firm. Remove the roulade from
    the oven, let stand 5 minutes, then turn it out onto a second piece of baking
    paper and remove the lining paper. Cut away any crisp edges, cover the roulade
    with a clean dish towel, and let cool completely.
4   In a large bowl, whisk the cream, powdered sugar, and cinnamon together until
    soft peaks form, using an electric hand mixer, then spread over the roulade.
5   Using the paper to help you, but making sure that it does not get trapped inside
    the roulade, gradually roll up the roulade jelly-roll style from a short end. Transfer
    carefully to a serving plate and dust with powdered sugar before serving.

055 Passionfruit, white chocolate & strawberry meringue roulade

PREPARATION TIME 25 minutes, plus cooling   **COOKING TIME** 15 to 18 minutes
SERVES 4 to 6

melted butter, for greasing
4 egg whites
pinch salt
1 cup plus 4 tsp. sugar
1 cup plus 2 tbsp. heavy cream,
  whipped to soft peaks

5¹/₂oz. white chocolate,
  melted and left to cool
2 cups strawberries, hulled
  and sliced
4 passionfruit
powdered sugar, sifted, for dusting

1   Preheat the oven to 325°F. Line a 9 x 13in. jelly roll pan with baking paper, so that the paper hangs over the edge. Lightly grease the paper with melted butter.

2   In a large bowl, whisk the egg whites with the salt until soft peaks form, using an electric hand mixer, then gradually add the sugar and continue whisking until stiff. Spread the meringue mixture over the prepared pan, using a palette knife.

3   Bake in the hot oven 15 to 18 minutes, or until the surface is crisp. Remove from the oven and let cool completely in the pan.

4   Turn the roulade out onto a large piece of baking paper and peel off the lining paper. In a large bowl, fold the cream and melted chocolate together, using a metal spoon. Using a palette knife, spread the cream mixture evenly over the roulade, then cover with the strawberries. Remove the pulp from the passionfruit, using a sharp knife, and scatter it over the strawberries.

5   Using the paper to help you, but making sure that it does not get trapped inside the roulade, gradually roll up the meringue jelly-roll style from a short end. Transfer carefully to a serving plate and dust with powdered sugar before serving.

056 Raspberry & chocolate meringue roulade

PREPARATION TIME 20 minutes, plus cooling   **COOKING TIME** 15 to 18 minutes
SERVES 4 to 6

melted butter, for greasing
4 egg whites
pinch salt
1 cup plus 4 tsp. sugar
2 tbsp. unsweetened cocoa powder

1 cup plus 2 tbsp. heavy cream,
  whipped to soft peaks
2 cups raspberries
powdered sugar, sifted, for dusting

1   Preheat the oven to 325°F. Line a 9 x 13in. jelly roll pan with baking paper, so that the paper hangs over the edge. Lightly grease the paper with the melted butter.

2   In a large bowl, whisk the egg whites with the salt, using an electric hand mixer, until soft peaks form, then gradually add the sugar and continue whisking until stiff. Lastly, whisk in the cocoa until just combined. Spread the meringue mixture over the prepared pan, using a palette knife.

3   Bake in the hot oven 15 to 18 minutes, or until the surface is crisp. Remove from the oven and let cool completely in the pan.

4   Turn the roulade out onto a large piece of baking paper and peel off the lining paper. Cover the roulade with the whipped cream, spreading it over evenly with a palette knife, then sprinkle with the raspberries.

5   Using the paper to help you, but making sure that it does not get trapped inside the roulade, gradually roll up the roulade jelly-roll style from a short end. Transfer carefully to a serving plate and dust with powdered sugar before serving.

057 Chocolate pavlova

PREPARATION TIME 20 minutes, plus cooling   **COOKING TIME** 70 minutes   **SERVES** 4 to 6

4 egg whites
1 cup plus 4 tsp. sugar
2 tsp. cornstarch
1 tsp. white vinegar
1³/₄oz. bittersweet chocolate, grated

1 recipe quantity Chocolate Chantilly
   Cream (see page 208)
1³/₄oz. bittersweet or milk chocolate,
   melted and left to cool

1   Preheat the oven to 325°F. Draw a 9in. circle on a sheet of baking paper, turn
    it over, and use to line a baking sheet.
2   In a bowl, whisk the egg whites until stiff peaks form, using an electric hand
    mixer, then gradually whisk in the sugar until the mixture is thick and shiny
    and the sugar dissolves. Add the cornstarch, vinegar, and grated chocolate and
    whisk until just combined. Spoon onto the prepared sheet and, using a palette
    knife, spread the mixture over the circle on the baking paper.
3   Bake in the hot oven 10 minutes, then turn the oven down to 275°F and continue
    cooking 1 hour. Turn the oven off and let the pavlova cool completely in the oven.
4   Remove the pavlova from the oven and transfer to a serving plate. Top with the
    chocolate chantilly cream and drizzle with melted chocolate just before serving.

058 Pavlova with white chocolate & passionfruit cream

PREPARATION TIME 15 minutes, plus cooling   **COOKING TIME** 30 minutes   **SERVES** 4 to 6

3 egg whites
1¹/₃ cups sugar
1 tsp. cornstarch
1 tsp. vanilla extract

3½oz. white chocolate, melted
   and left to cool
1 cup plus 2 tbsp. heavy cream,
   whipped to soft peaks
2 to 3 passionfruit

1   Preheat the oven to 300°F. Draw a 10in. circle on a sheet of baking paper, turn
    it over, and use to line a baking sheet.
2   In a large bowl, whisk the egg whites, sugar, cornstarch, vanilla extract, and
    ¼ cup boiling water, using an electric hand mixer, about 10 minutes until the
    mixture is very stiff. Spoon on to the prepared sheet and, using a palette knife,
    spread the mixture over the circle on the baking paper.
3   Bake in the warm oven 30 minutes, then turn the oven off and let the pavlova
    cool completely in the oven.
4   In a large bowl, gently fold the melted chocolate into the cream, using a metal
    spoon. Remove the pavlova from the oven, transfer to a serving plate, and
    spread the chocolate cream over the top. Remove the pulp from the
    passionfruit, using a sharp knife, and scatter evenly over the surface of the
    pavlova before serving.

059 Mini strawberry pavlovas with chocolate drizzle

PREPARATION TIME 20 minutes, plus cooling   **COOKING TIME** 45 minutes

2 egg whites
1/2 cup plus 2 tsp. sugar
1/2 tsp. white vinegar
1/2 tsp. vanilla extract
1/2 tsp. cornstarch
3/4 cup plus 1 tbsp. heavy cream

2 tbsp. powdered sugar
1 cup strawberries
31/2oz. bittersweet chocolate,
   melted and cooled

1   Preheat the oven to 200°F. Line a large baking sheet with baking paper.
2   In a bowl, whisk the egg whites until stiff peaks form, using an electric hand mixer, then gradually whisk in the sugar until the mixture is thick and shiny and the sugar dissolves. Fold in the vinegar, vanilla extract, and cornstarch, using a metal spoon. Make 4 circles of the mixture on the prepared sheet, forming a small indent in the middle of each one with the back of the spoon to create a cradle for the cream.
3   Bake in the warm oven 45 minutes, then turn the oven off and let the pavlovas cool completely in the oven.
4   In a clean bowl, whip the cream to soft peaks with the powdered sugar, using clean attachments for the electric hand mixer. Remove the pavlovas from the oven, transfer them to 4 plates, and divide the whipped cream between them. Divide the strawberries evenly between the pavlovas, placing them on top of the cream, then drizzle over the melted chocolate.

060 Mini mallow meringues with chocolate cream

PREPARATION TIME 15 minutes, plus cooling   **COOKING TIME** 55 to 60 minutes
MAKES 12 to 16 meringues

2 egg whites
1/2 cup plus 2 tsp. sugar
1/2 tsp. white vinegar
1/2 tsp. vanilla extract
1/2 tsp. cornstarch

1 recipe quantity Chocolate Chantilly
   Cream (see page 208)
powdered sugar, sifted, for dusting

1   Preheat the oven to 200°F. Line 2 baking sheets with baking paper.
2   In a bowl, whisk the egg whites until stiff peaks form, using an electric hand mixer, then gradually whisk in the sugar until the mixture is thick and shiny and the sugar dissolves. Add the vinegar, vanilla extract, and cornstarch and whisk for a few seconds until just combined. Place heaped teaspoonfuls of the mixture on the prepared baking sheets.
3   Bake in the warm oven 25 minutes. Turn the oven down to 170°F and leave the meringues in the oven an extra 30 to 35 minutes. Remove the meringues from the oven and let cool completely on the baking sheets, then place a spoonful of chocolate chantilly cream on top of each one and dust with powdered sugar.

061 Chocolate meringues with blackberries

PREPARATION TIME 15 minutes, plus cooling   **COOKING TIME** 40 minutes
MAKES 8 to 10 meringues

3 egg whites
2/3 cup sugar
1³/₄oz. bittersweet chocolate, grated,
   plus 1³/₄oz. melted and left to cool

1 recipe quantity Chocolate Chantilly
   Cream (see page 208)
1¹/₂ cups blackberries
powdered sugar, sifted, for dusting

1 Preheat the oven to 275°F. Line 2 baking sheets with baking paper.
2 In a bowl, whisk the egg whites until stiff peaks form, using an electric hand
    mixer, then gradually whisk in the sugar until the mixture is thick and shiny and
    the sugar dissolves. Gently fold in the grated chocolate and cocoa, using a metal
    spoon. Place 16 to 20 heaped tablespoonfuls of the meringue mixture on the
    prepared sheets.
3 Bake in the warm oven 40 minutes, then turn the oven off and let the meringues
    cool completely in the oven.
4 Remove the meringues from the oven and sandwich them together in pairs
    with the chocolate chantilly cream. Divide between 4 plates and drizzle with the
    melted chocolate. Serve with the blackberries, dusted with powdered sugar.

062 Chocolate hazelnut meringues

PREPARATION TIME 20 minutes, plus cooling   **COOKING TIME** 30 minutes
MAKES 10 meringues

3 egg whites
$^3/_4$ cup plus 2 tbsp. sugar
1 tsp. cornstarch
$^2/_3$ cup toasted hazelnuts, chopped

$5^1/_2$oz. bittersweet chocolate, melted
   and cooled
1 recipe quantity Chocolate Chantilly
   Cream (see page 208)

1   Preheat the oven to 300°F. Line 2 large baking sheets with baking paper.
2   In a bowl, whisk the egg whites until stiff peaks form, using an electric hand mixer, then gradually whisk in the sugar until the mixture is thick and shiny and the sugar dissolves. Using a metal spoon, fold in the cornstarch, half the hazelnuts, and the melted chocolate, to create a swirled effect. Place 20 heaped tablespoonfuls of the meringue mixture on the prepared sheets and top with the remaining hazelnuts.
3   Bake in the warm oven 30 minutes, then turn off the oven and let the meringues cool completely in the oven.
4   To serve, sandwich the chocolate hazelnut meringues together in pairs, using the chocolate chantilly cream.

063 Poached meringues with chocolate sauce

PREPARATION TIME 20 minutes   **COOKING TIME** 8 minutes

4 egg whites
$^3/_4$ cup plus 2 tbsp. sugar
1 tsp. vanilla extract

1 recipe quantity Rich Chocolate
   Sauce (see page 204)
3 tbsp. slivered almonds, roasted

1   In a bowl, whisk the egg whites until stiff peaks form, using an electric hand mixer, then gradually whisk in the sugar until the mixture is thick and shiny and the sugar dissolves. Whisk in the vanilla extract.
2   Bring a large, wide pan of water to a boil and turn down to a simmer. Shape the meringue into rounded ovals, using 2 large spoons (you will need to make 8 in all), and poach them 4 at a time in the water for 2 minutes on each side.
3   Remove the meringues from the water with a slotted spoon and set aside to drain on paper towel. Place 2 meringues on each plate and top with the rich chocolate sauce. Sprinkle with slivered almonds and serve immediately.

064 Chocolate ganache meringues

PREPARATION TIME 20 minutes, plus cooling **COOKING TIME** 55 minutes
MAKES 4 to 6 meringues

3 egg whites
¾ cup sugar
1 tsp. cornstarch
1 tsp. vinegar

½ recipe quantity Dark Chocolate
  Ganache (see page 209)
powdered sugar, sifted, for dusting

1 Preheat the oven to 350°F. Line a large baking sheet with baking paper.
2 In a bowl, whisk the egg whites until stiff peaks form, using an electric hand mixer, then gradually whisk in the sugar until the mixture is thick and shiny and the sugar dissolves. Fold in the cornstarch and vinegar until well combined, using a metal spoon. Spoon 8 to 12 flattish rounds onto the prepared sheet.
3 Bake in the hot oven 5 minutes, then turn the oven down to 250°F and continue to cook 45 minutes. Remove from the oven and transfer the meringues to a wire rack to cool completely.
4 Spread a spoonful of the dark chocolate ganache over half of the meringues and top with a spoonful of crème fraîche to complete the filling. Sandwich a second meringue on top of the filling and dust all the meringues with powdered sugar just before serving.

065 Irish coffee meringue with chocolate

PREPARATION TIME 30 minutes, plus cooling **COOKING TIME** 60 minutes
MAKES 1 x 9in. meringue

6 egg whites
1⅓ cups sugar
1 tbsp. instant coffee powder
1 tbsp. unsweetened cocoa powder

1½ cups plus 2 tbsp. heavy cream
2 tbsp. coffee liqueur
3½oz. bittersweet chocolate, melted
  and cooled

1 Preheat the oven to 200°F. Line 2 baking sheets with baking paper and draw 2 x 9in. circles on the paper in pencil.
2 In a bowl, whisk the egg whites until stiff peaks form, using an electric hand mixer, then gradually whisk in the sugar until the mixture is thick and shiny and the sugar dissolves. Whisk in the coffee and cocoa. Spoon the mixture onto the prepared sheets and, using a palette knife, spread it over the circles on the baking paper.
3 Bake in the warm oven 60 minutes until the meringue is crisp but not brown. Remove from the oven and let the meringues cool completely on the sheets.
4 In a clean bowl, whisk the cream and liqueur together, using an electric hand mixer, to form soft peaks. To assemble the meringue, place 1 round on a serving tray, spread with half the liqueur cream and drizzle with half the melted chocolate. Repeat with the second meringue, remaining cream, and chocolate for the top layer, then refrigerate the meringue 2 hours before serving.

066 Chocolate floating islands

PREPARATION TIME 45 minutes, plus chilling   **COOKING TIME** 25 to 30 minutes
SERVES 4 to 6

4 eggs, separated
1$^1/_3$ cups sugar
1 tsp. vanilla extract
4$^1/_3$ cups milk
4$^1/_2$oz. bittersweet chocolate,
   broken into pieces

FOR THE TOPPING:
$^1/_2$ cup sugar
3 tbsp. slivered almonds, toasted

1   In a large bowl, beat the egg yolks together with $^1/_3$ cup plus 4 tsp. of the sugar
    and the vanilla extract, using an electric hand mixer. In a small saucepan, heat
    the milk and chocolate together over low heat until just melted. Remove from
    the heat and whisk the chocolate milk into the egg mixture, using an electric
    hand mixer.

2   Return the mixture to the saucepan and cook over low heat, stirring constantly
    with a wooden spoon until the mixture thickens and coats the back of the spoon.
    Do not allow to boil. Immediately remove from the heat and pour into a large,
    shallow serving bowl. Set the custard aside to cool 10 minutes. Cover the bowl
    with plastic wrap (to prevent a skin forming) and let cool completely, then
    refrigerate 2 hours or overnight.

3   For the floating islands, in a clean bowl, whisk the egg whites to soft peaks,
    using an electric hand mixer, then gradually whisk in the sugar until the mixture
    is thick and shiny and the sugar dissolves.

4   Bring a large, wide pan of water to a boil and turn down to a simmer. Shape the
    meringue into rounded ovals, the "floating islands," using 2 large spoons, and
    poach them 4 at a time in the water 2 minutes on each side. (You will need to
    make 8 to 12 in all, depending on the number of people.) Remove the meringues
    from the water with a slotted spoon and set aside to drain on absorbent paper.
    Place the meringues on top of the custard to create the floating islands.

5   For the topping, in a medium-sized saucepan, dissolve the sugar in 2 tbsp. water
    over low heat, then boil vigorously 10 to 12 minutes until the mixture becomes a
    dark golden color. Cool slightly, then pour the caramel over the floating islands
    and sprinkle with the almonds. Refrigerate the assembled dessert a further
    20 to 30 minutes before serving.

067 Chocolate meringue kisses

PREPARATION TIME 15 minutes   **COOKING TIME** 15 minutes   **MAKES** 12 meringues

2 egg whites
$^1/_3$ cup plus 4 tsp. sugar

$^1/_4$ tsp. vanilla extract
1$^3/_4$oz. bittersweet chocolate, grated

1   Preheat the oven to 275°F. Line a large baking sheet with baking paper.

2   In a bowl, whisk the egg whites until stiff peaks form, using an electric hand
    mixer, then gradually whisk in the sugar until the mixture is thick and shiny
    and the sugar dissolves. Whisk in the vanilla extract and chocolate just until
    combined. Place heaped teaspoons of the mixture on the prepared sheet.

3   Bake in the warm oven 15 minutes. Turn the oven off and let the kisses cool
    completely in the oven 1 hour before serving.

068 Hot chocolate soufflés

PREPARATION TIME 25 minutes   **COOKING TIME** 20 to 23 minutes

melted butter, for greasing
1/3 cup sugar, plus extra for coating
2 tbsp. cornstarch
1 cup plus 2 tbsp. milk

3½oz. bittersweet chocolate,
   broken into pieces
3 eggs, separated, plus 2 whites
powdered sugar, sifted, for dusting

1   Preheat the oven to 375°F. Grease 4 x 6oz. ramekins or ovenproof cups with
    melted butter and coat lightly with sugar.
2   In a small bowl, mix the cornstarch to a paste with 2 tbsp. of the milk.
    In a medium-sized saucepan, heat the remaining milk with the chocolate
    and 3 tbsp. plus 1 tsp. of the sugar over low heat. When the chocolate has
    melted, whisk in the cornstarch paste, using a hand whisk. Continue whisking
    until the mixture boils and thickens, then turn down to a simmer and cook
    1 minute more. Remove from the heat and allow to cool a few minutes before
    beating in the egg yolks. Set the mixture aside to cool completely.
3   In a large bowl, whisk all the egg whites to soft peaks, using an electric hand
    mixer, then add the remaining sugar and continue to whisk until stiff but not
    dry. Gently fold the whisked whites into the chocolate mixture, using a metal
    spoon, and divide equally between the prepared cups.
4   Bake in the hot oven 15 to 18 minutes, or until the soufflés rise well.
    Remove from the oven, dust with powdered sugar, and serve immediately.

069 Hot mocha & rum soufflés

PREPARATION TIME 25 minutes **COOKING TIME** 20 to 23 minutes

melted butter, for greasing
5 tbsp. plus 1 tsp. sugar,
  plus extra for coating
2 tbsp. cornstarch
1 cup plus 2 tbsp. milk

3½oz. bittersweet chocolate,
  broken into pieces
2 tsp. instant coffee powder
1 tbsp. dark rum
3 eggs, separated, plus 2 whites
powdered sugar, sifted, for dusting

1 Preheat the oven to 375°F. Grease 4 x 6oz. ramekins with melted butter
and coat lightly with sugar.
2 In a small bowl, mix the cornstarch to a paste with 2 tbsp. of the milk. In a
medium-sized saucepan, heat the remaining milk with 3 tbsp. plus 1 tsp.
of the sugar and the chocolate, coffee, and rum. When the chocolate is melted,
whisk in the cornstarch paste, using a hand whisk. Continue whisking until the
mixture boils and thickens, then turn down to a simmer and cook 1 minute
more. Remove from the heat and allow to cool a few minutes before beating
in the egg yolks. Set the mixture aside to cool completely.
3 In a large bowl, whisk all the egg whites to soft peaks, using an electric hand
mixer, then add the remaining sugar and continue to whisk until stiff but not
dry. Gently fold the whisked whites into the chocolate mixture, using a metal
spoon, and divide equally between the prepared ramekins.
4 Bake in the hot oven 15 to 18 minutes, or until the soufflés rise well. Remove
from the oven, dust with powdered sugar, and serve immediately.

070 White chocolate soufflés

PREPARATION TIME 30 minutes **COOKING TIME** 35 to 40 minutes

melted butter, for greasing
⅓ cup plus 4 tsp. sugar, plus
  extra for coating
7 tbsp. butter, softened

5½oz. white chocolate, broken
  into pieces
2 eggs, separated
½ cup plus 2 tbsp. all-purpose flour
powdered sugar, sifted, for dusting

1 Preheat the oven to 350°F. Grease 4 x 6oz. ramekins with melted butter and
coat lightly with sugar.
2 In a small saucepan, heat the butter and chocolate together until just melted,
remove from the heat, and set aside to cool.
3 In a large bowl, beat the egg yolks and remaining sugar together until light
and creamy, using an electric hand mixer, and stir in the cooled chocolate
mixture and flour. In a clean bowl, whisk the egg whites until they form stiff
peaks, using clean attachments for the electric hand mixer, then gently fold
into the chocolate mixture, using a metal spoon. Divide the mixture evenly
between the prepared ramekin dishes.
4 Bake in a bain marie (see page 10) in the hot oven 30 to 35 minutes, or until
slightly puffed and just firm. Remove from the oven and serve the soufflés
warm, dusted with powdered sugar.

071 Chestnut & chocolate soufflés

PREPARATION TIME 35 minutes   **COOKING TIME** 20 to 23 minutes

melted butter, for greasing
1/3 cup sugar, plus extra for coating
2 tbsp. cornstarch
1 cup plus 2 tbsp. milk
3½oz. bittersweet chocolate,
   broken into pieces

1/4 cup canned, sweetened
   chestnut purée
3 eggs, separated, plus 2 whites
powdered sugar, sifted, for dusting

1   Preheat the oven to 375°F. Grease 4 x 6oz. ramekins with melted butter and
    coat lightly with sugar.
2   In a small bowl, mix the cornstarch to a paste with 2 tbsp. of the milk. In a small
    saucepan, heat the remaining milk with the chocolate and 3 tbsp. plus 1 tsp. of
    the sugar over low heat. When the chocolate has melted, whisk in the cornstarch
    paste, using a hand whisk. Continue whisking until the mixture boils and
    thickens, then turn down to a very low heat and cook 1 minute more. Remove
    the pan from the heat and allow the mixture to cool a few minutes before
    beating in the egg yolks and chestnut purée.
3   In a large bowl, whisk all the egg whites to soft peaks, using an electric hand
    mixer, then add the remaining sugar and continue to whisk until stiff but not
    dry. Gently fold the whisked whites into the chocolate mixture, using a metal
    spoon, and divide equally between the prepared ramekins.
4   Bake in the hot oven 15 to 18 minutes, or until the soufflés rise well.
    Remove from the oven, dust with powdered sugar, and serve immediately.

072 Chilled dark mocha soufflés

PREPARATION TIME 30 minutes, plus chilling   **COOKING TIME** 5 minutes

1¼ cups plus 1 tbsp. milk
2¾oz. bittersweet chocolate,
   broken into pieces
2 tsp. instant coffee powder
3 egg yolks
1/4 cup sugar

3 sheets leaf gelatin
1½ cups heavy cream, whipped
   to soft peaks
chocolate-coated coffee beans,
   to decorate (optional)
cocoa powder, sifted, for dusting

1   Prepare 4 x 5oz. soufflé dishes by wrapping a 2in. wide strip of foil around
    the outside of each dish and tying it in place with string. The foil should stand
    ¾in. above the rim of the dish.
2   In a small saucepan, heat the milk, chocolate, and coffee together over low heat
    until just melted, then remove the pan from the heat and stir with a wooden
    spoon until smooth. In a large bowl, beat the yolks and sugar together, using an
    electric hand mixer, then whisk in the warm chocolate milk. Return the mixture
    to the pan, return to the heat and continue cooking, stirring constantly with a
    wooden spoon, until the mixture thickens into a custard and coats the back of
    the spoon. Do not allow to boil.
3   Meanwhile, in a bowl, soak the gelatin sheets in cold water 5 to 10 minutes until
    soft, then remove them, wring out any excess water, and stir into the warm
    custard until they dissolve. Pour the mixture into a clean bowl and let cool.
    Gently fold three-quarters of the cream into the cooled mixture, using a metal
    spoon, then divide evenly between the prepared dishes. Refrigerate 2 hours
    or overnight.
4   To serve, remove the foil collars and decorate the soufflés with the remaining
    cream, chocolate-coated coffee beans, if using, and a sprinkling of cocoa.

073 Chilled chocolate & raspberry soufflés

PREPARATION TIME 30 minutes, plus chilling **COOKING TIME** 5 minutes

1 cup plus 2 tbsp. milk
2¾oz. bittersweet chocolate,
  broken into pieces
3 egg yolks
¼ cup sugar

3 sheets leaf gelatin
½ cup puréed raspberries
¾ cup plus 1 tbsp. heavy cream,
  whipped to soft peaks

1 Prepare 4 x 5oz. soufflé dishes by wrapping a 2in. wide strip of foil around the outside of each dish and tying it in place with string. The foil should stand ¾in. above the rim of the dish.

2 In a small saucepan, heat the milk and chocolate together over low heat until just melted, then remove the pan from the heat and stir with a wooden spoon until smooth. In a large bowl, whisk the yolks and sugar together, using an electric hand mixer, then whisk in the warm chocolate milk. Return the pan to the heat and continue cooking, stirring constantly with a wooden spoon, until the mixture thickens and coats the back of the spoon. Do not allow to boil.

3 Meanwhile, in a bowl, soak the gelatin sheets in cold water 5 to 10 minutes until soft, then remove them, wring out any excess water, and stir into the warm custard until they dissolve. Pour the mixture into a clean bowl and let cool.

4 Gently fold the raspberry purée and cream into the cooled custard, using a metal spoon, then divide equally between the prepared dishes. Refrigerate 2 hours or overnight. Remove the foil collars before serving.

074 Chilled white chocolate & passionfruit soufflés

PREPARATION TIME 30 minutes, plus chilling **COOKING TIME** 5 minutes

1¼ cups plus 1 tbsp. milk
3½oz. white chocolate,
  broken into pieces
1 tsp. vanilla extract
3 egg yolks

3 tbsp. sugar
3 sheets leaf gelatin
1¾ cups plus 2 tbsp. heavy cream,
  whipped to soft peaks
3 passionfruit

1 Prepare 4 x 5oz. soufflé dishes by wrapping a 2in. wide strip of foil around the outside of each dish and tying it in place with string. The foil should stand ¾in. above the rim of the dish.

2 In a medium-sized saucepan, heat the milk, chocolate, and vanilla together over low heat until just melted. Remove the pan from the heat and stir the mixture with a wooden spoon until smooth. In a large bowl, beat the yolks and sugar together, using an electric hand mixer, and whisk in the warm milk. Return the mixture to the pan, return to the heat, and continue cooking, stirring constantly with a wooden spoon, until the mixture thickens and coats the back of the spoon. Do not allow to boil.

3 Meanwhile, in a bowl, soak the gelatin sheets in cold water 5 to 10 minutes until soft, then remove them, wring out any excess water, and stir into the warm custard until they dissolve. Pour the mixture into a clean bowl and let cool. Gently fold two-thirds of the whipped cream into the cooled mixture, using a metal spoon.

4 Half-fill each of the prepared dishes with soufflé mix, reserving half of the mix for later. Remove the pulp from the passionfruit, using a sharp knife, and place a spoonful in each half-filled dish, reserving some for decoration. Spoon over the remaining soufflé mixture. Refrigerate 2 hours or overnight.

5 To serve, remove the foil collars and decorate the soufflés with the remaining whipped cream and the reserved passionfruit pulp.

075 Chocolate fondue

PREPARATION TIME 10 minutes   **COOKING TIME** 5 minutes

10½oz. bittersweet chocolate,
  broken into pieces
¾ cup plus 1 tbsp. heavy cream
1 tsp. vanilla extract

assorted fruits, cut into pieces,
  for dipping, such as apples, pears,
  peaches, bananas

1   In a small saucepan, heat the chocolate and cream together over low heat until melted. Remove the pan from the heat and stir the mixture with a wooden spoon until smooth. Stir in the vanilla extract.
2   Pour the warm fondue into a serving bowl (a purpose-made fondue bowl with a small candlewarmer underneath would be ideal) or small dish and surround it with your choice of fresh fruit pieces.

076 Chocolate & coconut cream fondue

PREPARATION TIME 10 minutes **COOKING TIME** 5 minutes

10½oz. bittersweet chocolate,
  broken into pieces
¾ cup plus 1 tbsp. coconut cream
1 tbsp. white or dark rum

1 tsp. vanilla extract
1 pineapple, cored, peeled, and cut
  into bite-size cubes, for dipping

1   In a small saucepan, heat the chocolate and coconut cream together over low heat until the chocolate is just melted. Remove the pan from the heat and stir the mixture with a wooden spoon until smooth. Add the rum and vanilla extract.
2   Pour the fondue into a fondue bowl (see recipe 075) or small dish and serve with pineapple pieces for dipping.

077 Marbled chocolate fondue

PREPARATION TIME 10 minutes   **COOKING TIME** 5 minutes

9oz. bittersweet chocolate,
  broken into pieces
¾ cup plus 1 tbsp. heavy cream

1 tsp. vanilla extract
1¾oz. white chocolate, grated
strawberries, for dipping

1   In a small saucepan, heat the chocolate and cream together over low heat until the chocolate is just melted. Remove the pan from the heat and stir the mixture with a wooden spoon until smooth. Stir in the vanilla extract.
2   Pour the chocolate mixture into a fondue bowl (see recipe 075) or small dish and sprinkle over the grated white chocolate. As the white chocolate starts to melt, gently run a knife through the mixture to create a marbled effect. Serve the fondue immediately, with strawberries for dipping.

078 Chocolate liqueur fondue

PREPARATION TIME 10 minutes **COOKING TIME** 5 minutes

10½oz. bittersweet chocolate,
    broken into pieces
¾ cup plus 1 tbsp. heavy cream
1 tsp. instant coffee powder

1 tbsp. coffee or hazelnut liqueur
1 tsp. vanilla extract
ladyfinger cookies, for dipping

1   In a medium-sized saucepan, heat the chocolate, cream, and coffee together over low heat until the chocolate is just melted. Remove the pan from the heat and stir the mixture with a wooden spoon until smooth. Stir in the liqueur and the vanilla extract.

2   Pour the fondue into a fondue bowl (see recipe 075) or small dish and serve immediately with the ladyfingers for dipping.

079 Italian chocolate custard cake

PREPARATION TIME 20 minutes, plus chilling   **COOKING TIME** 15 to 18 minutes
MAKES 1 x 9in. cake

½ stick butter, melted and left
   to cool, plus extra for greasing
4 eggs, separated
½ cup plus 2 tsp. sugar
1 cup all-purpose flour

1 recipe quantity Chocolate Pastry
   Cream (see page 12)
1 recipe quantity Chocolate Rum
   Frosting (see page 212)

1   Preheat the oven to 375°F. Grease 2 x 9in. round pans with butter and line the bottoms with baking paper.
2   In a large bowl, beat the yolks and sugar together with an electric hand mixer until thick and creamy. In a clean bowl, whisk the egg whites, using clean attachments for the electric hand mixer, and fold into the mixture with the flour and melted butter until just combined. Divide the mixture evenly between the prepared pans.
3   Bake in the hot oven 15 to 18 minutes, or until the cakes rise and turn golden brown. Remove from the oven and let the cakes cool 10 minutes in the pans, before turning out to cool completely on a wire rack.
4   Sandwich the cakes together with the chocolate pastry cream. Using a palette knife, spread the chocolate rum frosting over the top and sides of the cake. Refrigerate 1 hour before serving.

080 Chocolate mousse cake

PREPARATION TIME 30 minutes   **COOKING TIME** 25 to 30 minutes   **MAKES** 1 x 8in. cake

7 tbsp. butter, chopped,
   plus extra for greasing
5½oz. bittersweet chocolate,
   broken into pieces
5 eggs, separated
½ cup plus 2 tsp. sugar

⅔ cup heavy cream, whipped
   to soft peaks
2 tbsp. powdered sugar
1 tbsp. orange liqueur (optional)
chocolate curls, for decorating

1   Preheat the oven to 325°F. Grease an 8in. springform pan with butter and line the bottom with baking paper.
2   In a small saucepan, heat the chocolate and butter together over low heat until just melted, stirring with a wooden spoon until smooth. Set aside to cool 10 minutes. In a large bowl, beat the egg yolks and sugar together until thick and creamy, using an electric hand mixer, then stir in the melted chocolate mixture to form the cake mixture. Put ¼ cup of this mixture in a small bowl and set aside for making the mousse later. In a clean bowl, whisk the egg whites until stiff but not dry, using clean attachments for the electric hand mixer, then fold them into the cake mixture. Pour into the prepared pan.
3   Bake in the hot oven 20 to 25 minutes, or until the cake is firm around the edges but still soft in the middle. Remove from the oven and let cool in the pan completely (the middle will fall, but this will later be filled by the mousse).
4   To make the mousse, fold the cream, powdered sugar, and liqueur (if using) into the reserved cake mixture, using a metal spoon, until just combined. Spoon the mousse into the middle of the chocolate cake, then decorate with chocolate curls before serving.

081 Chocolate celebration tarts

PREPARATION TIME 25 minutes, plus chilling **COOKING TIME** 15 to 17 minutes
MAKES 18 tarts

1 recipe quantity Chocolate
   Shortcrust Pastry, uncooked
   (see page 13)
³/₄ cup plus 2 tbsp. heavy cream

7oz. bittersweet chocolate,
   broken into pieces
8 tsp. Marsala wine or Kahlua
1 sheet edible gold leaf (optional)
powdered sugar, sifted, for dusting

1 Preheat the oven to 400°F.
2 Roll the pastry dough out to ¼in. thick on a lightly floured surface. Using an
   appropriately sized round pastry cutter, cut out 18 circles to fit the holes of
   2 x 12-hole tartlette pans and place them in the holes. Prick the bottoms of the
   tart shell circles with a fork, then refrigerate 30 minutes.
3 Bake in the hot oven 10 to 12 minutes, or until firm. Remove from the oven
   and let the baked tart shells cool 5 minutes in the pans, then remove from
   the pans.
4 For the filling, heat the cream in a small saucepan over low heat until almost
   simmering, then remove from the heat. Add the chocolate, stir until smooth,
   and then add the liqueur. Set aside to cool. Spoon the cooled mixture into the
   prepared tart shells, top with a small piece of gold leaf, if using, and dust with
   powdered sugar.

082 Chocolate meringue tart

PREPARATION TIME 30 minutes **COOKING TIME** 50 to 55 minutes **MAKES** 1 x 9in. tart

1 x 9in. Chocolate Shortcrust
   Pastry shell, baked (see page 13)
1 cup plus 2 tbsp. sweetened
   condensed milk
1 tsp. vanilla extract

2 tbsp. unsweetened cocoa powder,
   sifted
2 tbsp. all-purpose flour
3 eggs, separated
½ stick butter, chopped
150g/5¹/₂oz/²/₃ cup sugar

1 Preheat the oven to 350°F. Place the baked tart shell on a baking sheet.
2 In a medium-sized saucepan, heat the condensed milk and vanilla extract over
   low heat 3 minutes, stirring constantly with a wooden spoon. Add the cocoa and
   flour, stirring well until combined, then remove the pan from the heat and stir
   in the egg yolks and butter. Pour the mixture into the prepared tart shell, being
   careful not to overfill it.
3 Bake in the hot oven 35 to 40 minutes, or until the filling is just set. Remove the
   tart from the oven and set aside in the pan.
4 In a clean bowl, whisk the egg whites to stiff peaks, using an electric hand mixer,
   then gradually whisk in the sugar until thick and glossy. Spread the meringue
   over the chocolate filling and return the tart to the hot oven 8 to 10 minutes,
   or until the meringue is golden brown. Remove from the oven and serve warm.

083   Chocolate raspberry ganache torte

PREPARATION TIME 40 minutes, plus setting   **COOKING TIME** 25 to 30 minutes
MAKES 1 x 9in. torte

butter, for greasing
3 eggs, separated, plus 3 yolks
$^1/_3$ cup plus 4 tsp. sugar
¼ cup all-purpose flour
¼ cup unsweetened cocoa powder

$^1/_2$ tsp. baking powder
2 x recipe quantity Dark Chocolate
  Ganache (see page 209)
3 tbsp. raspberry jam

1   Preheat the oven to 375°F. Grease 2 x 9in. round pans with butter and line the bottoms with baking paper.
2   In a large bowl, beat all the egg yolks and the sugar together until thick and creamy, using an electric mixer. In a separate bowl, sift the flour, cocoa, and baking powder together and fold into the egg mixture. In a third bowl, whisk the egg whites until stiff but not dry, using clean attachments for the electric hand mixer, and fold into the cake mixture. Divide the mixture evenly between the prepared pans.
3   Bake in the hot oven 25 to 30 minutes, or until the cakes rise and turn dark brown. Remove from the oven and let the cakes cool in the pans 10 minutes, then remove from the pans and transfer to a wire rack to cool completely.
4   Using a palette knife, sandwich the cakes together with a thick layer of dark chocolate ganache and then a layer of raspberry jam. Spread the remaining ganache over the top and sides of the torte. Leave the iced cake to set 1 hour at room temperature before serving.

084   Mocha truffle tart

PREPARATION TIME 40 minutes, plus chilling   **COOKING TIME** 5 minutes   **MAKES** 1 x 9in. tart

9oz. bittersweet chocolate,
  broken into pieces
1 stick plus 3 tbsp. butter, chopped
2 tbsp. instant coffee powder
4 egg yolks
$^1/_3$ cup plus 4 tsp. sugar

1 x 9in. Chocolate Shortcrust
  Pastry shell, baked (see page 13)
½ cup plus 2 tbsp. heavy cream,
  whipped to soft peaks
cocoa powder, sifted, for dusting

1   In a small saucepan, melt the chocolate, butter, and coffee together over low heat until just melted. Remove the pan from the heat and stir until smooth, then pour into a clean bowl and set aside to cool.
2   In a large bowl, beat the egg yolks and sugar together until thick and creamy, using an electric hand mixer. Stir in half the chocolate mixture, using a wooden spoon, and pour into the baked tart shell. Fold the cream into the remaining chocolate mixture, using a metal spoon, and pour into the tart shell, over the first layer. Refrigerate 1 hour. Dust cocoa over the top of the tart before serving.

085 White chocolate & lime tart

PREPARATION TIME 15 minutes, plus chilling   **COOKING TIME** 5 minutes   **MAKES** 1 x 9in. tart

¾ cup plus 1 tbsp. heavy cream
10½oz. white chocolate, broken
   into pieces

zest of 2 limes, plus 1 lime,
   thinly sliced
1 Chocolate Crumb Crust, baked
   (see page 13)

1   In a small saucepan, heat the cream and chocolate together over low heat until
    the chocolate is just melted, then remove from the heat and stir until smooth,
    using a wooden spoon. Stir in the lime zest, then set aside to cool 10 minutes.
2   Pour the mixture into the baked crumb crust and refrigerate 2 hours or until
    set. Decorate with lime slices before serving.

086 White chocolate mousse cake

PREPARATION TIME 25 minutes   **COOKING TIME** 35 to 40 minutes   **MAKES** 1 x 9in. cake

2 tbsp. butter, chopped,
   plus extra for greasing
7oz. white chocolate, half broken
   into pieces, and half melted
   and left to cool, plus shavings
   to decorate

1¼ cups plus 1 tbsp. heavy cream
4 eggs, separated
3 tbsp. plus 1 tsp. sugar
2½ tbsp. all-purpose flour
1 cup raspberries

1   Preheat the oven to 300°F. Grease a 9in. springform pan with butter and line the
    bottom with baking paper.
2   In a small saucepan, heat the chocolate pieces, butter, and ¼ cup of the cream
    together over low heat until the chocolate just melts. Remove the pan from the
    heat and stir until smooth, using a wooden spoon, then set aside to cool.
3   In a large bowl, beat the egg yolks and sugar together, using an electric hand
    mixer, until pale and creamy. Stir in the flour and the chocolate mixture, using
    a wooden spoon. In a clean bowl, whisk the egg whites until stiff but not dry,
    using clean attachments for the electric hand mixer. Gently fold the whisked
    whites into the chocolate cake mixture, using a metal spoon, then pour into the
    prepared pan.
4   Bake in the hot oven 30 to 35 minutes, or until the cake is just firm. Remove
    from the oven and let the cake cool completely in the pan. When cool, remove
    the cake from the pan and transfer to a serving plate.
5   In a clean bowl, lightly whip the remaining cream, using clean attachments for
    the electric hand mixer. (It will thicken when the chocolate is added, so be
    careful not to make it too stiff.) Gently fold the melted chocolate into it, using
    a metal spoon, then spoon the chocolate cream into the middle of the cake.
    Top the cake with raspberries and white chocolate shavings.

087 Chocolate lava cakes

PREPARATION TIME 10 minutes   **COOKING TIME** 15 to 18 minutes

7 tbsp. butter, chopped, plus extra
   for greasing
5½oz. bittersweet chocolate, broken
   into pieces

4 eggs
½ cup plus 2 tsp. sugar
1 cup plus 3 tbsp. all-purpose flour

1   Preheat the oven to 350°F. Grease 4 x 6oz. ramekins with butter.
2   In a small saucepan, heat the chocolate and butter together over low heat
    until just melted. Remove the pan from the heat and stir until smooth, using
    a wooden spoon, then set aside to cool. In a large bowl, beat the eggs and sugar
    together until thick and pale, using an electric hand mixer. Stir in the flour, then
    gently fold in the chocolate mixture, using a metal spoon. Divide the mixture
    evenly between the ramekins.
3   Bake in the hot oven 8 to 10 minutes. Remove from the oven and let the
    lava cakes cool in the ramekins a few minutes before turning out onto plates.
    Serve warm.

088 Sinful chocolate cake

PREPARATION TIME 35 minutes, plus chilling   **COOKING TIME** 5 minutes
SERVES 4 to 6

1 recipe quantity Chocolate Crumb
   Crust (see page 13)
¾ cup plus 1 tbsp. heavy cream
1 tsp. vanilla extract
7oz. bittersweet chocolate,
   broken into pieces

2⅓ cups raspberries, lightly crushed
2 eggs, separated
unsweetened cocoa powder, sifted,
   for dusting

1   Press the prepared chocolate crumb crust into the bottom of a 9in. square,
    loose-bottomed, fluted flan pan. You may not need all of the crust mixture.
    Refrigerate the prepared crust 15 minutes.
2   In a small saucepan, heat the cream, vanilla extract, and chocolate together
    over low heat until the chocolate is just melted. Remove the pan from the heat
    and stir with a wooden spoon until smooth. Set aside to cool. Spread the
    raspberries over the top of the chilled crumb crust.
3   In a clean bowl, whisk the egg whites until stiff, using an electric hand mixer.
    Stir the egg yolks into the cooled chocolate mixture, using a wooden spoon,
    then fold in the egg whites, using a metal spoon. Pour the mixture into the
    crumb crust, over the raspberries.
4   Refrigerate the cake 2 hours. Remove from the pan and dust with unsweetened
    cocoa before serving.

089 Sticky chocolate cake

PREPARATION TIME 25 minutes   **COOKING TIME** 50 to 55 minutes   **MAKES** 1 x 9in. cake

2 sticks plus 2 tbsp. butter,
   plus extra for greasing
1 cup plus 2 tbsp. heavy cream
6oz. bittersweet chocolate, broken
   into pieces
1 tsp. instant coffee powder
1$\frac{1}{3}$ cups packed light brown sugar
4 eggs, lightly beaten

2 tsp. vanilla extract
1$\frac{1}{2}$ cups plus 2 tbsp. self-rising flour
1 tsp. ground cinnamon
1 tsp. ground nutmeg
1 cup raisins
$\frac{3}{4}$ cup plus 2 tbsp. walnuts, chopped
1 recipe quantity Rich Chocolate
   Sauce (see page 204)

1   Preheat the oven to 325°F. Grease a 9in. springform pan with butter and line
    the bottom with baking paper.
2   In a small saucepan, heat the cream, chocolate, and coffee over low heat until
    the chocolate is just melted. Remove the pan from the heat and stir the mixture
    with a wooden spoon until smooth, then let cool. In a large bowl, beat the butter
    and sugar together, using an electric hand mixer, until light and creamy, then
    beat in the eggs gradually. Stir in the vanilla extract and chocolate mixture,
    using a wooden spoon. Gently fold in the flour, cinnamon, nutmeg, raisins, and
    walnuts, using a metal spoon, then pour the mixture into the prepared pan.
3   Bake in the hot oven 45 to 50 minutes, or until a skewer inserted into the middle
    comes out with just a few moist crumbs on it. Remove from the oven and let the
    cake cool in the pan 10 minutes.
4   Remove the cake from the pan and serve warm with the rich chocolate sauce.

090 Lemon roulade with chocolate drizzle

PREPARATION TIME 25 minutes, plus setting **COOKING TIME** 18 to 20 minutes
SERVES 4 to 6

butter, for greasing
¾ cup plus 1 tbsp. sugar
6 eggs, separated
8oz. bittersweet chocolate,
  melted and left to cool
2 tbsp. unsweetened cocoa powder

¼ cup lemon curd
juice and rind of 1 lemon,
  finely grated
1 cup plus 2 tbsp. heavy cream,
  whipped to soft peaks

1   Preheat the oven to 350°F. Grease a 9 x 13in. jelly roll pan with butter and line the bottom and sides with baking paper.
2   In a large bowl, beat the sugar and egg yolks together, using an electric hand mixer, until thick and creamy. Stir in 6oz. of the melted chocolate and the cocoa, using a wooden spoon. In a clean bowl, whisk the egg whites until stiff but not dry, using clean attachments for the electric hand mixer, then gently fold into the chocolate mixture, using a metal spoon. Pour the mixture into the prepared pan and spread evenly, using a palette knife.
3   Bake in the hot oven 18 to 20 minutes, or until firm. Remove from the oven and let cool completely in the pan. When cool, turn out onto a clean dish towel and remove the lining paper.
4   In a large bowl, mix the lemon curd with the lemon rind and juice, then fold into the cream, using a metal spoon. Spread the lemon cream evenly over the roulade.
5   Using the dish towel to help you, but making sure that it does not get trapped inside the roulade, gradually roll up the roulade jelly-roll style from a short end. Transfer carefully to a serving plate and drizzle the remaining melted chocolate over the top. Let set 30 minutes at room temperature before serving.

091 White chocolate roulade with raspberries

PREPARATION TIME 30 minutes **COOKING TIME** 15 to 18 minutes **SERVES** 4 to 6

butter, for greasing
½ cup plus 2 tsp. sugar
6 eggs, separated
6oz. white chocolate, melted
  and left to cool
2 tbsp. all-purpose flour

1 cup plus 2 tbsp. heavy cream,
  whipped to soft peaks
1½ cups raspberries, lightly crushed
bittersweet chocolate, grated,
  to sprinkle

1   Preheat the oven to 350°F. Grease a 9 x 13in. jelly roll pan with butter and line the bottom and sides with baking paper.
2   In a large bowl, beat the sugar and egg yolks together, using an electric hand mixer, until thick and creamy. Stir in the melted chocolate and flour, using a wooden spoon. In a clean bowl, whisk the egg whites until stiff but not dry, using clean attachments for the electric hand mixer, then gently fold into the chocolate mixture, using a metal spoon. Pour the mixture into the prepared pan and spread evenly, using a palette knife.
3   Bake in the hot oven 15 to 18 minutes, or until firm. Remove from the oven and let cool completely in the pan. When cool, turn out onto a clean dish towel and remove the lining paper.
4   Spread the cream evenly over the roulade and scatter over the raspberries. Using the dish towel to help you, but making sure that it does not get trapped inside the roulade, gradually roll up the roulade jelly-roll style from a short end. Transfer carefully to a serving plate. Sprinkle over the grated chocolate before serving.

092 Chocolate roulade with mixed berries & white chocolate cream

PREPARATION TIME 25 minutes   **COOKING TIME** 18 to 20 minutes   **SERVES** 4 to 6

butter, for greasing
³/₄ cup plus 1 tbsp. sugar
6 eggs, separated
6oz. bittersweet chocolate,
   melted and left to cool
2 tbsp. unsweetened cocoa powder

1 cup plus 2 tbsp. heavy cream,
   whipped to soft peaks
3¹/₂oz. white chocolate, melted
   and left to cool
1¹/₂ cups mixed berries
powdered sugar, sifted, for dusting

1   Preheat the oven to 350°F. Grease a 9 x 13in. jelly roll pan with butter and line the bottom and sides with baking paper.

2   In a large bowl, beat the sugar and egg yolks together, using an electric hand mixer, until thick and creamy. Stir in the melted bittersweet chocolate and cocoa, using a wooden spoon. In a clean bowl, whisk the egg whites until stiff but not dry, using clean attachments for the electric hand mixer, then gently fold into the chocolate mixture, using a metal spoon. Pour the mixture into the prepared pan and spread evenly, using a palette knife.

3   Bake in the hot oven 18 to 20 minutes, or until firm. Remove from the oven and let cool completely in the pan. When cool, turn out onto a clean dish towel and remove the lining paper.

4   In a large bowl, fold the cream and the melted white chocolate together, using a metal spoon, and spread evenly over the roulade. Scatter over the mixed berries, slicing any strawberries.

5   Using the dish towel to help you, but making sure that it does not get trapped inside the roulade, gradually roll up the roulade jelly-roll style from a short end. Transfer carefully to a serving plate, and dust with powdered sugar before serving.

093 Mocha roulade with chocolate mascarpone cream

PREPARATION TIME 20 minutes   **COOKING TIME** 18 to 20 minutes   **SERVES** 4 to 6

butter, for greasing
³/₄ cup plus 1 tbsp. sugar
6 eggs, separated
6oz. bittersweet chocolate, melted
   and left to cool
2 tbsp. unsweetened cocoa powder

3 tsp. instant coffee powder
1 recipe quantity Chocolate
   Mascarpone Cream (see page 208)
1 tbsp. heavy cream
2 tbsp. coffee liqueur
powdered sugar, sifted, for dusting

1   Preheat the oven to 350°F. Grease a 9 x 13in. jelly roll pan with butter and line the bottom and sides with baking paper.

2   In a large bowl, beat the sugar and egg yolks together, using an electric hand mixer, until thick and creamy. Stir in the melted chocolate, cocoa, and coffee, using a wooden spoon. In a clean bowl, whisk the egg whites until stiff but not dry, using clean attachments for the electric hand mixer, then gently fold into the chocolate mixture, using a metal spoon. Pour the mixture into the prepared pan and spread evenly, using a palette knife.

3   Bake in the hot oven 18 to 20 minutes, or until firm. Remove from the oven and let cool completely in the pan. When cool, turn out onto a clean dish towel and remove the lining paper.

4   In a large bowl, mix together the Chocolate Mascarpone Cream, cream, and liqueur, then spread evenly over the roulade. Using the dish towel to help you, but making sure that it does not get trapped inside the roulade, gradually roll up the roulade jelly-roll style from a short end. Transfer carefully to a serving plate and dust with powdered sugar before serving.

CHAPTER 2

Baking

There is nothing more wonderful than the smell of freshly
baked cakes, cookies, or tarts. For me, it brings back
precious memories of childhood—coming home after
school to a homemade chocolate cake or perhaps
a delicious muffin or cookie. I passed the tradition down
to the next generation, surprising my own children with
unexpected treats. And on birthdays, I would always
make sure there was a magnificent chocolate cake,
decorated with a creamy chocolate icing and dotted
with the appropriate number of candles.

Baking can be seen as complicated and time-consuming.
However, it really is a very simple skill to master and requires
only a light touch and good-quality, fresh ingredients.

I've put a large selection of recipes in this chapter,
including cakes, tarts, brownies, muffins, and cookies, so
you will find something for every occasion. Whether it is Rocky
Road Brownies for a casual family get-together or a Chocolate
Angel Food Cake as a centerpiece for a memorable birthday,
they're all here—just waiting for you to try them out!

094 Warm chocolate & nut torte

PREPARATION TIME 20 minutes   **COOKING TIME** 40 to 45 minutes   **MAKES** 1 x 9in. torte

1 stick plus 5 tbsp. butter, softened,
  plus extra for greasing
3/4 cup plus 1 tbsp. superfine sugar
1 tsp. vanilla extract
3 eggs, lightly beaten
13/4 cups ground almonds

3/4 cup walnuts, roasted
  and finely chopped
1/4 cup all-purpose flour
1/2 tsp. baking powder
1/4 cup Marsala wine
1 recipe quantity Dark Chocolate
  Ganache (see page 209)

1   Preheat the oven to 325°F. Grease a 9in. springform pan with butter and line
    the bottom with baking paper.
2   In a large bowl, beat the butter, sugar, and vanilla extract together until light
    and creamy, using an electric hand mixer. Beat in the eggs, one at a time.
    In a clean bowl, mix together the nuts, flour, and baking powder, using
    a wooden spoon. Fold into the butter mixture with the Marsala, then pour
    into the prepared pan.
3   Bake in the hot oven 40 to 45 minutes, or until the torte is lightly browned
    and firm in the middle. Remove from the oven and let the torte cool in the
    pan 10 minutes. Turn the torte out onto a wire rack and let cool completely.
4   To ice the torte, use a palette knife to spread the dark chocolate ganache
    over the top.

095 Chocolate chestnut cake

PREPARATION TIME 20 minutes   **COOKING TIME** 25 to 30 minutes   **MAKES** 1 x 9in. cake

butter, for greasing
4 eggs, separated
2/3 cup plus 11/2 tsp. superfine sugar
1 tsp. vanilla extract
9oz. canned, unsweetened chestnut
  purée

23/4oz. bittersweet chocolate, melted
  and left to cool
1 recipe quantity Shiny Chocolate
  Icing (see page 213)

1   Preheat the oven to 350°F. Grease a 9in. springform pan with butter and line
    the bottom with baking paper.
2   In a large bowl, beat the egg yolks, sugar, and vanilla extract until creamy,
    using an electric hand mixer. Add the chestnut purée, mixing well to combine,
    then stir in the melted chocolate. In a clean bowl, using clean attachments for
    the electric hand mixer, whisk the egg whites until stiff but not dry, and fold
    into the chocolate mixture with a metal spoon. Pour into the prepared pan.
3   Bake in the hot oven 25 to 30 minutes, or until a skewer inserted into the middle
    of the cake comes out dry. Remove from the oven and let the cake cool in the
    pan 10 minutes, then turn out onto a wire rack to cool completely.
4   To ice the cake, use a palette knife to spread the shiny chocolate icing over the top.

096 Chocolate berry torte

PREPARATION TIME 25 minutes   **COOKING TIME** 35 to 40 minutes   **MAKES** 1 x 9in. torte

2 tbsp. butter, chopped,
   plus extra for greasing
3¹/₂oz. bittersweet chocolate,
   broken into pieces
2 tbsp. heavy cream
4 eggs, separated

¹/₃ cup plus 2 tbsp. superfine sugar
2¹/₂ tbsp. all-purpose flour
2 tbsp. unsweetened cocoa powder
1 cup blueberries
powdered sugar, sifted, for dusting

1   Preheat the oven to 300°F. Grease a 9in. springform pan with butter and line the bottom with baking paper.
2   In a small saucepan, heat the butter, chocolate, and cream together over low heat until the chocolate is just melted. Remove the pan from the heat and set aside to cool.
3   In a large bowl, beat the egg yolks and 5 tbsp. of the sugar together until pale and creamy, using an electric hand mixer. Stir in the chocolate mixture, flour, and cocoa. In a clean bowl, whisk the egg whites until foamy, using clean attachments for the electric hand mixer, then gradually whisk in the remaining sugar until the mixture is thick and shiny. Gently fold the meringue mixture into the chocolate mixture and pour into the prepared pan. Sprinkle the blueberries over the top.
4   Bake in the warm oven 30 to 35 minutes, or until the torte is just firm to the touch. Remove the torte from the oven and let cool completely in the pan before turning out, then dust with powdered sugar.

097 Chocolate hazelnut torte

PREPARATION TIME 25 minutes   **COOKING TIME** 40 to 45 minutes   **MAKES** 1 x 9in. torte

1¹/₂ sticks butter, chopped,
   plus extra for greasing
6oz. bittersweet chocolate,
   broken into pieces
3 eggs, separated
³/₄ cup plus 1 tbsp. superfine sugar

³/₄ cup roasted hazelnuts,
   very finely chopped
2 tbsp. all-purpose flour
zest of 1 orange, grated
powdered sugar, sifted, for dusting

1   Preheat the oven to 325°F. Grease a 9in. springform pan with butter and line the bottom with baking paper.
2   In a small saucepan, heat the butter and chocolate together over low heat until just melted. Remove the pan from the heat and stir until smooth, using a wooden spoon, then set aside to cool.
3   In a large bowl, beat the egg yolks and half the sugar until light and creamy, using an electric hand mixer. Mix in the chocolate mixture, hazelnuts, flour, and orange zest. In a clean bowl, whisk the egg whites to soft peaks, using clean attachments for the electric hand mixer, then gradually whisk in the remaining sugar until the mixture is thick and shiny. Gently fold the meringue mixture into the chocolate mixture and pour into the prepared pan
4   Bake in the hot oven 35 to 40 minutes, or until the torte is just firm in the middle. Remove the torte from the oven, and let cool completely in the pan before turning out, then dust with powdered sugar.

098   Chocolate cake with Marsala

PREPARATION TIME 30 minutes   **COOKING TIME** 25 to 30 minutes   **MAKES** 1 x 9in. cake

1 stick plus 3 tbsp. butter, softened,
   plus extra for greasing
1 cup plus 4 tsp. superfine sugar
3 eggs, lightly beaten
3¹/₂oz. bittersweet chocolate, melted
   and left to cool
2 cups self-rising flour

2 tbsp. unsweetened cocoa powder
³/₄ cup milk
8 tbsp. Marsala wine
1 recipe quantity Chocolate Marsala
   Cream (see page 207)
1 recipe quantity Dark Chocolate
   Ganache (see page 209)

1   Preheat the oven to 325°F. Grease 2 x 9in. round pans with butter and line the
    bottoms with baking paper.
2   In a large bowl, beat the butter and sugar together until light and creamy,
    using an electric hand mixer, then beat in the eggs, one at a time, and the
    melted chocolate. In a clean bowl, sift together the flour and cocoa, then fold
    into the chocolate mixture with the milk and half of the Marsala until just
    blended. Pour into the prepared pans.
3   Bake in the hot oven 25 to 30 minutes, or until a skewer inserted into the middle
    of the cakes comes out with just a few moist crumbs on it. Remove from the
    oven. Pierce the top of the cakes 5 or 6 times with a skewer and brush over
    the remaining Marsala while they are still warm. Let the cakes cool in the
    pans 10 minutes, then remove from the pans and transfer to a wire rack
    to cool completely.
4   To finish the cake, sandwich the 2 halves together with the chocolate marsala
    cream, then transfer the cake to a serving plate and spread the dark chocolate
    ganache over the cake with a palette knife.

099   Mississippi mud cake

PREPARATION TIME 35 minutes   **COOKING TIME** 60 to 65 minutes   **MAKES** 1 x 9in. cake

1 stick plus 6 tbsp. butter, chopped,
   plus extra for greasing
3¹/₂oz. bittersweet chocolate, broken
   into pieces
1¹/₄ cups plus 1 tbsp. superfine sugar
2 tbsp. whisky

1 cup plus 3 tbsp. all-purpose flour
1 tbsp. self-rising flour
2 tbsp. unsweetened cocoa powder
2 eggs, lightly beaten
1 recipe quantity Chocolate Fudge
   Frosting (see page 212)

1   Preheat the oven to 325°F. Grease a 9in. springform pan with butter and line
    the bottom with baking paper.
2   In a small saucepan, melt the butter, chocolate, sugar, whisky, and scant
    ²/₃ cup water together over low heat until the chocolate is just melted. Pour into
    a clean bowl and stir with a wooden spoon until smooth, then set aside to cool
    10 minutes. In a clean bowl, mix the flours and cocoa together, then fold into
    the chocolate mixture with the eggs. Pour into the prepared pan.
3   Bake in the hot oven 55 to 60 minutes, or until a skewer inserted into the middle
    of the cake comes out slightly moist. Remove from the oven and let cool in the
    pan 15 minutes, then turn out onto a wire rack to cool completely.
4   To ice the cake, use a palette knife to spread the chocolate fudge frosting
    over the cake.

100 Chocolate banana bread

PREPARATION TIME 20 minutes **COOKING TIME** 50 to 55 minutes
MAKES 1 x 9 x 4½in. loaf

1 stick plus 1 tbsp. butter,
  softened, plus extra for greasing
  and to serve
²/₃ cup packed light brown sugar
2 eggs, lightly beaten

5½oz. bittersweet chocolate,
  melted and left to cool
3 ripe bananas, mashed
1 tsp. vanilla extract
1½ cups plus 2 tbsp. self-rising flour

1   Preheat the oven to 350°F. Grease a 9 x 4½in. loaf pan with butter and line the
    bottom with baking paper.

2   In a large bowl, beat the butter and sugar together until light and fluffy, using
    an electric hand mixer. Add the eggs, beating well, then stir in the melted
    chocolate, bananas, vanilla extract, and flour until just combined, using a
    wooden spoon. Spoon into the prepared pan.

3   Bake in the hot oven 50 to 55 minutes, or until a skewer inserted into the middle
    of the cake comes out with just a few crumbs clinging to it. Remove from the
    oven and let the cake cool in the pan 10 minutes, then turn out onto a wire rack
    to cool completely. Serve with butter for spreading.

101 Banana & chocolate loaf cake with liqueur

PREPARATION TIME 20 minutes   **COOKING TIME** 45 to 50 minutes
MAKES 1 x 9 x 4½in. loaf cake

6 tbsp. butter, softened, plus extra
  for greasing
⅓ cup plus 4 tsp. superfine sugar
1 egg, lightly beaten
1 tsp. vanilla extract
2 bananas, peeled and mashed

1 cup plus 3 tbsp. self-rising flour
2 tbsp. unsweetened cocoa powder
1 tsp. cinnamon
2 tbsp. Irish cream liqueur
2 tbsp. milk

1 Preheat the oven to 350°F. Grease a 9 x 4½in. loaf pan with butter and line the bottom with baking paper.
2 In a large bowl, beat the butter and sugar together until light and fluffy, using an electric hand mixer, and then beat in the egg. Add the vanilla extract and bananas and mix well with a wooden spoon to combine. Fold in the flour, cocoa, cinnamon, liqueur, and milk and pour into the prepared pan.
3 Bake in the hot oven 45 to 50 minutes, or until a skewer inserted into the middle of the cake comes out clean. Remove from the oven and let the cake cool in the pan 10 minutes, then turn out onto a wire rack to cool completely.

102 Chocolate banana swirl cake

PREPARATION TIME 30 minutes   **COOKING TIME** 30 to 35 minutes   **MAKES** 1 x 9in. cake

1½ sticks butter, softened,
  plus extra for greasing
1 cup plus 4 tsp. superfine sugar
3 eggs, lightly beaten
2 cups self-rising flour

1 tbsp. unsweetened cocoa powder
2 tbsp. milk
2 ripe bananas, mashed
powdered sugar, sifted, for dusting

1 Preheat the oven to 350°F. Grease a 9in. springform pan with butter and line the bottom with paper.
2 In a large bowl, whisk the butter and sugar together until pale and creamy, using an electric hand mixer, then add the eggs a little at a time until well combined. Fold in the flour, using a metal spoon. Divide the mixture in half. Mix the cocoa with the milk to make a paste and stir into one half, using a wooden spoon. Stir the banana into the remaining cake mixture. Spoon tablespoonfuls of the mixtures into the prepared pan so that both flavors are evenly distributed. Carefully drag a skewer through the mixture to create a swirl effect.
3 Bake in the hot oven 30 to 35 minutes, or until the cake is just firm. Remove from the oven and let the cake cool in the pan 10 minutes, then turn out onto a wire rack to cool completely and dust with powdered sugar.

103   Chocolate bundt cake

PREPARATION TIME 20 minutes   **COOKING TIME** 55 to 60 minutes   **MAKES** 1 x 10in. cake

1 stick plus 6 tbsp. butter, softened,
   plus extra for greasing
1³/₄ cups superfine sugar
3 eggs, lightly beaten
2 cups plus 4 tsp. self-rising flour
2 tbsp. unsweetened cocoa powder

²/₃ cup milk
1 tsp. vanilla extract
4¹/₂oz. bittersweet or milk
   chocolate chips
1 recipe quantity Shiny Chocolate
   Icing (see page 213)

1   Preheat the oven to 325°F. Grease a 10in. bundt pan with butter.
2   In a large bowl, beat the butter and sugar together until light and creamy, using
an electric hand mixer, then gradually whisk in the eggs. Fold in the flour, cocoa,
milk, vanilla extract, and chocolate chips until just combined, using a metal
spoon. Spoon into the prepared pan.
3   Bake in the hot oven 55 to 60 minutes, or until a skewer inserted into the middle
of the cake comes out clean. Remove from the oven and let the cake cool in the
pan 10 minutes. Turn the cake out on to a wire rack and, while still warm,
drizzle over the shiny chocolate icing.

104   All-in-one chocolate & sour cream cake

PREPARATION TIME 15 minutes   **COOKING TIME** 40 to 45 minutes   **MAKES** 1 x 9in. cake

butter, for greasing
2 cups self-rising flour
1 tsp. baking powder
3 tbsp. unsweetened cocoa powder
³/₄ cup plus 2 tbsp. superfine sugar
¹/₂ cup plus 1 tsp. packed light
   brown sugar
3¹/₂oz. bittersweet chocolate chips

1 cup plus 2 tbsp. sour cream
3 tbsp. vegetable oil
2 eggs
scant ¹/₂ cup milk
1 tsp. vanilla extract
1 recipe quantity Creamy Chocolate
   Icing (see page 212)

1   Preheat the oven to 350°F. Grease a 9in. springform pan with butter and line the
bottom with baking paper.
2   Place all of the ingredients, apart from the icing, in a large bowl and beat with
an electric hand mixer on low speed 2 minutes until just combined. Pour into
the prepared pan.
3   Bake in the hot oven 40 to 45 minutes, or until a skewer inserted in the middle
of the cake comes out with just a few crumbs on it. Remove from the oven
and let the cake cool in the pan 15 minutes, then turn out onto a wire rack
to cool completely.
4   To ice the cake, use a palette knife to spread over the creamy chocolate icing.

105   Simple chocolate & raspberry jam cake

PREPARATION TIME 20 minutes   **COOKING TIME** 50 to 55 minutes   **MAKES** 1 x 9in. cake

1½ sticks butter, chopped,
   plus extra for greasing
2 tbsp. raspberry jam
1 cup plus 4 tsp. superfine sugar
3 eggs, lightly beaten
2 cups self-rising flour

1 cup plus 2 tbsp. chocolate
   drink mix
scant ½ cup milk
1 recipe quantity Creamy Chocolate
   Icing (see page 212)

1   Preheat the oven to 350°F. Grease a 9in. springform pan with butter and line the bottom with baking paper.
2   In a small saucepan, melt the butter and raspberry jam together over low heat, then remove from the heat and set aside to cool slightly. In a large bowl, beat the sugar and eggs together until thick and pale, using an electric hand mixer. In a clean bowl, mix together the flour and chocolate drink mix, using a wooden spoon. Fold into the egg mixture with the melted butter and jam, and the milk. Pour into the prepared pan.
3   Bake in the hot oven 45 to 50 minutes until the cake is browned and just firm to the touch. Remove from the oven and let the cake cool in the pan 10 minutes, then turn out onto a wire rack to cool completely.
4   To ice the cake, use a palette knife to spread over the creamy chocolate icing.

106   Flourless chocolate & citrus cake

PREPARATION TIME 25 minutes   **COOKING TIME** 45 to 50 minutes   **MAKES** 1 x 9in. cake

1½ sticks butter, melted and left
   to cool, plus extra for greasing
6 eggs, separated
¾ cup plus 2 tbsp. superfine sugar
zest of 1 orange, finely grated
zest of 1 lemon, finely grated

½ cup orange juice
1¼ cups ground almonds
2 tbsp. unsweetened cocoa powder
9oz. bittersweet chocolate, melted
   and left to cool
powdered sugar, sifted, for dusting

1   Preheat the oven to 350°F. Grease a deep 9in. springform round cake pan with butter and line the bottom with baking paper.
2   In a large bowl, beat the egg yolks, sugar, and orange and lemon zest together until thick and pale, using an electric hand mixer. Stir in the melted butter and the orange juice. In a clean bowl, combine the ground almonds and cocoa, then fold into the egg mixture. In a clean bowl, whisk the egg whites to soft peaks, using clean attachments for the electric hand mixer, then pour in the melted chocolate and stir together. Fold into the cake mixture until just combined, using a metal spoon, then pour into the prepared pan.
3   Bake in the hot oven 45 to 50 minutes, or until the cake is firm around the edges but still slightly soft in the middle. Remove from the oven and let the cake cool completely in the pan, then remove the cake from the pan and dust with powdered sugar.

107 Pear, pistachio & chocolate loaf cake

PREPARATION TIME 30 minutes **COOKING TIME** 55 to 60 minutes
MAKES 1 x 9 x 4½in. loaf cake

1 stick plus 3 tbsp. butter, softened,
  plus extra for greasing
²/₃ cup plus 1½ tsp. superfine sugar
3 eggs, lightly beaten
1 tsp. vanilla extract

7oz. bittersweet chocolate,
  finely chopped
1 pear, peeled, cored, and diced
¹/₃ cup pistachio nuts
1 cup plus 3 tbsp. self-rising flour

1   Preheat the oven to 350°F. Grease a 9 x 4½in. loaf pan with butter.
2   In a large bowl, beat the butter and sugar together until light and fluffy, using
    an electric hand mixer. Add the eggs one at a time, whisking well in between,
    then add the vanilla extract. Fold in the chocolate, pear, pistachio nuts, and
    flour until just combined, using a wooden spoon. Pour into the prepared pan.
3   Bake in the hot oven 55 to 60 minutes, or until a skewer inserted into the middle
    of the cake comes out clean. Remove from the oven and let the cake cool in the
    pan 10 minutes, then turn out onto a wire rack to cool completely.

108 Devil's food cake

PREPARATION TIME 25 minutes   COOKING TIME 20 to 25 minutes   MAKES 1 x 9in. cake

1½ sticks butter, softened,
  plus extra for greasing
1 cup unsweetened cocoa powder
1⅔ cups superfine sugar
1 tsp. vanilla extract

1 tbsp. chocolate liqueur
4 eggs, lightly beaten
2¼ cups self-rising flour
1 recipe quantity Creamy Chocolate
  Icing (see page 212)

1   Preheat the oven to 350°F. Grease 2 x 9in. round pans with butter and line the
    bottoms with baking paper.
2   Place the cocoa in a small bowl and blend with ¾ cup boiling water to form
    a paste. Set aside to cool. In a large bowl, beat the butter, sugar, and vanilla
    extract until light and creamy, using an electric hand mixer. Gradually add the
    liqueur and eggs. Stir in some of the flour with a wooden spoon, then add the
    cocoa mixture and finally the remaining flour until just combined. Divide the
    mixture evenly between the prepared pans.
3   Bake in the hot oven 20 to 25 minutes, or until a skewer inserted in the middle
    of the cakes comes out clean. Remove from the oven and let the cakes cool in
    the pans 10 minutes, then turn out onto a wire rack to cool completely.
4   To finish the cake, sandwich both halves together with some of the creamy
    chocolate icing and use a palette knife to spread the remainder over the top.

109 Bourbon chocolate cake

PREPARATION TIME 20 minutes   COOKING TIME 35 to 40 minutes   MAKES 1 x 9in. cake

1 stick plus 1 tbsp. butter, softened,
  plus extra for greasing
9oz. bittersweet chocolate, broken
  into pieces
4 eggs, separated
½ cup plus 1 tsp. packed light
  brown sugar

2 tbsp. all-purpose flour
3 tbsp. bourbon whiskey
1 tsp. vanilla extract
powdered sugar, sifted, for dusting
light cream, for serving (optional)

1   Preheat the oven to 350°F. Grease a 9in. round springform pan with butter and
    line the bottom with baking paper.
2   In a small saucepan, melt the butter and chocolate together over low heat, then
    remove from the heat and set aside to cool slightly. In a large bowl, beat the egg
    yolks with the brown sugar until pale and thick, using an electric hand mixer.
    Add the chocolate mixture and stir with a wooden spoon until just combined.
    Fold in the flour, whiskey, and vanilla extract, using a metal spoon. In a clean
    bowl, whisk the egg whites to soft peaks, using clean attachments for the
    electric hand mixer. Fold gently into the chocolate mixture, using a metal spoon,
    then pour into the prepared pan.
3   Bake in the hot oven 30 to 35 minutes, or until the cake is just set in the middle.
    Remove from the oven and let cool in the pan 10 to 15 minutes, then remove
    the cake from the pan. Dust with powdered sugar and serve with cream,
    if desired.

110 Easy fudge cake

PREPARATION TIME 15 minutes   **COOKING TIME** 25 to 30 minutes   **MAKES** 1 x 9in. cake

6 tbsp. butter, melted,
  plus extra for greasing
200g/7oz/1 cup plus 1 tbsp.
  packed light brown sugar
2 eggs, lightly beaten

1 tsp. vanilla extract
140g/5oz/1¼ cups self-rising flour
2 tbsp. unsweetened cocoa powder
1 recipe quantity Creamy Chocolate
  Icing (see page 212)

1 Preheat the oven to 350°F. Grease a 9in. springform pan with butter and line the
   bottom with baking paper.
2 In a large bowl, beat the butter and sugar together, using an electric hand
   mixer, then add the eggs and vanilla extract, beating until well combined.
   In another bowl, combine the flour and cocoa, then add to the sugar mixture
   with ½ cup hot water, stirring with a wooden spoon just until everything is
   moist. Pour into the prepared pan.
3 Bake in the hot oven 25 to 30 minutes, or until a skewer inserted into the middle
   of the cake comes out clean. Remove from the oven and let the cake cool in the
   pan 10 minutes, then turn out onto a wire rack to cool completely.
4 To ice the cake, use a palette knife to spread over the creamy chocolate icing.

111 Sour cream chocolate cake

PREPARATION TIME 25 minutes   **COOKING TIME** 20 to 25 minutes   **MAKES** 1 x 9in. cake

1 stick plus 1 tbsp. butter, softened,
  plus extra for greasing
¾ cup plus 2 tbsp. superfine sugar
1 tsp. vanilla extract
3 eggs, lightly beaten

175g/6oz/1⅓ cups plus 4 tsp
  self-rising flour
3 tbsp. unsweetened cocoa powder
⅔ cup sour cream
1 recipe quantity Shiny Chocolate
  Icing (see page 213)

1 Preheat the oven to 325°F. Grease a deep 9in. springform pan with butter
   and line the bottom with baking paper.
2 In a large bowl, whisk the butter, sugar, and vanilla extract together until
   light and pale, using an electric hand mixer, then gradually whisk in the eggs.
   In a clean bowl, combine the flour and cocoa, using a wooden spoon, then fold
   into the butter mixture with the sour cream. Spoon into the prepared pan.
3 Bake in the hot oven 20 to 25 minutes, or until firm and a skewer inserted
   in the middle of the cake comes out just dry. Remove from the oven and let
   the cake cool in the pan 10 minutes, then turn out onto a wire rack to
   cool completely.
4 To ice the cake, use a palette knife to spread over the shiny chocolate icing.

112 Chocolate ricotta cake

PREPARATION TIME 20 minutes   **COOKING TIME** 30 to 35 minutes   **MAKES** 1 x 9in. cake

1 stick plus 3 tbsp. butter, softened,
  plus extra for greasing
$^1/_3$ cup plus 4 tsp. superfine sugar
$5^1/_2$oz. bittersweet chocolate, melted
  and left to cool

3 eggs, separated
9oz. ricotta cheese
1 cup ground almonds
2 tbsp. all-purpose flour
powdered sugar, sifted, for dusting

1   Preheat the oven to 325°F. Grease a 9in. springform pan with butter and line
    the bottom with baking paper.
2   In a large bowl, beat the butter and sugar together until light and fluffy, using
    an electric hand mixer. Add the melted chocolate, egg yolks, and ricotta, stirring
    with a wooden spoon until just combined, then stir in the ground almonds and
    flour. In a clean bowl, whisk the egg whites to soft peaks, using clean attachments
    for the electric hand mixer, then fold into the chocolate mixture. Pour into the
    prepared pan.
3   Bake in the hot oven 30 to 35 minutes until the cake is just firm around the
    edges but still wobbly in the middle. Remove from the oven and let cool in the
    pan 10 to 15 minutes, then remove the cake from the pan and transfer to a
    serving plate. Dust with powdered sugar and serve warm.

113 Chocolate beer cake

PREPARATION TIME 30 minutes   **COOKING TIME** 20 to 25 minutes   **MAKES** 1 x 8in. cake

1 stick plus 1 tbsp. butter, softened,
  plus extra for greasing
1 cup plus 4 tsp. packed light
  brown sugar
2 eggs, lightly beaten
$1^1/_3$ cups plus 4 tsp. self-rising flour
2 tbsp. unsweetened cocoa powder

scant 1 cup beer
1 recipe quantity Chocolate Chantilly
  Cream (see page 208)
1 recipe quantity Chocolate Fudge
  Frosting (see page 212)
$^1/_2$ cup walnuts, roasted,
  finely chopped

1   Preheat the oven to 350°F. Grease 2 x 8in. round pans with butter.
2   In a large bowl, beat the butter and sugar together until light and creamy, using
    an electric hand mixer, then beat in the eggs, one at a time. In another bowl,
    combine the flour and cocoa, using a wooden spoon, then fold into the butter
    mixture with the beer, using a metal spoon. Divide the mixture equally between
    the pans.
3   Bake in the hot oven 20 to 25 minutes, or until the cakes just start to pull away
    from the sides of the pans and a skewer inserted into the middle of the cakes
    comes out clean. Remove from the oven and let the cakes cool in the pans
    10 minutes, then turn out onto a wire rack to cool completely.
4   To finish the cake, sandwich the halves together with the Chocolate Chantilly
    Cream, then, using a palette knife, spread the Chocolate Fudge Frosting
    over the top and sides. Transfer to a serving plate and sprinkle with the
    chopped walnuts.

114   Chocolate angel food cake

PREPARATION TIME 15 minutes   **COOKING TIME** 45 to 50 minutes
MAKES 1 x 8½ x 4in. cake

6 eggs, separated
1 cup plus 2 tbsp. vegetable oil
1¼ cups chocolate drink mix

2¼ cups self-rising flour
1¾ cups superfine sugar
powdered sugar, sifted, for dusting

1   Preheat the oven to 300°F. Place an ungreased, loose-bottomed angel food cake pan on a baking sheet. (If you do not have an angel food cake pan, use a ring pan of the same diameter, but make only half of the recipe.)

2   Place the egg yolks, oil, chocolate drink mix, flour, sugar, and 1 cup plus 2 tbsp. water in a large bowl and mix on low speed with an electric hand mixer until just combined. Then beat at the highest setting 10 minutes. In a clean bowl, whisk the egg whites until stiff, using clean attachments for the electric hand mixer, then fold gently into the chocolate mixture using a metal spoon. Pour into the prepared pan.

3   Bake in the warm oven 45 to 50 minutes, or until the cake is firm when touched. Remove from the oven and turn the cake pan upside down on to a wire rack, then let the cake cool completely in the pan.

4   When cold, loosen the cake from the pan with a sharp knife, turn out onto a serving plate and dust with powdered sugar.

115 Chocolate pear upside-down cake

PREPARATION TIME 20 minutes   **COOKING TIME** 30 to 35 minutes   **MAKES** 1 x 9in. cake

1 stick plus 6 tbsp. butter, softened,
  plus extra for greasing
7oz. bittersweet chocolate, broken
  into pieces
$^2/_3$ cup plus 1$^1/_2$ tsp. superfine sugar
3 eggs, lightly beaten

1 tsp. vanilla extract
$^3/_4$ cup plus 4 tsp. self-rising flour
3 tbsp. packed light brown sugar
3 pears, ripe but firm, peeled,
  cored, and sliced into quarters

1   Preheat the oven to 350°F. Grease a 9in. springform pan with butter and line
    the bottom with baking paper.
2   In a small saucepan, combine the butter, chocolate, and sugar over low heat
    until just melted, stirring with a wooden spoon. Remove from the heat and set
    aside to cool completely. Stir in the eggs, vanilla extract, and flour until just
    combined. Sprinkle the brown sugar over the bottom of the pan, arrange the
    pear quarters over the top in a spiral shape, and pour the chocolate batter over.
3   Bake in the hot oven 25 to 30 minutes, or until a skewer inserted in the middle
    of the cake comes out with just a few moist crumbs on it. Remove from the oven
    and let the cake cool in the pan 15 minutes, then turn out onto a wire rack to cool
    completely, pear side up.

116 Chocolate raisin cake

PREPARATION TIME 30 minutes   **COOKING TIME** 35 to 40 minutes   **MAKES** 1 x 9in. cake

1 stick plus 3 tbsp. butter, melted,
  plus extra for greasing
$^1/_2$ cup raisins
2 tbsp. Marsala wine
10$^1/_2$oz. bittersweet chocolate,
  melted and left to cool

$^1/_3$ cup plus 4 tsp. superfine sugar
3 tbsp. self-rising flour
2 tbsp. unsweetened cocoa powder,
  sifted
4 eggs, separated

1   Preheat the oven to 350°F. Grease a 9in. springform pan with butter and line the
    bottom with baking paper.
2   Place the raisins in a bowl, and cover with the wine. Microwave on high for
    1 minute, then set aside to cool. Place the melted chocolate in a large bowl
    and stir in the butter, sugar, flour, cocoa, and egg yolks just until combined.
    In a clean bowl, whisk the egg whites until stiff but not dry, using an electric
    hand mixer, then fold into the chocolate mixture with the raisins, using a metal
    spoon. Pour into the prepared pan.
3   Bake in the hot oven 35 to 40 minutes, or until a skewer inserted into the middle
    of the cake comes out dry. Remove from the oven and let the cake cool in the
    pan 15 minutes, then turn out onto a wire rack to cool completely.

117 Chocolate polenta cake

PREPARATION TIME 20 minutes   **COOKING TIME** 30 to 35 minutes   **MAKES** 1 x 9in. cake

1 stick plus 1 tbsp. butter, softened,
    plus extra for greasing
9oz. bittersweet chocolate, broken
    into pieces
5 eggs, separated

²/₃ cup plus 1½ tsp. superfine sugar
¹/₄ cup dark rum
³/₄ cup plus 1 tbsp. fine polenta
powdered sugar, sifted, for dusting

1   Preheat the oven to 350°F. Grease a 9in. springform pan with butter and line
    the bottom with baking paper.
2   In a small saucepan, combine the butter and chocolate over low heat until
    the chocolate is just melted. Remove from the heat and set aside to cool.
    In a large bowl, beat the egg yolks and sugar together until pale and light,
    using an electric hand mixer. Stir in the chocolate mixture using a wooden
    spoon. In a clean bowl, whisk the egg whites until stiff, using clean attachments
    for the electric hand mixer, then fold into the chocolate mixture with the rum
    and polenta. Pour into the prepared pan.
3   Bake in the hot oven 25 to 30 minutes, or until the cake is just set but still
    slightly wobbly in the middle. Remove from the oven and let the cake cool
    in the pan 15 minutes, then turn out onto a wire rack to cool completely.
    Dust with powdered sugar.

118 Chocolate zucchini loaf cake

PREPARATION TIME 30 minutes   **COOKING TIME** 50 to 55 minutes
MAKES 1 x 9 x 4½in. loaf cake

1 stick butter, softened,
    plus extra for greasing
³/₄ cup plus 2 tbsp. superfine sugar
1 tsp. orange zest, finely grated
2 eggs, lightly beaten
175g/6oz/1¹/₃ cups plus 4 tsp
    self-rising flour

1 tbsp. unsweetened cocoa powder
1 tsp. cinnamon
¹/₃ cup milk
1 cup grated zucchini
¹/₂ cup roasted pecan nuts, chopped
1 recipe quantity Chocolate Sour
    Cream Frosting (see page 210)

1   Preheat the oven to 350°F. Grease a 9½ x 4½in. loaf pan with butter and line
    the bottom with baking paper.
2   In a large bowl, beat together the butter, sugar, and orange zest until light
    and creamy, using an electric hand mixer. Gradually beat in the eggs until well
    combined. In a clean bowl, mix together the flour, cocoa, and cinnamon with
    a wooden spoon and fold into the cake mixture with the milk, using a metal
    spoon. Stir in the grated zucchini and pecan nuts until just combined. Spoon the
    mixture into the prepared pan.
3   Bake in the hot oven 50 to 55 minutes, or until a skewer inserted in the middle
    of the cake comes out just moist. Remove from the oven and let the cake cool in
    the pan 10 minutes, then turn out onto a wire rack to cool completely before
    transferring to a serving plate.
4   To ice the cake, use a palette knife to spread the chocolate sour cream frosting
    over the cake.

119 White chocolate Sauternes cake

PREPARATION TIME 20 minutes   **COOKING TIME** 30 to 35 minutes   **MAKES** 1 x 9in. cake

1½ sticks butter, softened,
  plus extra for greasing
¾ cup plus 2 tbsp. superfine sugar
3 eggs, lightly beaten
1 cup all-purpose flour
¾ cup plus 4 tsp. self-rising flour

½ cup milk
⅓ cup Sauternes
7oz. white chocolate, melted
  and left to cool
1 recipe quantity White Chocolate
  Frosting (see page 210)

1   Preheat the oven to 350°F. Grease a 9in. springform pan with butter and line
    the bottom with baking paper.
2   In a large bowl, beat the butter and sugar together until light and creamy,
    using an electric hand mixer, then gradually beat in the eggs until smooth.
    In a clean bowl, combine the flours using a wooden spoon, then fold into the
    butter mixture with the milk and half of the Sauternes, using a metal spoon.
    Stir in the melted chocolate and pour the mixture into the prepared pan.
3   Bake in the hot oven 30 to 35 minutes, or until a skewer inserted into the middle
    of the cake comes out clean. Remove from the oven and let the cake cool in the
    pan 10 minutes, then turn out onto a wire rack to cool completely. Pierce a few
    holes in the top of the cake with a skewer, then drizzle with the remaining
    Sauternes. Let the cake cool completely.
4   To ice the cake, use a palette knife to spread the white chocolate frosting
    over the cake.

120 White chocolate cake

PREPARATION TIME 25 minutes   **COOKING TIME** 35 to 40 minutes   **MAKES** 1 x 9in. cake

1 stick plus 1 tbsp. butter, softened,
   plus extra for greasing
¾ cup plus 2 tbsp. superfine sugar
1 tsp. vanilla extract
3 eggs, lightly beaten
5½oz. white chocolate, melted
   and left to cool

1⅓ cups plus 4 tsp. self-rising flour
½ cup heavy cream
1 recipe quantity White Chocolate
   Ganache (see page 210)
raspberries, for serving (optional)

1   Preheat the oven to 325°F. Grease a 9in. springform pan with butter and line
    the bottom with baking paper.
2   In a large bowl, beat the butter, sugar, and vanilla extract together until
    light and fluffy, using an electric hand mixer, then gradually beat in the eggs.
    Stir in the melted chocolate, using a wooden spoon, then fold in the flour with
    the cream until just combined, using a metal spoon. Pour into the prepared pan.
3   Bake in the hot oven 35 to 40 minutes, or until a skewer inserted in the middle
    of the cake comes out with just a few crumbs sticking to it. Remove from the
    oven and let the cake cool in the pan 10 minutes, then turn out onto a wire rack
    to cool completely.
4   To ice the cake, use a palette knife to spread the white chocolate ganache over
    the cake. Serve with raspberries, if using.

121 Lemon & chocolate drizzle loaf cake

PREPARATION TIME 15 minutes   **COOKING TIME** 35 to 40 minutes
MAKES 1 x 9 x 4½in. loaf cake

1½ sticks butter, softened,
   plus extra for greasing
¾ cup plus 1 tbsp. superfine sugar,
   plus 2 tbsp. for sprinkling
2 eggs, lightly beaten
1⅓ cups plus 4 tsp. self-rising flour

zest of 1 lemon, grated
1 tbsp. milk
3½oz. bittersweet chocolate,
   melted and left to cool
juice of 1 lemon

1   Preheat the oven to 350°F. Grease a 9 x 4½in. loaf pan, and line the bottom with
    baking paper.
2   In a large bowl, beat the butter and sugar together until light and creamy, using
    an electric hand mixer, then beat in the eggs, a little at a time. Fold in the flour,
    lemon zest, milk, and melted chocolate, using a metal spoon, and pour into the
    prepared pan.
3   Bake in the hot oven 35 to 40 minutes, or until the cake is just firm in the middle.
    Remove from the oven and let the cake cool in the pan 5 minutes. Using a
    skewer, pierce the top of the cake in 5 or 6 places, then brush over the lemon
    juice until it is absorbed. Sprinkle over the extra sugar. Leave the cake in the
    pan a further 5 minutes, then turn out onto a wire rack to cool completely.

122   Chocolate & almond marble cake

PREPARATION TIME 20 minutes   **COOKING TIME** 18 to 20 minutes   **MAKES** 1 x 9in. cake

1$^1/_2$ sticks butter, softened,
   plus extra for greasing
$^3/_4$ cup superfine sugar
1 egg, lightly beaten
1 tsp. vanilla extract
1 cup ground almonds

$^3/_4$ cup plus 4 tsp. self-rising flour
$^1/_4$ cup milk
5$^1/_2$oz. milk chocolate, melted
   and left to cool
1 recipe quantity Dark Chocolate
   Ganache (see page 209)

1   Preheat the oven to 350°F. Grease an 9in. square cake pan with butter and line the bottom with baking paper.

2   In a large bowl, beat the butter and sugar together until light and fluffy, using an electric hand mixer. Gradually beat in the egg and vanilla extract until well combined. In a clean bowl, mix together the almonds and flour, using a wooden spoon, then gently fold into the butter mixture with the milk, using a metal spoon. Place half of the cake mixture into the prepared pan. Fold the melted chocolate into the remaining mixture and pour into the pan. Gently draw a fork through the mix to create a swirled effect.

3   Bake in the hot oven 18 to 20 minutes, or until the cake is just firm. Remove from the oven and let the cake cool in the pan 10 minutes, then turn out onto a wire rack to cool completely.

4   To ice the cake, use a palette knife to spread the dark chocolate ganache over the cake.

123   Chocolate & orange loaf cake

PREPARATION TIME 30 minutes   **COOKING TIME** 55 to 60 minutes
MAKES 1 x 9 x 4$^1/_2$in. loaf cake

1 stick plus 3 tbsp. butter, softened,
   plus extra for greasing
$^3/_4$ cup plus 2 tbsp. superfine sugar
1 tsp. vanilla extract
2 eggs, lightly beaten
2$^1/_3$ cups plus 4 tsp. self-rising flour

$^1/_2$ cup milk
3$^1/_2$oz. bittersweet chocolate,
   melted and left to cool
2 tbsp. orange juice
zest of 1 orange, finely grated
powdered sugar, sifted, for dusting

1   Preheat the oven to 350°F. Grease a 9 x 4$^1/_2$in. loaf pan with butter and line the bottom with baking paper.

2   In a large bowl, beat the butter and sugar together until light and fluffy, using an electric hand mixer, then add the vanilla extract and eggs a little at a time, beating well between additions. Fold in the flour and milk until just combined, using a metal spoon. Stir in the melted chocolate and the orange juice and zest and pour into the prepared pan.

3   Bake in the hot oven 55 to 60 minutes, or until a skewer inserted in the middle of the cake comes out dry. Remove from the oven and let the cake cool in the pan 10 minutes, then turn out onto a wire rack to cool completely. Dust with powdered sugar.

124 Nutty chocolate, rum & fig cake

PREPARATION TIME 30 minutes **COOKING TIME** 35 to 40 minutes **MAKES** 1 x 9in. cake

1 stick plus 6 tbsp. butter, softened,
plus extra for greasing
¾ cup plus 2 tbsp. superfine sugar
3 eggs, lightly beaten
7oz. bittersweet chocolate, melted
and left to cool
1 cup ground almonds

½ cup plus 2 tbsp. self-rising flour
½ cup dried soft figs, stalks
removed and roughly chopped
2 tbsp. dark rum
1 recipe quantity Chocolate Rum
Frosting (see page 212)

1 Preheat the oven to 350°F. Grease a 9in. springform pan with butter and line the bottom with baking paper.
2 In a large bowl, beat the butter and sugar together until light and fluffy, using an electric hand mixer, then add the eggs one at a time. Stir in the melted chocolate, almonds, flour, figs, and rum, using a wooden spoon, then spoon the mixture into the prepared pan.
3 Bake in the hot oven 35 to 40 minutes, or until a skewer inserted into the middle of the cake comes out clean. Remove from the oven and let the cake cool in the pan 10 minutes, then turn out onto a wire rack to cool completely.
4 To ice the cake, use a palette knife to spread the chocolate rum frosting over the cake.

125 Orange loaf cake with chocolate chips

PREPARATION TIME 20 minutes **COOKING TIME** 40 to 45 minutes
MAKES 1 x 9 x 4½in. loaf cake

1½ sticks butter, softened,
plus extra for greasing
¾ cup plus 1 tbsp. superfine sugar
2 eggs, lightly beaten
1⅓ cups plus 4 tsp. self-rising flour

3½oz. bittersweet or milk
chocolate chips
zest of 1 orange, grated, plus juice
1 tbsp. milk
1 recipe quantity Chocolate
Buttercream (see page 208)

1 Preheat the oven to 350°F. Grease a 9 x 4½in. loaf pan with butter and line the bottom with baking paper.
2 In a large bowl, beat the butter and sugar together until light and fluffy, using an electric hand mixer, then gradually beat in the eggs. Fold in the flour, chocolate chips, orange zest, and milk until just combined and pour into the prepared pan.
3 Bake in the hot oven 40 to 45 minutes, or until a skewer inserted into the center comes out with just a few moist crumbs on it. Remove from the oven.
4 Pierce the top of the cake in 3 or 4 places with the skewer and brush over the orange juice. Cool 10 minutes, then turn out onto a wire rack and top with the chocolate buttercream.

126 Chocolate brownie cake

PREPARATION TIME 25 minutes **COOKING TIME** 40 to 45 minutes **MAKES** 1 x 9in. cake

1½ sticks butter, softened,
  plus extra for greasing
6oz. bittersweet chocolate,
  broken into pieces
3 eggs, separated
¾ cup plus 1 tbsp. superfine sugar

1 cup walnuts, chopped
3½oz. bittersweet or milk
  chocolate chips
2 tbsp. all-purpose flour
powdered sugar, sifted, for dusting

1 Preheat the oven to 325°F. Grease a 9in. springform pan with butter and line the bottom with baking paper.
2 In a small saucepan, heat the butter and chocolate together over low heat until just melted. Remove the pan from the heat and stir until smooth, using a wooden spoon. Set aside to cool. In a large bowl, beat the egg yolks and half the sugar together until light and creamy, using an electric hand mixer. Using a wooden spoon, mix in the chocolate mixture, then stir in the walnuts, chocolate chips, and flour.
3 In a clean bowl, whisk the egg whites to soft peaks, using clean attachments for the electric hand mixer, then continue whisking, gradually adding the remaining sugar, until thick and shiny. Gently fold the whisked whites into the chocolate mixture, then pour into the prepared pan.
4 Bake in the hot oven 35 to 40 minutes, or until the cake is just firm in the middle. Let the cake cool completely in the pan before turning out, then dust with powdered sugar.

127 Peanut butter chocolate cake

PREPARATION TIME 20 minutes **COOKING TIME** 30 to 35 minutes **MAKES** 1 x 9in. cake

1 stick plus 1 tbsp. butter, chopped,
  plus extra for greasing
1 tsp. vanilla extract
1 cup plus 3 tbsp. superfine sugar
3 eggs, separated
4½oz. bittersweet chocolate, melted
  and left to cool

2 tbsp. smooth peanut butter
1 cup plus 2 tbsp. self-rising flour
¾ cup plus 4 tsp. all-purpose flour
1 cup plus 2 tbsp. milk
1 recipe quantity Chocolate Fudge
  Frosting (see page 212)

1 Preheat the oven to 325°F. Grease a deep 9in. square cake pan with butter and line the bottom with baking paper.
2 In a large bowl, beat the butter, vanilla extract, and sugar together until light and creamy, using an electric hand mixer. Whisk in the egg yolks, then stir in the melted chocolate and peanut butter. In a clean bowl, combine the flours and fold into the chocolate mixture with the milk, using a metal spoon. In a clean bowl, whisk the egg whites to stiff peaks, using clean attachments for the electric hand mixer, then gently fold into the cake mixture. Pour into the prepared pan.
3 Bake in the hot oven 30 to 35 minutes, or until the cake is dark brown and firm. Remove from the oven and let the cake cool in the pan 15 minutes, then turn out onto a wire rack to cool completely.
4 Using a large knife, split the cake in half and sandwich the two halves back together with half of the chocolate fudge frosting. To ice the cake, use a palette knife to spread the remaining frosting over the top.

128 Chocolate cream roll with strawberries

PREPARATION TIME 35 minutes   **COOKING TIME** 10 to 12 minutes   **MAKES** 1 x cream roll

butter, for greasing
4 eggs, separated
³/₄ cup plus 2 tbsp. superfine
   sugar, plus 2 tbsp. for sprinkling
2³/₄oz. bittersweet or milk
   chocolate, grated

¹/₂ cup plus 2 tbsp. self-rising flour
1 recipe quantity Chocolate Chantilly
   Cream (see page 208)
1 cup strawberries, hulled and sliced

1   Preheat the oven to 350°F. Grease a 9 x 13in. jelly roll pan with butter and line
    the bottom and sides with baking paper.
2   In a large bowl, beat the egg yolks and half the sugar together until thick and
    creamy, using an electric hand mixer. Stir in 2 tbsp. water, the grated chocolate,
    and flour, using a wooden spoon. In a clean bowl, whisk the egg whites to soft
    peaks, using clean attachments for the electric hand mixer, then continue
    whisking, gradually adding the remaining sugar, until thick and shiny. Fold into
    the chocolate mixture until just combined, using a metal spoon. Pour the mixture
    into the prepared pan and spread evenly, using a palette knife.
3   Bake in the hot oven 10 to 12 minutes, or until just firm. Remove from the oven
    and turn out onto a large sheet of baking paper that has been sprinkled with
    sugar. Remove the lining paper, then, using the baking paper to help you, roll
    up from a short side, enclosing the paper in the cake. Let cool completely.
4   When cool, unroll the cake carefully, spread with the chocolate chantilly cream
    and scatter over the strawberries. Re-roll, transfer to a serving plate, and
    refrigerate until ready to serve.

129 Chocolate Lamingtons

PREPARATION TIME 40 minutes   **COOKING TIME** 15 to 20 minutes   **MAKES** 16 Lamingtons

2 tbsp. butter, melted,
  plus extra for greasing
4 eggs
1/3 cup plus 4 tsp. superfine sugar
3/4 cup plus 4 tsp. self-rising flour
1 tbsp. cornstarch

FOR THE COATING:
4 cups powdered sugar, sifted
3 tbsp. unsweetened cocoa powder,
  sifted
2 tbsp. butter, melted
1/2 cup milk
2 cups flaked coconut

1   Preheat the oven to 350°F. Grease a shallow 9in. square cake pan with butter
    and line the bottom with baking paper.
2   In a large bowl, beat the eggs and sugar together, using an electric hand mixer,
    until thick and pale (about 5 to 10 minutes). In a clean bowl, combine the flour
    and cornstarch and fold into the egg mixture with the melted butter until just
    mixed, using a metal spoon. Pour into the prepared pan.
3   Bake in the hot oven 15 to 20 minutes until the cake is firm and lightly golden.
    Remove from the oven and let the cake cool in the pan 10 minutes, then turn
    out onto a wire rack to cool completely. With a sharp knife, cut the cooled cake
    into 16 squares, removing the crusts.
4   For the coating, combine the powdered sugar and cocoa in a large bowl.
    Using a wooden spoon, stir in the melted butter, milk, and as much of 1/2 cup
    hot water as is needed to make the mixture the consistency of thick cream.
    Dip each piece of cake into the coating until it is well covered, then toss the
    coated cake in the coconut until completely covered. Place on a wire rack to set.

130 Double chocolate Lamingtons

PREPARATION TIME 40 minutes   **COOKING TIME** 15 to 20 minutes   **MAKES** 16 Lamingtons

2 tbsp. butter, melted,
  plus extra for greasing
4 eggs
1/3 cup plus 4 tsp. superfine sugar
3/4 cup plus 4 tsp. self-rising flour
1 tbsp. cornstarch
2 tbsp. unsweetened cocoa powder

FOR THE COATING:
4 cups powdered sugar, sifted
3 tbsp. unsweetened cocoa powder,
  sifted
2 tbsp. butter, melted
1/2 cup milk
2 cups flaked coconut

1   Preheat the oven to 350°F. Grease a shallow 9in. square cake pan with butter
    and line the bottom with baking paper.
2   In a large bowl, beat the eggs and sugar together, using an electric hand mixer,
    until thick and pale (about 5 to 10 minutes). In a clean bowl, combine the flour,
    cornstarch, and cocoa and fold into the egg mixture with the melted butter until
    just mixed, using a metal spoon. Pour into the prepared pan.
3   Bake in the hot oven 15 to 20 minutes until the cake is firm and lightly golden.
    Remove from the oven and let the cake cool in the pan 10 minutes, then turn
    out onto a wire rack to cool completely. Using a sharp knife, cut the cooled cake
    into 16 squares, removing the crusts.
4   For the coating, combine the powdered sugar and cocoa in a large bowl.
    Using a wooden spoon, stir in the melted butter, milk, and as much of 1/2 cup
    hot water as is needed to make the mixture the consistency of thick cream.
    Dip each piece of cake into the coating until it is well covered, then toss the
    coated cake in the coconut until completely covered. Allow to set on a wire rack.

131 White chocolate Lamingtons

PREPARATION TIME 40 minutes   **COOKING TIME** 15 to 20 minutes   **MAKES** 16 Lamingtons

2 tbsp. butter, melted,
  plus extra for greasing
4 eggs
$^1/_3$ cup plus 4 tsp. superfine sugar
$^3/_4$ cup plus 4 tsp. self-rising flour
1 tbsp. cornstarch

FOR THE COATING:
4 cups powdered sugar,
  sifted
2 tbsp. butter, melted
$^1/_2$ cup milk
$4^1/_2$oz. white chocolate, melted
  and left to cool
1 tbsp. coconut liqueur
2 cups flaked coconut, toasted

1   Preheat the oven to 350°F. Grease a 9in. square pan with butter and line
    the bottom with baking paper.
2   In a large bowl, beat the eggs and sugar together, using an electric hand mixer,
    until thick and pale (about 5 to 10 minutes). In a clean bowl, combine the flour
    and cornstarch and fold into the egg mixture with the melted butter until just
    mixed, using a metal spoon. Pour into the prepared pan.
3   Bake in the hot oven 15 to 20 minutes until the cake is firm and lightly golden.
    Remove from the oven and let the cake cool in the pan 10 minutes, then turn
    out onto a wire rack to cool completely. With a sharp knife, cut the cooled cake
    into 16 squares, removing the crusts.
4   For the coating, place the powdered sugar in a large bowl and add the melted
    butter and milk. Using a wooden spoon, stir in the white chocolate and liqueur.
    Dip each piece of cake into the coating until it is well covered, then toss the
    coated cake in the coconut until completely covered. Place on a wire rack to set.

132 Apple chocolate cake

PREPARATION TIME 20 minutes   **COOKING TIME** 30 to 35 minutes   **MAKES** 1 x 9in. cake

$1^1/_2$ sticks butter, softened,
  plus extra for greasing
$^3/_4$ cup plus 2 tbsp. superfine sugar
3 eggs, lightly beaten
2 tbsp. unsweetened cocoa powder

$^1/_4$ tsp. baking soda
2 large apples, peeled and chopped
2 cups self-rising flour
1 recipe quantity Chocolate Cream
  Cheese Frosting (see page 211)

1   Preheat the oven to 325°F. Grease a shallow 9in. square cake pan with butter
    and line the bottom with baking paper.
2   Place the butter, sugar, eggs, cocoa, baking soda, apples, flour, and $^1/_3$ cup
    water in the bowl of a processor and pulse until just smooth. Pour into the
    prepared pan.
3   Bake in the hot oven 30 to 35 minutes, or until the cake is dark brown and
    firm in the middle. Remove from the oven and let the cake cool in the pan
    15 minutes, then turn out onto a wire rack to cool completely.
4   To ice the cake, use a palette knife to spread the chocolate cream cheese
    frosting over the cake.

133 Chocolate ginger cake

PREPARATION TIME 25 minutes   **COOKING TIME** 35 to 40 minutes   **MAKES** 1 x 9in. cake

1 stick plus 3 tbsp. butter, softened,
   plus extra for greasing
3/4 cup plus 2 tsp. packed light
   brown sugar
2 eggs, lightly beaten
2 tbsp. chopped candied ginger
1 tbsp. honey

3 1/2 oz. bittersweet chocolate, melted
   and left to cool
1 cup plus 3 tbsp. self-rising flour
2 tsp. ground ginger
1 tbsp. dark rum
1 recipe quantity Chocolate Rum
   Frosting (see page 212)

1   Preheat the oven to 350°F. Grease a 9in. square cake pan with butter and line
    the bottom with baking paper.
2   In a large bowl, beat the butter and sugar together until light and fluffy, using
    an electric hand mixer, then add the eggs and beat until smooth. Stir in the
    chopped ginger, honey, and melted chocolate until just combined, using a
    wooden spoon. Sift the flour and ground ginger together and fold into the cake
    mixture with the rum, using a metal spoon. Spoon into the prepared pan.
3   Bake in the hot oven 35 to 40 minutes, or until the cake is just firm in the
    middle. Remove from the oven and let the cake cool in the pan 10 minutes,
    then turn out onto a wire rack to cool completely.
4   To ice the cake, use a palette knife to spread the chocolate rum frosting
    over the cake.

134 White chocolate, ginger & apricot loaf cake

PREPARATION TIME 30 minutes   **COOKING TIME** 50 to 55 minutes
MAKES 1 x 9 x 4 1/2 in. loaf cake

1 stick plus 1 tbsp. butter, softened,
   plus extra for greasing
1/2 cup plus 1 tsp. superfine sugar
3 eggs, lightly beaten

6oz. white chocolate, melted
   and left to cool
1 1/2 cups plus 2 tbsp. self-rising flour
2 tbsp. chopped candied ginger
1/2 cup soft dried apricots, chopped

1   Preheat the oven to 350°F. Grease a 9 x 4 1/2 in. loaf pan with butter and line
    the bottom with baking paper.
2   In a large bowl, beat the butter and sugar together until light and fluffy, using
    an electric hand mixer. Gradually beat in the eggs. Using a wooden spoon, stir
    in the melted chocolate, then fold in the flour, ginger, and apricots with a metal
    spoon until just combined. Spoon into the prepared pan.
3   Bake in the hot oven 50 to 55 minutes, or until the loaf is just firm to the touch.
    Remove from the oven and let the cake cool in the pan 10 minutes, then turn out
    onto a wire rack to cool completely.

135 Chocolate cupcakes

PREPARATION TIME 20 minutes   **COOKING TIME** 12 to 15 minutes   **MAKES** 12 cupcakes

1 stick plus 1 tbsp. butter, softened
$\frac{1}{2}$ cup plus 1 tsp. superfine sugar
2 eggs, lightly beaten
1 cup self-rising flour
3 tbsp. unsweetened cocoa powder

2 tbsp. milk
$\frac{1}{2}$ tsp. vanilla extract
1 recipe quantity Creamy Chocolate
   Icing (see page 212)

1   Preheat the oven to 350°F. Line a 12-hole muffin pan with 12 paper muffin liners.

2   In a large bowl, beat the butter and sugar until light and creamy, using an electric hand mixer, then gradually whisk in the eggs until well blended. In a clean bowl, sift the flour and cocoa together, then fold into the butter mixture, using a metal spoon, along with the milk and vanilla extract. Divide the mixture evenly between the muffin liners.

3   Bake in the hot oven 12 to 15 minutes, or until the cupcakes are firm to the touch. Remove from the oven and transfer to wire racks to cool completely.

4   To ice the cupcakes, use a palette knife to spread the creamy chocolate icing over the cupcakes.

136 Dark & white chocolate cupcakes

PREPARATION TIME 20 minutes   **COOKING TIME** 12 to 15 minutes   **MAKES** 12 cupcakes

1 stick plus 1 tbsp. butter, softened
$^1/_3$ cup plus 4 tsp. superfine sugar
2 eggs, lightly beaten
1 cup self-rising flour
3 tbsp. unsweetened cocoa powder

3oz. white chocolate chips
2 tbsp. milk
$^1/_2$ tsp. vanilla extract
1 recipe quantity Creamy Chocolate
  Icing (see page 212)

1   Preheat the oven to 350°F. Line a 12-hole muffin pan with 12 paper
    muffin liners.
2   In a large bowl, beat the butter and sugar together until light and creamy, using
    an electric hand mixer, then gradually whisk in the eggs. In a clean bowl, sift
    the flour and cocoa together, then fold into the butter mixture with the white
    chocolate chips, milk, and vanilla extract, using a metal spoon. Divide the
    mixture evenly between the cake cases.
3   Bake in the hot oven 12 to 15 minutes, or until the cupcakes are firm to the
    touch. Remove from the oven and transfer to wire racks to cool completely.
4   To ice the cupcakes, use a palette knife to spread the creamy chocolate
    icing over the cupcakes.

137 Chocolate surprise cupcakes

PREPARATION TIME 15 minutes   **COOKING TIME** 12 to 15 minutes   **MAKES** 12 cupcakes

1 stick plus 1 tbsp. butter, softened
$^1/_2$ cup plus 1 tsp. superfine sugar
2 eggs, lightly beaten
1 cup self-rising flour
3 tbsp. unsweetened cocoa powder

$^1/_4$ cup milk
$^1/_2$ tsp. vanilla extract
24 small dark chocolate buttons
powdered sugar, sifted, for dusting

1   Preheat the oven to 350°F. Line a 12-hole muffin pan with 12 paper
    muffin liners.
2   In a large bowl, beat the butter and sugar until light and creamy, using
    an electric hand mixer, then gradually whisk in the eggs until well blended.
    In a clean bowl, sift the flour and cocoa together, then fold into the butter
    mixture, using a metal spoon, along with the milk and vanilla extract.
3   Place a small spoonful of the mixture into the bottom of each paper case.
    Place 2 chocolate buttons on top of each spoonful, then divide the remaining
    mixture evenly between the cake cases, to cover the chocolate buttons.
4   Bake in the hot oven 12 to 15 minutes, or until the cupcakes are firm to
    the touch. Remove from the oven and transfer to wire racks to cool a little.
    Dust with powdered sugar and serve warm.

138 White chocolate cupcakes

PREPARATION TIME 20 minutes **COOKING TIME** 17 to 20 minutes **MAKES** 16 cupcakes

4¹/₂oz. white chocolate, broken
  into pieces
7 tbsp. butter, chopped
¹/₂ cup milk
¹/₃ cup plus 4 tsp. superfine sugar

1 tsp. vanilla extract
1 egg, lightly beaten
1 cup self-rising flour
1 recipe quantity White Chocolate
  Ganache (see page 210)

1 Preheat the oven to 350°F. Line 2 x 12-hole muffin pans with 16 paper
muffin liners.
2 In a medium-sized saucepan, melt the chocolate, butter, milk, and sugar
together over low heat, stirring occasionally. When smooth, remove from the
heat and set aside to cool 15 minutes. In a bowl, whisk the vanilla extract and
egg together and add to the chocolate mixture. Place the flour in a large bowl
and whisk in the chocolate and egg mixture until well combined. Divide the
mixture evenly between the muffin liners.
3 Bake in the hot oven 12 to 15 minutes, or until the cupcakes are firm to the
touch. Remove from the oven and transfer to wire racks to cool completely.
4 To ice the cupcakes, use a palette knife to spread the white chocolate ganache
over the cupcakes.

139 White chocolate, lime & coconut cupcakes

PREPARATION TIME 20 minutes **COOKING TIME** 18 to 20 minutes **MAKES** 12 cupcakes

1 cup plus 3 tbsp. self-rising flour
3 tbsp. plus 1 tsp. superfine sugar
¹/₂ stick butter, melted
1 egg, lightly beaten
scant ¹/₂ cup milk
1 tsp. vanilla extract

juice and zest of 1 lime
3¹/₂oz. white chocolate, broken
  into pieces
¹/₂ cup flaked coconut
1 recipe quantity White Chocolate
  Frosting (see page 210)

1 Preheat the oven to 350°F. Line a 12-hole muffin pan with 12 paper
muffin liners.
2 In a large bowl, combine the flour and sugar and make a well in the middle.
Mix together the butter, egg, milk, vanilla extract, and lime juice and zest,
using a wooden spoon, and stir into the flour mixture until just combined.
Stir in the white chocolate and coconut, then divide the mixture evenly between
the muffin liners.
3 Bake in the hot oven 18 to 20 minutes, or until the cupcakes are firm to the
touch. Remove from the oven and transfer to wire racks to cool completely.
4 To ice the cupcakes, use a palette knife to spread the white chocolate
frosting over the cupcakes.

140   Butterfly cakes with chocolate cream

PREPARATION TIME 20 minutes   **COOKING TIME** 15 to 20 minutes   **MAKES** 12 cakes

1 stick plus 1 tbsp. butter, softened
1/2 cup plus 1 tsp. superfine sugar
2 eggs, lightly beaten
1 tsp. vanilla extract
1 1/2 cups plus 2 tbsp. self-rising flour

2 tbsp. unsweetened cocoa powder
3 tbsp. milk
1 recipe quantity Chocolate Chantilly
    Cream (see page 208)
powdered sugar, sifted, for dusting

1   Preheat the oven to 350°F. Line a 12-hole muffin pan with 12 paper
muffin liners.

2   In a large bowl, beat the butter and sugar together until light and fluffy, using
an electric hand mixer, then gradually beat in the eggs and vanilla extract until
combined. In a clean bowl, sift the flour and cocoa together and fold into the
mixture with the milk, using a metal spoon. Divide the mixture evenly between
the muffin liners.

3   Bake in the hot oven 15 to 20 minutes, or until the cakes are firm to the touch.
Remove from the oven and lift the cakes out to cool on a wire rack.

4   Using a sharp knife, make a small circular incision in the top of each cake and
remove the small circle of cake, then cut the circle in half, to form two semi-
circular pieces. Place a spoonful of the chocolate chantilly cream in the middle
of each cake, then replace the two pieces of cake on the top at an angle to form
"wings" and dust with powdered sugar.

141   Apple & chocolate upside-down cakes

PREPARATION TIME 25 minutes   **COOKING TIME** 15 to 20 minutes   **MAKES** 12 cakes

7 tbsp. butter, softened, plus extra
    for greasing
2 apples, peeled, cored, and diced
3 tbsp. plus 1 tsp. superfine sugar
1/4 cup powdered sugar, plus extra,
    sifted, for dusting

2 eggs, lightly beaten
1 cup plus 3 tbsp. self-rising flour
2 tbsp. unsweetened cocoa powder
3 tbsp. milk

1   Preheat the oven to 350°F. Grease a 12-hole muffin pan with butter and
distribute the diced apple evenly between the muffin holes.

2   In a large bowl, beat the butter and sugars together, using an electric hand
mixer, then add the eggs one at a time until well combined. In a clean bowl,
sift the flour and cocoa together, then fold into the cake mixture with the milk,
using a metal spoon. Divide the mixture evenly between the muffin holes.

3   Bake in the hot oven 15 to 20 minutes, or until the cakes are just firm in the
middle. Remove from the oven and let the cakes cool in the pan 10 minutes,
then turn out onto a wire rack, apple side up, and let cool completely. Dust with
powdered sugar.

142 Chocolate madeleines

PREPARATION TIME 15 minutes   **COOKING TIME** 15 to 17 minutes
MAKES 12 to 14 madeleines

7 tbsp. butter, chopped, plus extra for greasing	$\frac{1}{2}$ tsp. baking powder
2$\frac{3}{4}$oz. bittersweet chocolate, broken into pieces	pinch salt
$\frac{1}{2}$ cup plus 2 tbsp. all-purpose flour	2 eggs
	$\frac{1}{3}$ cup plus 4 tsp. superfine sugar
	powdered sugar, sifted, for dusting

1   Preheat the oven to 350°F. Grease a 12-hole madeleine pan with butter.
2   In a small saucepan, heat the butter and chocolate together over low heat until just melted, then set aside to cool. Sift the flour and baking powder into a bowl, and add the salt. In a large bowl, beat the eggs and sugar together until the mixture is light in color, using an electric hand mixer, then whisk in the chocolate mixture. Using a metal spoon, gently fold in the flour mix, then divide the mixture between the holes in the prepared pan, taking care not to overfill.
3   Bake in the hot oven 10 to 12 minutes until the cakes are firm to the touch. Remove from the oven and let the madeleines cool in the pan 10 minutes, then turn out onto a wire rack to cool completely and dust with powdered sugar.

143   White chocolate, coconut & blueberry friands

PREPARATION TIME 15 minutes   **COOKING TIME** 17 to 20 minutes   **MAKES** 24 friands

7 tbsp. butter, softened, plus
    extra for greasing
3¹/₂oz. white chocolate, broken
    into pieces
1 cup flaked coconut

1³/₄ cups plus 1 tbsp. powdered
    sugar
¹/₂ cup plus 2 tsp. all-purpose flour
6 egg whites
1 tsp. vanilla extract
24 blueberries

1   Heat the oven to 350°F. Grease 24 friand molds or 2 x 12-hole mini muffin pans
with butter.

2   In a small saucepan, combine the butter and chocolate and melt together over
low heat. Remove from the heat and set aside to cool slightly. Mix together the
coconut, sugar, and flour, using a wooden spoon, then stir in the egg whites,
vanilla extract, and chocolate mixture until well combined. Divide the mixture
between the holes in the prepared pan, taking care not to overfill, and place
a blueberry on top of each friand.

3   Bake in the hot oven 12 to 15 minutes until the friands are lightly browned.
Remove from the oven and let the friands cool in the pans 5 minutes, then
turn out onto a wire rack to cool completely.

144   Chocolate-almond friands with raspberries

PREPARATION TIME 15 minutes   **COOKING TIME** 12 to 15 minutes   **MAKES** 24 friands

7 tbsp. butter, melted, plus extra
    for greasing
³/₄ cup plus 1 tbsp. ground almonds
1³/₄ cups plus 1 tbsp. powdered sugar
¹/₂ cup plus 2 tsp. all-purpose flour

2 tbsp. unsweetened cocoa powder
6 egg whites
1 tsp. vanilla extract
24 raspberries

1   Heat the oven to 350°F. Grease 24 friand molds or 2 x 12-hole mini muffin pans
with butter.

2   In a large bowl, mix the butter, ground almonds, sugar, flour, cocoa, egg whites,
and vanilla extract together until combined, using a wooden spoon. Divide the
mixture between the molds or holes in the prepared pan, taking care not to
overfill, and place a raspberry on top of each friand.

3   Bake in the hot oven 12 to 15 minutes until the friands are lightly browned.
Remove from the oven and let the friands cool in the pans 5 minutes, then turn
out onto a wire rack to cool completely.

145 Cream liqueur brownies

PREPARATION TIME 20 minutes   **COOKING TIME** 20 to 25 minutes   **MAKES** 12 brownies

7 tbsp. butter, chopped, plus extra
  for greasing
3¹/₂oz. bittersweet chocolate, broken
  into pieces
2 eggs, lightly beaten
³/₄ cup plus 2 tbsp. superfine sugar
3 tbsp. Irish cream liqueur
³/₄ cup plus 4 tsp. all-purpose flour

FOR THE ICING:
3 cups plus 2 tbsp. powdered sugar
2 tbsp. unsweetened cocoa powder
2 tbsp. Irish cream liqueur

1   Preheat the oven to 350°F. Grease a shallow 9in. square pan with butter and line the bottom with baking paper, leaving some hanging over the edges to make removing the brownies easier.
2   In a small saucepan, heat the butter and chocolate together over low heat until just melted, then remove from the heat. In a large bowl, beat the eggs and sugar together until light and creamy, using an electric hand mixer. Stir in the chocolate mixture, liqueur, and flour until just combined, using a wooden spoon. Pour into the prepared pan.
3   Bake in the hot oven 15 to 20 minutes, or until the brownie is firm around the edges and still slightly soft in the middle. Remove from the oven and let cool in the pan.
4   For the icing, sift the powdered sugar and cocoa into a bowl and make a well in the middle. Add the liqueur, then, using a wooden spoon, mix in just enough boiling water to make a spreading consistency. Ice the brownies while still warm, using a palette knife. Allow to set, then cut into 12 squares.

146 Chocolate cream cheese brownies

PREPARATION TIME 20 minutes   **COOKING TIME** 20 to 25 minutes   **MAKES** 12 brownies

3 sticks butter, chopped, plus extra
  for greasing
12oz. bittersweet chocolate, broken
  into pieces
1¹/₄ cups plus 1 tbsp. superfine sugar
3 eggs, lightly beaten

1 tsp. vanilla extract
1¹/₂ cups plus 2 tbsp. all-purpose
  flour
pinch salt
10¹/₂oz. cream cheese, cut into thin
  slices and chilled

1   Preheat the oven to 350°F. Grease a shallow 9in. square pan with butter and line the bottom with baking paper, leaving some hanging over the edges to make removing the brownies easier.
2   In a medium-sized saucepan, melt the butter and chocolate together over low heat, stirring constantly, until the chocolate is just melted. Remove from the heat. Add the sugar and mix well, using a wooden spoon, then set aside to cool to room temperature. Gradually mix the beaten eggs into the chocolate mixture with the vanilla extract, using a wooden spoon, then fold in the flour and salt. Pour half the mixture into the prepared pan and top with the chilled cream cheese slices. Pour over the remaining brownie mixture.
3   Bake in the hot oven 15 to 20 minutes, or until the brownie is firm around the edges and still slightly soft in the middle. Remove from the oven and let cool completely in the pan, then cut into 12 squares.

147 Chocolate fudge brownies

PREPARATION TIME 15 minutes   **COOKING TIME** 20 to 25 minutes   **MAKES** 12 brownies

1 stick plus 6 tbsp. butter, chopped,
   plus extra for greasing
7oz. bittersweet chocolate, broken
   into pieces
1 cup plus 4 tsp. superfine sugar

3 eggs, lightly beaten
1 tsp. vanilla extract
1 cup all-purpose flour
pinch salt

1 Preheat the oven to 350°F. Grease a shallow 9in. square pan with butter and line the bottom with baking paper, leaving some hanging over the edges to make removing the brownies easier.

2 In a medium-sized saucepan, melt the butter and chocolate over low heat until the chocolate is just melted, stirring constantly with a wooden spoon, then remove the pan from the heat. Add the sugar, and mix well, then let cool to room temperature. In a large bowl, gradually mix the eggs into the chocolate mixture, with the vanilla extract, then fold in the flour and salt, using a metal spoon. Pour the mixture into the prepared pan.

3 Bake in the hot oven 15 to 20 minutes, or until the brownie is firm around the edges and still slightly soft in the middle. Remove from the oven and let cool completely in the pan, then cut into 12 squares.

148 Cashew & chocolate-chip brownies

PREPARATION TIME 20 minutes   **COOKING TIME** 20 to 25 minutes   **MAKES** 12 brownies

1¹/₂ sticks butter, chopped,
   plus extra for greasing
2 tbsp. unsweetened cocoa powder
1 cup plus 4 tsp. superfine sugar
pinch salt
2 eggs, lightly beaten

1 tsp. vanilla extract
1 cup plus 3 tbsp. all-purpose flour
4¹/₂oz. bittersweet or milk
   chocolate chips
²/₃ cup unsalted cashew nuts, roasted
   and roughly chopped

1 Preheat the oven to 350°F. Grease a shallow 9in. square pan with butter and line the bottom with baking paper, leaving some hanging over the edges to make removing the brownies easier.

2 In a small saucepan, heat the butter with the cocoa and sugar over low heat until just melted, then remove from the heat and set aside to cool. When cool, add the salt, eggs, vanilla extract, flour, and chocolate chips and stir with a wooden spoon until just combined. Pour into the prepared pan and scatter the cashew nuts over the top.

3 Bake in the hot oven 15 to 20 minutes, or until the brownie is firm around the edges and still slightly soft in the middle. Remove from the oven and let cool completely in the pan, then cut into 12 squares.

149 Dark & white chocolate brownies

PREPARATION TIME 25 minutes   **COOKING TIME** 20 to 25 minutes   **MAKES** 12 brownies

1½ sticks butter, chopped,
  plus extra for greasing
2 tbsp. unsweetened cocoa powder
1¼ cups plus 1 tbsp. superfine sugar
2 eggs, lightly beaten

1 tsp. vanilla extract
1 cup plus 3 tbsp. all-purpose flour
2¼oz. white chocolate chips
2¼oz. bittersweet chocolate chips
⅔ cup walnuts, roughly chopped

1   Preheat the oven to 350°F. Grease a shallow 9in. square pan with butter and line the bottom with baking paper, leaving some hanging over the edges to make removing the brownies easier.
2   In a large saucepan, heat the butter with the cocoa and sugar over low heat until just melted, remove from the heat and set aside to cool. When cool, add the remaining ingredients and stir with a wooden spoon until just combined. Pour into the prepared pan.
3   Bake in the hot oven 15 to 20 minutes, or until the brownie is firm around the edges and still slightly soft in the middle. Remove from the oven and let cool in the pan completely, then cut into 12 squares.

150 Cakey chocolate brownies

PREPARATION TIME 20 minutes   **COOKING TIME** 12 to 15 minutes   **MAKES** 12 brownies

1/2 stick butter, softened, plus extra
  for greasing
2/3 cup plus 1 1/2 tsp. superfine sugar
2 eggs, lightly beaten
1 tsp. vanilla extract
1/4 cup milk

4 1/2 oz. bittersweet chocolate, melted
  and left to cool
1/2 cup plus 2 tbsp. self-rising flour
powdered sugar, sifted, for dusting
  (optional)

1   Preheat the oven to 350°F. Grease a shallow 9in. square pan with butter and line the bottom with baking paper, leaving some hanging over the edges to make removing the brownies easier.

2   In a large bowl, whisk the butter and sugar together, using an electric hand mixer, then add the eggs, whisking well until combined. Stir in the vanilla extract, milk, melted chocolate, and flour, using a wooden spoon, then pour into the prepared pan.

3   Bake in the hot oven 12 to 15 minutes, or until the brownie is firm around the edges and still slightly soft in the middle. Remove from the oven and let cool completely in the pan, then cut into 12 squares. Dust with powdered sugar, if desired.

151 Cappuccino brownies

PREPARATION TIME 20 minutes   **COOKING TIME** 20 to 25 minutes   **MAKES** 12 brownies

1 1/2 sticks butter, chopped,
  plus extra for greasing
2 tbsp. unsweetened cocoa powder
2 tsp. instant coffee powder
1 cup plus 4 tsp. superfine sugar
2 eggs, lightly beaten

1 tsp. vanilla extract
1 cup plus 3 tbsp. all-purpose flour
1 recipe quantity White Chocolate
  Frosting (see page 210)
1 tbsp. unsweetened cocoa powder,
  sifted

1   Preheat the oven to 350°F. Grease a shallow 9in. square pan with butter and line the bottom with baking paper, leaving some hanging over the edges to make removing the brownies easier.

2   In a small saucepan, heat the butter with the cocoa, coffee, and sugar over low heat until just melted, remove from the heat and set aside to cool. When cool, add the eggs, vanilla extract, and flour and stir with a wooden spoon until just combined. Pour into the prepared pan.

3   Bake in the hot oven 15 to 20 minutes, or until the brownie is firm around the edges and still slightly soft in the middle. Remove from the oven and let cool completely in the pan.

4   To ice the brownie, use a palette knife to spread the white chocolate frosting over the top. Sprinkle with the cocoa, then cut into 12 squares.

152 Rocky road brownies

PREPARATION TIME 20 minutes, plus setting **COOKING TIME** 20 to 25 minutes
MAKES 12 brownies

1½ sticks butter, chopped,
  plus extra for greasing
2 tbsp. unsweetened cocoa powder
1 cup plus 4 tsp. superfine sugar
2 eggs, lightly beaten
1 tsp. vanilla extract
1 cup plus 3 tbsp. all-purpose flour
3½oz. bittersweet or milk
  chocolate chips

FOR THE TOPPING:
7oz. white and pink marshmallows,
  chopped
1 recipe quantity Shiny Chocolate
  Icing (see page 213)

1 Preheat the oven to 350°F. Grease a shallow 9in. square pan with butter and
   line the bottom with baking paper, leaving some hanging over the edges to
   make removing the brownies easier.
2 In a small saucepan, heat the butter with the cocoa and sugar over low heat
   until just melted, then remove from the heat and set aside to cool. When cool,
   add the eggs, vanilla extract, flour, and chocolate chips and stir with a wooden
   spoon until just combined. Pour the mixture into the prepared pan.
3 Bake in the hot oven 15 to 20 minutes, or until the edges of the brownie are firm
   and the middle is still moist. Remove from the oven and let the brownie cool
   completely in the pan.
4 Stir the marshmallows into the Shiny Chocolate Icing until they are well coated,
   then spread the mixture evenly over the top of the brownie. Let the icing set
   30 minutes, then cut the brownie into 12 squares.

153 Brown sugar brownies

PREPARATION TIME 25 minutes **COOKING TIME** 25 to 30 minutes **MAKES** 24 brownies

1 stick plus 1 tbsp. butter, softened,
  plus extra for greasing
1½ cups plus 2 tbsp. packed light
  brown sugar
2 eggs, lightly beaten
1½ cups plus 2 tbsp. all-purpose
  flour
1 tsp. vanilla extract
1¼ cups pecan nuts, chopped

FOR THE TOPPING:
6oz. bittersweet chocolate, melted
  and left to cool
¾ cup sour cream

1 Preheat the oven to 350°F. Grease a shallow 9in. square pan with butter and
   line the bottom with baking paper, leaving some hanging over the edges to
   make removing the brownies easier.
2 In a large bowl, beat the butter and sugar together until light, using an electric
   hand mixer, then beat in the eggs. Fold in the flour, vanilla extract, and pecan
   nuts, using a metal spoon, and pour into the prepared pan.
3 Bake in the hot oven 25 to 30 minutes, or until the brownie is firm around the
   edges and still slightly soft in the middle. Remove the brownie from the oven
   and let cool in the pan 10 minutes while making the topping.
4 Mix the melted chocolate and sour cream together in a small bowl, then spread
   over the brownie. Let the brownie cool completely in the pan, then cut into
   24 small squares.

154 Blondies

PREPARATION TIME 20 minutes   **COOKING TIME** 25 to 30 minutes   **MAKES** 12 blondies

7 tbsp. butter, chopped, plus extra
    for greasing
4$\frac{1}{2}$oz. white chocolate, broken
    into pieces
$\frac{3}{4}$ cup plus 2 tbsp. superfine sugar
3 eggs, lightly beaten

1 tsp. vanilla extract
$\frac{3}{4}$ cup hazelnuts, skinned
    and chopped
3$\frac{1}{2}$oz. white chocolate chips
1$\frac{1}{3}$ cups plus 4 tsp. all-purpose flour

1   Preheat the oven to 350°F. Grease a shallow 9in. square pan with butter
    and line the bottom with baking paper.
2   In a small saucepan, heat the butter and chocolate together over low heat
    until the chocolate is just melted, then remove from the heat and stir gently
    until smooth. In a large bowl, combine the sugar and eggs, then stir in the
    chocolate mixture, vanilla extract, hazelnuts, chocolate chips, and flour, using
    a wooden spoon. Pour into the prepared pan.
3   Bake in the hot oven 20 to 25 minutes, or until the cake is firm around the edges
    but still moist in the middle. Remove from the oven and let the cake cool in the
    pan completely. Remove the cake from the pan and cut into 12 squares.

155 Chewy chocolate cookies

PREPARATION TIME 15 minutes   **COOKING TIME** 12 to 15 minutes   **MAKES** 18 cookies

butter, for greasing	3 tbsp. unsweetened cocoa powder
4 egg whites	2 tbsp. all-purpose flour
2³/₄ cups plus 4 tsp. powdered sugar	1 cup walnuts, finely chopped

1   Preheat the oven to 350°F. Grease 2 large baking sheets with butter.
2   In a large bowl, whisk the egg whites to soft peaks, using an electric hand mixer, then whisk in the powdered sugar, cocoa, and flour until well combined. Add 1 tbsp. water and continue to whisk until the mixture becomes very thick and shiny. Gently fold in the walnuts, using a metal spoon. Place 18 tablespoonfuls of the mixture on the prepared sheets, leaving about 4in. between them to allow for spreading.
3   Bake in the hot oven 12 to 15 minutes, or until the tops are firm but not dry (they will look cracked). (You may need to cook them in batches.) Remove the cookies from the oven and let cool on the sheets 10 minutes before transferring to a wire rack to cool completely.

156 Double chocolate cookies

PREPARATION TIME 15 minutes   **COOKING TIME** 10 to 12 minutes   **MAKES** 24 cookies

1 stick plus 1 tbsp. butter, softened, plus extra for greasing	1 egg, lightly beaten
1 tsp. vanilla extract	1¹/₂ cups all-purpose flour
¹/₃ cup plus 1 tbsp. packed light brown sugar	1 tbsp. unsweetened cocoa powder
5 tbsp. superfine sugar	3¹/₂oz. bittersweet or milk chocolate chips
	3¹/₂oz. white chocolate chips

1   Preheat the oven to 350°F. Grease 2 large baking sheets with butter.
2   In a large bowl, beat together the butter, vanilla extract, and both sugars until light and creamy, using an electric hand mixer. Add the egg until well combined. Fold in the flour, cocoa, and both kinds of chocolate chips, using a metal spoon. Place 24 tablespoonfuls of the mixture on the prepared sheets, leaving about 4in. between them to allow for spreading.
3   Bake in the hot oven 10 to 12 minutes, or until the cookies are dark brown. (You may need to cook them in batches.) Remove the cookies from the oven and let cool on the sheets 10 minutes before transferring to a wire rack to cool completely.

157 Chocolate macaroons

PREPARATION TIME 20 minutes   **COOKING TIME** 10 to 15 minutes   **MAKES** 24 macaroons

butter, for greasing
3 egg whites
¾ cup plus 2 tbsp. superfine sugar

1½ tbsp. all-purpose flour
2 tbsp. unsweetened cocoa powder
1½ cups ground almonds

1   Preheat the oven to 350°F. Line 2 large baking sheets with baking paper.
2   In a clean bowl, whisk the egg whites to soft peaks, using an electric hand
    mixer. Gradually add the sugar and continue to whisk until stiff and the sugar
    dissolves (about 5 minutes). In a clean bowl, combine the flour, cocoa, and
    ground almonds, using a wooden spoon, then gently fold into the egg whites
    until just combined. Place 24 tablespoonfuls of the mixture on the prepared
    sheets, leaving about 2in. between them to allow for spreading.
3   Bake in the warm oven 10 to 15 minutes, or until the macaroons are dry on the
    outside but still moist in the middle. (You may need to cook them in batches.)
    Remove the macaroons from the oven and let cool completely on the sheets.

158 Chocolate melting moments

PREPARATION TIME 20 minutes   **COOKING TIME** 8 to 10 minutes   **MAKES** 20 cookies

1 stick plus 1 tbsp. butter, softened,
   plus extra for greasing
¼ cup powdered sugar, plus extra,
   sifted, for dusting

1 cup all-purpose flour
3 tbsp. unsweetened cocoa powder

1   Preheat the oven to 350°F. Grease 2 large baking sheets with butter.
2   In a large bowl, mix the butter and sugar together, using a wooden spoon,
    until light and fluffy. In a clean bowl, combine the flour and cocoa, then stir into
    the butter mixture until just combined (the mixture will be soft). Place a little
    flour on your hands and roll the mixture into 20 balls. Place 10 balls of dough
    on each baking sheet, leaving about 2in. between them to allow for spreading,
    and press the top of each cookie down with a lightly floured fork.
3   Bake in the hot oven 8 to 10 minutes, or until the cookies are firm. (You may
    need to cook them in batches.) Remove the melting moments from the oven
    and let cool on the sheets 5 minutes before transferring to a wire rack
    to cool completely. Dust with the extra sugar.

159 Chocolate cherry macaroons

PREPARATION TIME 10 minutes, plus chilling **COOKING TIME** 18 to 20 minutes
MAKES 20 macaroons

butter, for greasing
1²/₃ cups flaked coconut
³/₄ cup plus 2 tbsp. coconut cream
2 tbsp. unsweetened cocoa powder

³/₄ cup plus 4 tsp. powdered sugar
2 large egg whites
¹/₂ cup candied cherries,
  finely chopped

1 Preheat the oven to 325°F. Line 2 large baking sheets with baking paper.
2 In a large bowl, mix all of the ingredients until well combined, using a wooden
   spoon. Refrigerate the mixture 30 minutes. Place 20 heaped teaspoonfuls
   of the mixture on the prepared baking sheet, leaving about 2in. between them
   to allow for spreading.
3 Bake in the hot oven 18 to 20 minutes, or until the macaroons look just firm.
   (You may need to cook them in batches.) Remove the macaroons from the
   oven and let cool on the sheets 5 minutes before transferring to a wire
   rack to cool completely.

160 Chocolate Anzac cookies

PREPARATION TIME 20 minutes   **COOKING TIME** 20 to 23 minutes   **MAKES** 20 cookies

6 tbsp. butter, chopped,
    plus extra for greasing
2 tbsp. honey
1/2 tsp. baking soda
1/2 cup rolled oats

1/2 cup plus 2 tbsp. all-purpose flour
1/3 cup plus 4 tsp. superfine sugar
3 tbsp. flaked coconut
2oz. milk or bittersweet chocolate
    chips

1   Preheat the oven to 325°F. Grease 2 large baking sheets with butter.
2   In a small saucepan, heat the butter and honey over low heat until just melted,
    then add the baking soda. The mixture should fizz up for a moment or two
    and then settle down. Remove from the heat and set aside to cool. In a large
    bowl, combine the remaining ingredients, using a wooden spoon, then pour over
    the cooled mixture and mix together. Place 20 large teaspoonfuls of the mixture
    on the prepared sheets, leaving about 4in. between them to allow for spreading.
3   Bake in the hot oven 15 to 18 minutes (the cookies will still look soft). (You may
    need to cook them in batches.) Remove the cookies from the oven and let cool
    on the sheet 5 minutes, then transfer to a wire rack to cool completely.

161 Dark chocolate & coffee cookies

PREPARATION TIME 20 minutes   **COOKING TIME** 15 to 20 minutes   **MAKES** 20 cookies

1 stick plus 3 tbsp. butter, softened,
    plus extra for greasing
1 1/3 cups plus 4 tsp. all-purpose flour
2 tbsp. unsweeetened cocoa powder
1 3/4oz. bittersweet chocolate, broken
    into very small pieces

1/4 tsp. instant coffee granules
1/2 cup plus 1 tsp. superfine sugar
2 tbsp. milk
1 tsp. vanilla extract
powdered sugar, for dusting

1   Preheat the oven to 350°F. Grease 2 large baking sheets with butter.
2   Place the flour, cocoa, chocolate, coffee, and sugar in the bowl of a food processor
    and process until combined. Add the butter, milk, and vanilla extract and pulse
    briefly until the mixture forms a dough. Roll 20 large teaspoonfuls of the dough
    into balls roughly the size of a walnut and place on the prepared sheets, leaving
    about 2in. between them to allow for spreading.
3   Bake in the hot oven 15 to 20 minutes, or until the cookies spread slightly and
    become firm, but are still soft in the middle. (You may need to cook them in
    batches.) Remove the cookies from the oven and let cool on the sheets
    5 minutes before transferring to a wire rack to cool completely. Dust with
    powdered sugar.

162 Chocolate & hazelnut cookies

PREPARATION TIME 20 minutes   **COOKING TIME** 10 to 12 minutes   **MAKES** 24 cookies

1 stick plus 1 tbsp. butter, softened,
  plus extra for greasing
1/3 cup plus 4 tsp. superfine sugar

1 cup all-purpose flour
1 tbsp. unsweetened cocoa powder
3 tbsp. roasted ground hazelnuts

1   Preheat the oven to 350°F. Grease 2 large baking sheets with butter.
2   In a large bowl, beat the butter and sugar together until light and creamy, using
    an electric hand mixer. In a clean bowl, mix together the flour, cocoa, and
    ground hazelnuts, using a metal spoon, and fold into the butter mixture until
    well blended. Roll 24 large teaspoonfuls of the mixture into balls between
    lightly floured hands and place on the prepared baking sheets, leaving about
    2in. between them to allow for spreading. Press down on each ball to flatten
    them slightly.
3   Bake in the hot oven 10 to 12 minutes, or until the cookies are firm. (You may
    need to cook them in batches.) Remove the cookies from the oven and let cool
    on the sheets 10 minutes, then transfer to a wire rack to cool completely.

163 Chocolate & peanut butter cookies

PREPARATION TIME 20 minutes, plus chilling   **COOKING TIME** 10 to 12 minutes
MAKES 18 cookies

1 stick plus 1 tbsp. butter, softened,
  plus extra for greasing
1/2 cup plus 1 tsp. superfine sugar
1/2 cup crunchy peanut butter
2 tbsp. light corn syrup

1 tbsp. milk
1 1/3 cups plus 4 tsp. all-purpose flour
2 tbsp. unsweetened cocoa powder
1/2 tsp. baking soda

1   Preheat the oven to 350°F. Grease 2 large baking sheets with butter.
2   In a large bowl, beat together the butter and sugar until light and creamy,
    using an electric hand mixer, then mix in the remaining ingredients with
    a wooden spoon. Mix together until well blended and the ingredients form
    a dough. Shape the dough into a log measuring about 12 x 1 1/2in. and wrap
    in plastic wrap. Refrigerate the dough 1 hour, or until firm but not solid.
3   Cut the dough into 1/4in slices and place the slices on the prepared sheets,
    leaving about 2in. between them to allow for spreading.
4   Bake in the hot oven 10 to 12 minutes, or until the cookies are firm. (You may
    need to cook them in batches.) Remove the cookies from the oven and let cool
    on the sheets 10 minutes, then transfer to a wire rack to cool completely.

164 Chocolate soufflé cookies

PREPARATION TIME 20 minutes   **COOKING TIME** 10 to 12 minutes   **MAKES** 20 cookies

1 egg white
pinch cream of tartar
1 tsp. vanilla extract
2 tbsp. superfine sugar

1/3 cup plus 2 tbsp. walnuts,
   finely chopped
31/2oz. bittersweet chocolate,
   melted and left to cool

1   Preheat the oven to 350°F. Line 2 large baking sheets with baking paper.
2   In a large bowl, whisk the egg white and cream of tartar to soft peaks, using
    an electric hand mixer, then add the vanilla extract. Gradually whisk in the
    sugar until the egg whites are stiff, but not dry. Fold in the walnuts and melted
    chocolate until just combined, using a metal spoon. Place 20 teaspoonfuls
    of the mixture on to the prepared sheets, leaving about 4in. between them
    to allow for spreading.
3   Bake in the hot oven 10 to 12 minutes until the cookies are shiny and cracked
    on the surface, but still moist in the middle. (You may need to cook them in
    batches.) Remove from the oven and transfer to wire racks to cool completely.

165 Orange chocolate-chip cookies

PREPARATION TIME 20 minutes   **COOKING TIME** 10 to 12 minutes   **MAKES** 24 cookies

1 stick plus 1 tbsp. butter, softened,
   plus extra for greasing
1 tsp. vanilla extract
1/3 cup plus 1 tbsp. packed light
   brown sugar
5 tbsp. superfine sugar
1 egg, lightly beaten

11/2 cups all-purpose flour
1 tsp. cardamom
1 tsp. cinnamon
zest of 1 orange, grated
7oz. orange-flavored chocolate,
   broken into pieces

1   Preheat the oven to 350°F. Grease 2 large baking sheets with butter.
2   In a large bowl, beat together the butter, vanilla extract, and both sugars until
    light and creamy, using an electric hand mixer. Add the egg until well combined,
    then stir in the remaining ingredients. Place 24 tablespoonfuls of the mixture
    on the prepared baking sheets, leaving about 2in. between them to allow
    for spreading.
3   Bake in the hot oven 10 to 12 minutes, or until the cookies are dark brown.
    (You may need to cook them in batches.) Remove the cookies from the oven
    and transfer to wire racks to cool completely.

166 Chocolate & pistachio biscotti

PREPARATION TIME 35 minutes **COOKING TIME** 50 to 65 minutes
MAKES about 20 biscotti

$^1/_2$ cup plus 1 tsp. superfine sugar
1 egg
1 cup all-purpose flour
2 tbsp. unsweetened cocoa powder

$^1/_2$ tsp. baking powder
$^3/_4$ cup pistachio nuts,
   roughly chopped

1 Preheat the oven to 325°F. Line a large baking sheet with baking paper.
2 In a large bowl, beat the sugar and egg together until pale and thick,
   using an electric hand mixer. In a separate bowl, combine the remaining
   ingredients, using a metal spoon, and fold into the egg mixture to form
   a dough. Remove the dough from the bowl and gently knead it on a lightly
   floured surface about 30 seconds. Form a log about 7 x 2in. in size and place
   on the prepared baking sheet.
3 Bake in the hot oven 20 to 25 minutes, or until the dough is firm to the touch.
   Remove from the oven, turning the temperature down to 275°F, and let cool
   completely. When the dough is cold, cut it into about 20 slices about $^1/_4$in. thick,
   using a serrated knife.
4 Place the biscotti slices on a fresh baking sheet and bake them in the warm
   oven 30 to 40 minutes, turning once, until they are very dry. Remove the biscotti
   from the oven and let cool completely.

167 Chocolate-chip biscotti

PREPARATION TIME 35 minutes **COOKING TIME** 50 to 65 minutes
MAKES about 20 biscotti

¹/₂ cup plus 1 tsp. superfine sugar
1 egg
1 cup all-purpose flour

¹/₂ tsp. baking powder
3¹/₂oz. bittersweet chocolate chips

1 Preheat the oven to 325°F. Line a baking sheet with baking paper.
2 In a large bowl, beat the sugar and egg together until pale and thick, using an electric hand mixer. In a separate bowl, combine the remaining ingredients, using a metal spoon, and fold into the egg mixture to form a dough. Remove the dough from the bowl and gently knead it on a lightly floured surface about 30 seconds. Form a dough log about 10 x 2in. in size and place on the prepared baking sheet.
3 Bake in the hot oven 20 to 25 minutes, or until the dough is firm to the touch. Remove from the oven, turning the temperature down to 275°F, and let cool completely. When the dough is cold, cut it into about 20 slices about ¹/₄in. thick, using a serrated knife.
4 Place the biscotti slices on a fresh baking sheet and bake them in the warm oven 30 to 40 minutes, turning once, until they are very dry. Remove the biscotti from the oven and let cool completely.

168 Double chocolate biscotti with hazelnuts

PREPARATION TIME 35 minutes **COOKING TIME** 50 to 65 minutes
MAKES about 20 biscotti

¹/₂ cup plus 1 tsp. superfine sugar
1 egg
1 cup all-purpose flour
2 tbsp. unsweetened cocoa powder
¹/₂ tsp. baking powder

1³/₄oz. bittersweet chocolate, broken into rough pieces
1³/₄oz. white chocolate, broken into rough pieces
³/₄ cup roasted hazelnuts, skinned and roughly chopped

1 Preheat the oven to 325°F. Line a large baking sheet with baking paper.
2 In a large bowl, beat the sugar and egg together until pale and thick, using an electric hand mixer. In a separate bowl, combine the remaining ingredients, using a metal spoon, and fold into the egg mixture to form a dough. Remove the dough from the bowl and gently knead it on a lightly floured surface about 30 seconds. Form a dough log about 10 x 2in. in size, and place on the prepared baking sheet.
3 Bake in the hot oven 20 to 25 minutes, or until the dough is firm to the touch. Remove from the oven, turning the temperature down to 275°F, and let cool completely. When the dough is cold, cut into about 20 slices about ¹/₄in. thick, using a serrated knife.
4 Place the biscotti slices on a fresh baking sheet and bake them in the warm oven 30 to 40 minutes, turning once, until they are very dry. Remove the biscotti from the oven and let cool completely.

169 Crispy chocolate chip cookies

PREPARATION TIME 15 minutes   **COOKING TIME** 10 to 12 minutes   **MAKES** 24 cookies

1 stick plus 1 tbsp. butter, softened,
    plus extra for greasing
1 tsp. vanilla extract
1/3 cup plus 1 tbsp. packed light
    brown sugar

5 tbsp. superfine sugar
1 egg, lightly beaten
1 1/2 cups all-purpose flour
7oz. bittersweet or milk
    chocolate chips

1   Preheat the oven to 350°F. Grease 2 large baking sheets with butter.
2   In a large bowl, beat the butter, vanilla extract, and both sugars together until
    light and creamy, using an electric hand mixer, then beat in the egg. Stir in
    the flour and chocolate chips, using a wooden spoon. Place 24 tablespoonfuls
    of the mixture on the prepared sheets, leaving about 4in. between them to allow
    for spreading.
3   Bake in the hot oven 10 to 12 minutes, or until the cookies are golden brown.
    (You may need to cook them in batches.) Remove the cookies from the oven
    and transfer to wire racks to cool completely.

170 Chocolate-chip pecan cookies

PREPARATION TIME 20 minutes   **COOKING TIME** 10 to 12 minutes   **MAKES** 30 cookies

1 stick plus 2 tbsp. butter, softened,
    plus extra for greasing
3 tbsp. superfine sugar
1/3 cup packed light brown sugar
1 egg, lightly beaten

1 cup all-purpose flour
1/2 tsp. baking soda
scant 1 cup bittersweet or
    milk chocolate chips
1 cup pecan nuts, finely chopped

1   Preheat the oven to 350°F. Grease 2 large baking sheets with butter.
2   In a large bowl, beat the butter and both sugars together until light and creamy,
    using an electric hand mixer, then beat in the egg. In a separate bowl, mix the
    remaining ingredients together using a wooden spoon, then stir into the butter
    mixture until well combined (do this in 2 batches). Roll 30 large teaspoonfuls
    of the mixture between floured hands to form balls. Place on the prepared
    sheets, leaving about 2in. between them to allow for spreading. Press down
    lightly to flatten the balls into rounds.
3   Bake in the hot oven 10 to 12 minutes until the cookies are lightly browned.
    (You may need to cook them in batches.) Remove the cookies from the oven
    and let cool on the baking sheets 10 minutes, then transfer the cookies
    to wire racks to cool completely.

171 Truffle dough cookies

PREPARATION TIME 15 minutes, plus chilling   **COOKING TIME** 10 to 12 minutes
MAKES 20 cookies

$^1/_3$ cup plus 4 tsp. superfine sugar
$^1/_2$ cup plus 2 tbsp. self-rising flour
3 tbsp. unsweetened cocoa powder
pinch salt
2 tbsp. butter, chopped

1 egg, lightly beaten
1 tsp. vanilla extract
powdered sugar, sifted, for rolling
   and dusting

1   Line a large baking sheet with baking paper.
2   Place the sugar, flour, cocoa, salt, and butter in the bowl of a food processor, and pulse 30 seconds. Add the egg and vanilla extract and pulse 15 seconds more, or until the mixture forms a dough. Remove the dough from the processor and refrigerate 30 minutes. Preheat the oven to 350°F.
3   Roll the dough into 20 balls about the size of a walnut, then roll these balls in powdered sugar and place on the prepared sheet, leaving about 4in. between them to allow for spreading.
4   Bake in the hot oven 10 to 12 minutes until the cookies are just set. (You may need to cook them in batches.) Remove the cookies from the oven and transfer to a wire rack to cool completely. Dust with powdered sugar.

172 White & dark truffle dough cookies

PREPARATION TIME 20 minutes, plus chilling **COOKING TIME** 10 to 12 minutes
MAKES 20 cookies

5 tbsp. superfine sugar
$^1/_2$ cup plus 2 tbsp. self-rising flour
3 tbsp. unsweetened cocoa powder
pinch salt
2 tbsp. butter, chopped

1 egg, lightly beaten
1 tsp. vanilla extract
$3^1/_2$oz. white chocolate chips
powdered sugar, sifted, for rolling

1   Line a large baking sheet with baking paper.
2   Place the sugar, flour, cocoa, salt, and butter in the bowl of a food processor, and pulse 30 seconds. Add the egg and vanilla extract and pulse 15 seconds more, or until the mixture forms a dough. Remove the dough from the processor, place in a bowl, and fold in the chocolate chips, then refrigerate 30 minutes. Preheat the oven to 350°F.
3   Roll the dough into 20 balls about the size of a walnut, then roll these balls in powdered sugar and place on the prepared sheet, leaving about 4in. between them to allow for spreading.
4   Bake in the hot oven 10 to 12 minutes until the cookies are just set. (You may need to cook them in batches.) Remove the cookies from the oven and transfer to a wire rack to cool completely.

173 Chocolate pine nut cookies

PREPARATION TIME 20 minutes   **COOKING TIME** 15 to 18 minutes   **MAKES** 20 cookies

1 stick plus 1 tbsp. butter, softened,
   plus extra for greasing
$^1/_2$ cup plus 2 tbsp. powdered sugar
1 tsp. vanilla extract

1 tbsp. unsweetened cocoa powder
1 cup all-purpose flour
$^1/_2$ cup pine nuts, finely chopped,
   plus $^1/_3$ cup for decorating

1   Preheat the oven to 325°F. Grease 2 large baking sheets with butter.
2   In a large bowl, beat the butter, sugar, and vanilla extract together until light and creamy, using an electric hand mixer. Fold in the cocoa, flour, and pine nuts until the mixture forms a soft dough, using a metal spoon.
3   Roll the dough into 20 balls about the size of a walnut and place on the prepared baking sheets, leaving about 4in. between them to allow for spreading. Press a few pine nuts on top of each cookie.
4   Bake in the hot oven 15 to 18 minutes, or until the cookies just begin to look dry. (You may need to cook them in batches.) Remove the cookies from the oven and let cool on the sheets 5 minutes, before transferring to a wire rack to cool completely.

174 Chocolate brownie cookies

PREPARATION TIME 15 minutes **COOKING TIME** 11 to 13 minutes **MAKES** 12 cookies

2 tbsp. butter, chopped
6oz. bittersweet chocolate,
   broken into pieces
1 egg, lightly beaten
1/3 cup plus 4 tsp. superfine sugar

1 tsp. vanilla extract
1/3 cup self-rising flour
2/3 cup pecan nuts, chopped
   and toasted

1   Preheat the oven to 350°F. Grease 2 large baking sheets with butter.
2   In a small saucepan, melt the butter and chocolate together over low heat and stir with a wooden spoon until smooth. Remove the pan from the heat and set aside to cool. In a large bowl, beat the egg and sugar together until thick and creamy, using an electric hand mixer. Stir in the chocolate mixture, vanilla extract, flour, and nuts, using a wooden spoon. Place tablespoonfuls of the mixture on the prepared sheets, leaving about 4in. between them to allow for spreading.
3   Bake in the hot oven 6 to 8 minutes, or until the cookies are puffed and cracked, but still moist. Remove the cookies from the oven and transfer them to a wire rack to cool completely.

175 Spiced chocolate cookies

PREPARATION TIME 20 minutes **COOKING TIME** 12 to 15 minutes **MAKES** 24 cookies

1 stick plus 1 tbsp. butter, softened,
   plus extra for greasing
1/3 cup plus 4 tsp. superfine sugar
1/2 cup plus 1 tsp. packed light
   brown sugar
1 tsp. vanilla extract
1 egg, lightly beaten

1 cup rolled oats
1 cup self-rising flour
2 tbsp. unsweetened cocoa powder
1/2 cup ground almonds
1 tsp. cinnamon
1 tsp. allspice

1   Preheat the oven to 350°F. Grease 2 large baking sheets with butter.
2   In a large bowl, beat the butter and both sugars together until light and creamy, using an electric hand mixer, then beat in the vanilla extract and egg. Stir in the remaining ingredients until just combined. Place tablespoonfuls of the mixture on the prepared sheets, leaving about 2in. between them to allow for spreading.
3   Bake in the hot oven 12 to 15 minutes, or until the cookies are golden brown. (You may need to cook them in batches.) Remove the cookies from the oven and transfer to wire racks to cool completely.

176 Hazelnut thumbprints

PREPARATION TIME 20 minutes **COOKING TIME** 10 to 12 minutes **MAKES** 24 cookies

1 stick plus 1 tbsp. butter, softened, plus extra for greasing
1/2 cup plus 1 tsp. superfine sugar
1 egg, lightly beaten
1/2 cup plus 2 tbsp. all-purpose flour
1/2 cup plus 2 tbsp. self-rising flour
2 tbsp. unsweetened cocoa powder
2/3 cup chocolate hazelnut spread
powdered sugar, sifted, for dusting

1 Preheat the oven to 350°F. Grease 2 large baking sheets with butter.
2 In a large bowl, beat the butter and sugar together until pale and creamy, using an electric hand mixer, then add the egg, beating well to combine. In a separate bowl, mix together both flours and the cocoa, using a wooden spoon, and stir into the butter mixture to form a dough.
3 Roll teaspoonfuls of the dough into 24 balls and place on the prepared sheets, leaving about 2in. between them to allow for spreading. Push the middle of each ball of dough down with your thumb to create an indentation, then place a teaspoonful of the chocolate hazelnut spread into each indented hole.
4 Bake in the hot oven 10 to 12 minutes, or until the cookies are firm. (You may need to cook them in batches.) Remove the thumbprints from the oven and let cool on the sheets 10 minutes before transferring to a wire rack to cool completely. Dust with powdered sugar.

177 Chocolate shortbread

PREPARATION TIME 15 minutes **COOKING TIME** 25 to 30 minutes **MAKES** 16 shortbreads

2 sticks butter, chopped
2 1/3 cups plus 4 tsp. all-purpose flour
1/3 cup plus 4 tsp. superfine sugar, plus extra for sprinkling
1 tbsp. unsweetened cocoa powder

1 Preheat the oven to 300°F. Line a large baking sheet with baking paper.
2 Place all the ingredients in the bowl of a food processor and pulse until the mixture just forms a dough. Divide the dough into 2 equal halves, place them on the prepared sheet, and press into 2 circles about 9in. in diameter. Mark each circle lightly into 8 pieces, using the back of a knife. Prick 6 or 7 times with a fork and sprinkle with some sugar.
3 Bake in the warm oven 35 to 40 minutes, or until the shortbreads are firm. Remove from the oven and let the shortbreads cool on the sheet 10 minutes before transferring to a wire rack to cool completely. Cut each shortbread round into 8 pieces along the scored lines.

178 Chocolate-dipped shortbreads

PREPARATION TIME 15 minutes   **COOKING TIME** 10 to 12 minutes   **MAKES** 18 shortbreads

1 stick plus 1 tbsp. butter, softened
1/2 cup plus 2 tbsp. powdered sugar
1 cup all-purpose flour

3 1/2 oz. bittersweet chocolate,
  melted and left to cool

1   Preheat the oven to 350°F. Line a large baking sheet with baking paper.
2   In a large bowl, mix together the butter, sugar, and flour until well combined, using a wooden spoon. Roll teaspoonfuls of the mixture into balls and place on the prepared sheet, flattening them slightly, leaving about 4in. between them to allow for spreading.
3   Bake in the hot oven 10 to 12 minutes, or until the shortbreads are lightly browned. Remove from the oven and transfer the shortbreads to a wire rack to cool completely.
4   Dip the cooled shortbreads into the melted chocolate and place on a clean sheet of baking paper to set.

179 Nutty white chocolate shortbreads

PREPARATION TIME 20 minutes   **COOKING TIME** 35 to 40 minutes   **MAKES** 16 shortbreads

1 cup plus 3 tbsp. all-purpose flour
3/4 cup plus 2 tbsp. rice flour
1/3 cup plus 4 tsp. superfine sugar
2 sticks chilled butter, chopped

4 1/2 oz. white chocolate, broken
  into small pieces
3/4 cup plus 2 tbsp. hazelnuts,
  roasted, skins removed,
  finely chopped

1   Preheat the oven to 300°F. Line a large baking sheet with baking paper.
2   Place both flours and the sugar in the bowl of a food processor and pulse briefly to combine. Add the butter, chocolate, and hazelnuts and pulse several times until all the ingredients are combined and the mixture begins to form a dough.
3   Remove from the food processor and shape the dough to form 2 x 8in. rounds, about 1/4in. thick, on the prepared sheet. Prick each round with a fork, then score each round into 8 pieces using the back of a knife.
4   Bake in the warm oven 35 to 40 minutes, or until the shortbreads are firm and lightly browned. Remove from the oven and let the shortbreads cool on the sheet 10 minutes before transferring to a wire rack to cool completely. Cut each shortbread round into 8 pieces along the scored lines.

180 Chocolate almond squares

PREPARATION TIME 15 minutes   **COOKING TIME** 20 to 25 minutes   **MAKES** 16 squares

7 tbsp. butter, softened, plus extra
   for greasing
5 tbsp. superfine sugar
4 eggs, separated
3$^{1}/_{2}$oz. bittersweet chocolate, grated

1$^{3}/_{4}$ cups ground almonds
$^{1}/_{4}$ cup all-purpose flour
1 tbsp. brandy
1 recipe quantity Shiny Chocolate
   Icing (see page 213)

1   Preheat the oven to 350°F. Grease a shallow 9in. square pan with butter, then
    line the bottom with baking paper.
2   In a large bowl, mix together the butter, sugar, egg yolks, chocolate, ground
    almonds, flour, and brandy, using a wooden spoon. In a clean bowl, whisk
    the egg whites to soft peaks, using an electric hand mixer, then fold into the
    chocolate mixture, using a metal spoon. Pour into the prepared pan.
3   Bake in the hot oven 20 to 25 minutes, or until the cake is firm and lightly
    browned. Remove from the oven and let cool completely in the pan.
4   To ice, use a palette knife to spread the shiny chocolate icing over the cake,
    then cut into 16 squares.

181 Crunchy chocolate-topped squares

PREPARATION TIME 20 minutes   **COOKING TIME** 17 to 20 minutes   **MAKES** 16 squares

6 tbsp. butter, melted, plus extra
   for greasing
3¹/₂oz. bittersweet chocolate,
   broken into pieces
1 cup plus 3 tbsp. self-rising flour
¹/₂ cup flaked coconut
¹/₄ cup cornflakes

¹/₃ cup plus 2 tbsp.
   packed light brown sugar

FOR THE TOPPING:
3¹/₂oz. bittersweet chocolate,
   broken into pieces
2 tbsp. butter, chopped

1 Preheat the oven to 350°F. Grease a shallow 9in. square cake pan with butter
   and line the bottom with baking paper.
2 In a small saucepan, heat the butter and chocolate together over low heat until
   just melted. Place the flour, coconut, cornflakes, brown sugar, and melted
   butter into a large bowl and mix together, using a wooden spoon. Add the
   chocolate mixture and stir until well combined. Spoon into the prepared pan.
3 Bake in the hot oven 12 to 15 minutes, or until the cake is just firm, then remove
   from the oven and let cool completely in the pan.
4 For the topping, heat the chocolate and butter together in a small saucepan
   over low heat until just melted. Set aside to cool 10 minutes. Spread the topping
   over the squares and allow to set before cutting into 16 squares.

182 Crunchy chocolate crisp squares

PREPARATION TIME 15 minutes, plus chilling   **COOKING TIME** 5 minutes
MAKES 18 squares

1¹/₂ sticks butter, plus extra
   for greasing
3 cups crisp rice cereal
2 tbsp. unsweetened cocoa powder

3¹/₂oz. bittersweet chocolate,
   broken into pieces
4¹/₂oz. marshmallows

1 Grease a shallow 8 x 12in. pan with butter and line with baking paper.
2 Mix the crisp rice cereal and cocoa together in a bowl until well combined.
   In a small saucepan, melt the butter and chocolate together over low heat,
   then remove from the heat and add the marshmallows. Using a wooden spoon,
   stir until melted, then pour over the rice cereal and stir well to combine.
3 Press the mixture into the prepared pan and let cool, then refrigerate
   1 hour before cutting into 18 squares.

183 Chocolate & coconut squares

PREPARATION TIME 20 minutes, plus chilling   **COOKING TIME** 12 to 15 minutes
MAKES 12 squares

1 stick plus 1 tbsp. butter, melted,
  plus extra, for greasing
1/2 cup plus 2 tbsp. self-rising flour
1/2 cup plus 2 tbsp. all-purpose flour
2 tbsp. unsweetened cocoa powder
5 tbsp. superfine sugar
1/2 cup flaked coconut

FOR THE TOPPING:
3/4 cup plus 4 tsp. powdered sugar
2 tbsp. unsweetened cocoa powder
1/2 cup flaked coconut
1/2 cup sweetened condensed milk

1   Preheat the oven to 350°F. Grease a shallow 9in. square cake pan with butter and line with baking paper.
2   In a large bowl, sift both flours and the cocoa together, then add the sugar and coconut. Add the melted butter and stir with a wooden spoon until well combined. Press the mixture into the prepared pan.
3   Bake in the hot oven 12 to 15 minutes, or until the cake is just firm. Remove from the oven and let cool completely in the pan.
4   For the topping, sift the powdered sugar and cocoa together into a clean bowl, add the remaining ingredients, and stir to combine. Spread the topping evenly over the slice using a palette knife. Refrigerate the iced cake 30 minutes or until set before cutting into 12 squares.

184 Chocolate & coconut cherry squares

PREPARATION TIME 20 minutes   **COOKING TIME** 15 to 20 minutes   **MAKES** 16 squares

butter, for greasing
7oz. bittersweet chocolate, melted
3/4 cup plus 2 tbsp. flaked coconut

5 tbsp. superfine sugar
1 cup candied cherries, chopped
1 egg white

1   Preheat the oven to 350°F. Grease a shallow 9in. square cake pan with butter. Line with baking paper, leaving a little overhanging the edges.
2   Spread the melted chocolate evenly over the base of the prepared pan and allow to set. In a large bowl, mix the coconut, sugar, cherries, and egg white together, using a wooden spoon, and spread over the chocolate.
3   Bake in the hot oven 15 to 20 minutes, or until the cake is just firm. Remove from the oven and let cool completely in the pan before removing and cutting into 16 squares.

185 Rocky road squares

PREPARATION TIME 20 minutes   **COOKING TIME** 15 to 17 minutes   **MAKES** 16 squares

1 stick plus 1 tbsp. butter, chopped,
  plus extra for greasing
2 tbsp. unsweetened cocoa powder
1/3 cup plus 4 tsp. superfine sugar
1 egg, lightly beaten
2/3 cup walnuts, chopped
9oz. graham crackers, crushed

FOR THE TOPPING:
5 1/2 oz. milk chocolate, melted
  and left to cool
7oz. marshmallows, chopped

1 Preheat the oven to 350°F. Grease a shallow 9in. square cake pan with butter and line with baking paper.
2 In a small saucepan, melt the butter over low heat , then stir in the cocoa and sugar, using a wooden spoon. Remove from the heat and set aside to cool. Whisk in the egg. In a large bowl, combine the walnuts and crushed crackers, then pour the butter mixture over the cracker mix. Stir until well combined, using a wooden spoon. Press the mixture into the prepared pan.
3 Bake in the hot oven 10 to 12 minutes, or until the cake is just firm, then remove from the oven.
4 For the topping, mix the melted chocolate and marshmallows together in a bowl and spread over the cake. Let the cake cool completely in the pan, then refrigerate 30 minutes before cutting into 16 squares.

186 Chocolate-chip & nut bars

PREPARATION TIME 15 minutes   **COOKING TIME** 20 to 25 minutes   **MAKES** 16 bars

7 tbsp. butter, melted, plus
  extra for greasing
4 1/2 oz. graham crackers,
  finely crushed

7oz. milk or bittersweet
  chocolate chips
1 cup flaked coconut
3/4 cup mixed nuts, chopped
14oz. can sweetened condensed milk

1 Preheat the oven to 350°F. Grease a shallow 9in. square cake pan with butter and line with baking paper.
2 Pour the melted butter into the pan and spread it over the paper lining to coat it evenly. Sprinkle over the crushed crackers, chocolate chips, coconut, and nuts, then pour over the sweetened condensed milk as evenly as possible.
3 Bake in the hot oven 20 to 25 minutes, or until lightly browned. Remove from the oven and let the cake cool completely in the pan before cutting into 16 bars and transferring to a serving plate.

187 White chocolate fruit & nut bars

PREPARATION TIME 20 minutes   **COOKING TIME** 35 to 40 minutes   **MAKES** 16 bars

butter, for greasing
1 cup slivered almonds
2 cups walnuts, chopped
1²/₃ cups desiccated coconut
³/₄ cup dried apricots, chopped
1 cup plus 2 tbsp. raisins

2 tbsp. plus 1 tsp. rice flour
¹/₄ cup ground almonds
¹/₂ cup apricot jam
¹/₂ cup honey
9oz. white chocolate,
    melted and left to cool

1   Preheat the oven to 325°F. Grease a shallow 8 x 12in. pan with butter and line with baking paper.

2   In a large bowl, mix the almonds, walnuts, coconut, apricots, raisins, flour, and ground almonds together. In a small saucepan, gently warm the jam and honey together over low heat until melted. Pour the jam and honey mixture into the fruit mixture, stir well to combine, then pour into the prepared pan.

3   Bake in the hot oven 30 to 35 minutes, or until the slice is lightly browned. Remove from the oven and let the cake cool completely in the pan before spreading the melted chocolate over the top. Allow to set before cutting into 16 bars.

188 Chocolate coconut bars

PREPARATION TIME 20 minutes   **COOKING TIME** 15 to 20 minutes   **MAKES** 16 bars

1 stick plus 1 tbsp. butter, melted,
plus extra for greasing
1/2 cup plus 1 tsp.
packed light brown sugar
1 cup flaked coconut, plus 2 tbsp.
for sprinkling

1 egg, lightly beaten
1/2 cup plus 2 tbsp. all-purpose flour
1/4 cup self-rising flour
1 tbsp. unsweetened cocoa powder
1 recipe quantity Chocolate Fudge
Frosting (see page 212)

1   Preheat the oven to 350°F. Grease a shallow 8 x 12in. pan with butter and line
with baking paper.
2   In a large bowl, mix together the melted butter, brown sugar, coconut,
egg, both flours, and the cocoa until well combined, using a wooden spoon.
Press the mixture into the prepared pan.
3   Bake in the hot oven 15 to 20 minutes until the cake is firm and golden brown.
Remove from the oven and let cool completely in the pan.
4   To decorate the cake, use a palette knife to spread the chocolate fudge frosting
over the cake, then sprinkle with the coconut before cutting into 16 bars.

189 Chocolate peppermint bars

PREPARATION TIME 30 minutes, plus chilling   **COOKING TIME** 12 to 15 minutes
MAKES 24 bars

2 tbsp. butter, melted, plus extra
for greasing
3/4 cup plus 4 tsp. self-rising flour
2 tbsp. unsweetened cocoa powder
1/4 tsp. baking soda
5 tbsp. superfine sugar
1 egg, lightly beaten

FOR THE FILLING
2 1/3 cups plus 1 tbsp. powdered
sugar
1 tbsp. vegetable oil
2 tbsp. milk (about)
1 tsp. peppermint extract

FOR THE TOPPING
4 1/2 oz. bittersweet chocolate,
broken into pieces
7 tbsp. butter, chopped

1   Preheat the oven to 350°F. Grease a shallow 9in. square cake pan with butter
and line with baking paper.
2   In a large bowl, mix the flour, cocoa, baking soda, sugar, butter, and 5 tbsp.
water together until smooth, using a wooden spoon. Add the egg and mix until
well combined. Pour into the prepared pan.
3   Bake in the hot oven 12 to 15 minutes, or until the cake is just firm, then remove
from the oven and let cool in the pan.
4   For the filling, sift the powdered sugar into a bowl and mix all of the ingredients
plus 1/4 cup hot water together until smooth, using as much of the milk as is
necessary for a soft consistency. Spread the filling evenly over the cake, using a
palette knife, and then refrigerate 1 hour until firm.
5   For the filling, melt the chocolate and butter together in a small saucepan until
the chocolate is just melted, stirring until smooth, using a wooden spoon.
Spread the topping over the filling, then refrigerate the cake 1 hour. Remove
from the refrigerator and cut into 24 bars.

190 Mincemeat & chocolate bars

PREPARATION TIME 15 minutes **COOKING TIME** 20 to 25 minutes **MAKES** 16 squares

1 stick plus 1 tbsp. butter, melted,
   plus extra for greasing
1 cup plus 3 tbsp. self-rising flour
2 tbsp. unsweetened cocoa powder
1/3 cup plus 4 tsp. superfine sugar

1 1/2 cups mincemeat
1 egg, lightly beaten
1 recipe quantity Shiny Chocolate
   Icing (see page 213)

1   Preheat the oven to 350°F. Grease a shallow 9in. square cake pan with butter and line with baking paper.
2   Mix together the butter, flour, cocoa, sugar, mincemeat, and egg until just combined, using a wooden spoon. Press the mixture into the prepared pan.
3   Bake in the hot oven 20 to 25 minutes until the cake is firm and lightly browned. Let cool completely in the pan.
4   To ice the cake, use a palette knife to spread the shiny chocolate icing over the cake before cutting into 16 bars.

191 Butterscotch & chocolate bars

PREPARATION TIME 15 minutes **COOKING TIME** 35 to 40 minutes **MAKES** 16 bars

2 sticks plus 2 tbsp. butter, softened,
   plus extra for greasing
3/4 cup plus 3 tbsp. packed light
   brown sugar
2 eggs, lightly beaten

1 tsp. vanilla extract
7oz. bittersweet or semi-sweet
   chocolate, finely chopped
2 3/4 cups plus 4 tsp. self-rising flour
1 cup walnuts, finely chopped

1   Preheat the oven to 325°F. Grease a shallow 9 x 13in. pan with butter and line with baking paper.
2   In a large bowl, beat together the butter and brown sugar, using an electric hand mixer, then add the eggs, a little at a time. Add the vanilla extract, then gently fold in the chocolate and flour until just combined, using a metal spoon. Spread the mixture evenly over the bottom of the prepared pan and scatter the walnuts evenly over the top of the mixture.
3   Bake in the hot oven 35 to 40 minutes, or until the middle is just firm and the top is golden brown. Remove from the oven and let the cake cool in the pan completely before cutting into 16 bars.

192 Chocolate oat bars

PREPARATION TIME 20 minutes   **COOKING TIME** 15 to 20 minutes   **MAKES** 18 bars

3 sticks butter, chopped,
  plus extra for greasing
3 tbsp. light corn syrup
³/₄ cup plus 3 tbsp. packed light
  brown sugar

¹/₃ cup plus 4 tsp. superfine sugar
5 tbsp. unsweetened cocoa powder
3¹/₂ cups rolled oats

1 Preheat the oven to 300°F. Grease a shallow 9in. square cake pan with butter
   and line the bottom with baking paper.
2 In a small saucepan, melt the butter with the light corn syrup, over low heat.
   Remove from the heat and set aside. In a large bowl, mix together both sugars,
   cocoa, and rolled oats, using a wooden spoon, then pour the butter mixture into
   the bowl. Stir until well combined then press the mixture into the prepared pan.
3 Bake in the warm oven 15 to 20 minutes, or until just firm in the middle.
   Remove from the oven and let cool completely in the pan before cutting
   into 18 bars.

193 Chocolate & almond tuiles

PREPARATION TIME 15 minutes   **COOKING TIME** 6 to 8 minutes   **MAKES** 18 tuiles

6 tbsp. butter, melted
1/2 cup ground almonds
1/4 cup all-purpose flour
1 tbsp. unsweetened cocoa powder

3 tbsp. plus 1 tsp. superfine sugar
pinch salt
2 egg whites
1/2 cup slivered almonds

1   Preheat the oven to 325°F. Line a large baking sheet with baking paper.
2   Place all of the ingredients except the slivered almonds in a large bowl and stir
until combined, using a wooden spoon. Place tablespoonfuls of the mixture
on the prepared sheet and spread thinly, using the back of a spoon or a knife.
Sprinkle with the slivered almonds.
3   Bake in the hot oven 6 to 8 minutes, or until the tuiles are golden brown.
Remove from the oven and let the tuiles cool on the sheet 5 minutes, then
transfer to a wire rack to cool completely.

194 Macadamia & chocolate wafers

PREPARATION TIME 15 minutes   **COOKING TIME** 8 to 10 minutes   **MAKES** 18 wafers

7 tbsp. butter, softened, plus extra
   for greasing
3/4 cup plus 1 tbsp. superfine sugar
3 tbsp. light corn syrup or honey
1 cup plus 3 tbsp. all-purpose flour

1 tbsp. unsweetened cocoa powder
2 egg whites
1/2 cup macadamia nuts, chopped
1/4 cup chocolate chips

1   Preheat the oven to 350°F. Line 2 large baking sheets with baking paper.
2   Place the butter, sugar, syrup, flour, cocoa, and egg whites in the bowl of a food
processor and pulse until smooth. Spoon 9 tablespoonfuls of the mixture on
each of the prepared sheets. Spread out each one thinly, using the back of the
spoon, leaving about 4in. between them to allow for spreading. Sprinkle with the
chopped nuts and chocolate chips.
3   Bake in the hot oven 8 to 10 minutes until the wafers are golden brown.
Remove from the oven and let the wafers cool completely on the sheets.

195 Chocolate scones

PREPARATION time 20 minutes   **COOKING TIME** 15 to 20 minutes   **MAKES** 6 large scones

6 tbsp. chilled butter, chopped,
 plus extra for greasing
2³/₄ cups plus 4 tsp. self-rising flour,
 plus extra for dusting
2 tbsp. unsweetened cocoa powder
1 tsp. cinnamon

¹/₃ cup plus 4 tsp. superfine sugar
scant ¹/₂ cup milk, plus extra
 for brushing
1 egg, lightly beaten
1 recipe quantity Chocolate Chantilly
 Cream (see page 208)

1   Preheat the oven to 375°F. Grease a large baking sheet with butter.
2   Sift the flour and cocoa into a large bowl, then add the cinnamon and sugar.
    Add the butter and, working lightly, rub it into the flour using your fingertips
    until the mixture resembles breadcrumbs. In a small bowl, beat together the
    milk and egg. Add the milk mixture to the flour mixture until it forms a soft
    dough, using a rounded knife and a cutting motion.
3   Turn the dough out onto a lightly floured board and pat it out until it is about
    1in. thick. Cut out 6 circles, using a round cookie cutter, and place on the
    prepared sheet. Brush the tops with a little extra milk, using a pastry brush.
4   Bake in the hot oven 15 to 20 minutes, or until the scones are golden brown.
    Remove from the oven and transfer to a wire rack to cool completely, then
    transfer to a serving plate and serve with the chocolate chantilly cream.

196 Chocolate chunk scones

PREPARATION TIME 20 minutes   **COOKING TIME** 15 to 20 minutes   **MAKES** 6 large scones

6 tbsp. chilled butter, chopped,
 plus extra for greasing
2³/₄ cups plus 4 tsp. self-rising flour,
 plus extra for dusting
5 tbsp. superfine sugar
3¹/₂oz. bittersweet or milk chocolate,
 broken into pieces

scant ¹/₂ cup milk, plus extra
 for brushing
1 egg, lightly beaten
1 recipe quantity Chocolate Chantilly
 Cream (see page 208)

1   Preheat the oven to 375°F. Grease a baking sheet with butter.
2   Place the flour and sugar in a large bowl and, working lightly, rub in the butter
    with your fingertips until the mixture resembles breadcrumbs. Stir in the
    chocolate with a wooden spoon. In a small bowl, beat together the milk and
    egg. Add the milk mixture to the flour mixture until it forms a soft dough, using
    a rounded knife and a cutting motion.
3   Turn the dough out on to a lightly floured board and pat it out until it is about
    1in. thick. Cut out 6 circles, using a round cookie cutter, and place on the
    prepared sheet. Brush the tops with a little extra milk, using a pastry brush.
4   Bake in the hot oven 15 to 20 minutes, or until the scones are golden brown.
    Remove from the oven and transfer to a wire rack to cool completely, then
    transfer to a serving plate and serve with the chocolate chantilly cream.

197 Cranberry and white chocolate scones

PREPARATION TIME 20 minutes   **COOKING TIME** 15 to 20 minutes   **MAKES** 6 large scones

6 tbsp. butter, chilled and chopped,
  plus extra for greasing and
  to serve
2 cups self-rising flour
3 tbsp. plus 1 tsp. superfine sugar

2³/₄oz. white chocolate chips
³/₄ cup plus 1 tbsp. dried cranberries
6 tbsp. milk, plus extra for brushing
1 egg, lightly beaten

1   Preheat the oven to 375°F. Grease a large baking sheet with butter.
2   Place the flour and sugar in a large bowl and, working lightly, rub in the butter
    with your fingertips until the mixture resembles breadcrumbs. Stir in the
    chocolate chips and cranberries, using a wooden spoon. In a small bowl, beat
    together the milk and egg. Add the milk mixture to the flour mixture until it
    forms a soft dough, using a rounded knife and a cutting motion.
3   Turn the dough out on to a lightly floured board and pat it out until it is about
    1in. thick. Cut out 6 circles, using a round cookie cutter, and place on the
    prepared sheet. Brush the tops with a little extra milk, using a pastry brush.
4   Bake in the hot oven 15 to 20 minutes, or until the scones are golden brown.
    Remove from the oven and transfer to a wire rack to cool completely, then
    transfer to a serving plate and serve warm or cold with butter.

198   Chocolate coconut drops

PREPARATION TIME 15 minutes   **COOKING TIME** 10 to 12 minutes   **MAKES** 20 cookies

butter, for greasing
2³/₄oz. bittersweet chocolate,
   melted and left to cool
1 cup flaked coconut

¹/₂ cup plus 1 tsp. superfine sugar
1 tbsp. unsweetened cocoa powder
1 egg white
1 tbsp. powdered sugar, sifted

1   Preheat the oven to 350°F. Grease 2 baking sheets with butter.
2   In a large bowl, mix together the melted chocolate, coconut, superfine sugar,
    cocoa, and egg white until well combined, using a wooden spoon. Shape large
    teaspoonfuls of the mixture into balls and place them on the prepared sheets,
    leaving about 2in. between them to allow for spreading. Flatten each ball
    slightly and sprinkle with the powdered sugar.
3   Bake in the hot oven 10 to 12 minutes, or until the cookies are just firm.
    Remove from the oven and let the cookies cool on the sheets 10 minutes,
    then transfer to wire racks to cool completely.

199   Chocolate donut mini-muffins

PREPARATION TIME 20 minutes   **COOKING TIME** 15 to 20 minutes   **MAKES** 24 mini muffins

6 tbsp. butter, softened, plus extra
   for greasing
²/₃ cup superfine sugar
1 egg, lightly beaten
1¹/₂ cups self-rising flour
2 tbsp. unsweetened cocoa powder

¹/₄ tsp. baking soda
1 tsp. ground nutmeg
¹/₂ cup milk
1 tsp. cinnamon
2 tbsp. butter, melted

1   Preheat the oven to 350°F. Grease 2 x 12-hole mini-muffin pans with butter.
2   In a large bowl, beat the butter and ¹/₃ cup plus 4 tsp. of the sugar together until
    pale and creamy, using an electric hand mixer, then whisk in the egg. In a clean
    bowl, combine the flour, cocoa, baking soda, and nutmeg, then fold into the
    butter mixture with the milk. Spoon the mixture evenly into the prepared pan.
3   Bake in the hot oven 15 to 20 minutes until the mini-muffins are firm and lightly
    browned. Remove from the oven and let the mini-muffins cool in the pans
    5 minutes.
4   In a clean bowl, combine the remaining sugar and the cinnamon. While still
    warm, brush the top of each mini-muffin with the melted butter, then sprinkle
    over the cinnamon sugar. Remove the mini-muffins from the pans and transfer
    to a wire rack to cool completely.

200 Chocolate-chip & coconut muffins

PREPARATION TIME 15 minutes   **COOKING TIME** 15 to 20 minutes   **MAKES** 12 muffins

7 tbsp. butter, melted, plus extra
   for greasing
3 cups self-rising flour
3/4 cup plus 1 tbsp. superfine sugar
1/2 cup flaked coconut

1/2 cup sour cream
1/4 cup milk
2 eggs, lightly beaten
31/2 oz. bittersweet chocolate chips

1 Preheat the oven to 375°F. Grease a 12-hole muffin pan with butter.
2 In a large bowl, mix all of the ingredients together, using a wooden spoon,
   until well combined. Spoon the mixture evenly into the prepared pan.
3 Bake in the hot oven 15 to 20 minutes until the muffins rise and are golden
   brown. Remove from the oven and let cool in the pan 5 to 10 minutes, then
   remove from the pan and transfer to a wire rack to cool completely.

201 Chocolate cherry muffins

PREPARATION TIME 15 minutes   **COOKING TIME** 18 to 20 minutes   **MAKES** 12 large muffins

1 tbsp. butter, melted, plus extra
   for greasing
1 cup plus 3 tbsp. self-rising flour
1/2 cup plus 2 tbsp. all-purpose flour
3 tbsp. unsweetened cocoa powder
1 cup plus 4 tsp. superfine sugar

1 egg, lightly beaten
1 cup plus 2 tbsp. milk
1/2 cup candied cherries,
   roughly chopped
31/2 oz. bittersweet chocolate chips
1/2 cup flaked coconut

1 Preheat the oven to 375°F. Grease a 12-hole muffin pan with butter.
2 In a large bowl, mix both flours, the cocoa, sugar, egg, butter, and milk until just
   combined, using a wooden spoon. Stir in the cherries, chocolate chips, and
   coconut and spoon the mixture evenly into the prepared pan.
3 Bake in the hot oven 18 to 20 minutes until the muffins rise and are dark brown.
   Remove from the oven and let cool in the pan 5 to 10 minutes, then remove from
   the pan and transfer to a wire rack to cool completely.

202 Banana & white chocolate muffins

PREPARATION TIME 15 minutes   **COOKING TIME** 15 to 20 minutes   **MAKES** 12 muffins

1 stick plus 1 tbsp. butter, melted,
  plus extra for greasing
3 cups self-rising flour
³/₄ cup plus 1 tbsp. superfine sugar
2 eggs lightly beaten

2 ripe bananas, mashed
4¹/₂oz. white chocolate chips
1 cup plus 2 tbsp. milk
powdered sugar, sifted, for dusting

1   Preheat the oven to 375°F. Grease a 12-hole muffin pan with butter.
2   In a large bowl, mix together all the ingredients until just combined, using
    a wooden spoon. Divide the mixture evenly into the prepared pan.
3   Bake in the hot oven 15 to 20 minutes until the muffins rise and are
    golden brown. Remove from the oven and let the muffins cool in the pan
    5 to 10 minutes, then remove from the pan and transfer to a wire rack to cool
    completely. Dust with powdered sugar.

203 White chocolate & blueberry muffins

PREPARATION TIME 15 minutes   **COOKING TIME** 15 to 20 minutes   **MAKES** 12 muffins

1 stick plus 1 tbsp. butter, melted,
  plus extra for greasing
2 cups self-rising flour
¹/₃ cup plus 4 tsp. superfine sugar
4¹/₂oz. white chocolate, broken
  into pieces

1 egg, lightly beaten
¹/₂ cup milk
1 tsp. vanilla extract
1 cup blueberries

1   Preheat the oven to 375°F. Grease a 12-hole muffin pan with butter.
2   In a large bowl, mix all the ingredients together until just combined, using
    a wooden spoon. Divide the mixture evenly into the prepared pan.
3   Bake in the hot oven 15 to 20 minutes until the muffins rise and are
    golden brown. Remove from the oven and let the muffins cool in the pan
    5 to 10 minutes, then remove from the pan and transfer to a wire rack to
    cool completely.

204 Orange chocolate-chip muffins

PREPARATION TIME 20 minutes   **COOKING TIME** 20 to 25 minutes   **MAKES** 12 muffins

6 tbsp. butter, melted, plus extra
  for greasing
2 cups self-rising flour
pinch salt
¹/₃ cup plus 4 tsp. superfine sugar
1 egg, lightly beaten

¹/₂ cup milk
¹/₂ cup plain yogurt
zest of 1 orange
3¹/₂oz. orange-flavored chocolate,
  broken into pieces

1   Preheat the oven to 350°F. Grease a 12-hole muffin pan with butter.
2   In a large bowl, combine the flour, salt, and sugar, using a wooden spoon.
    In a separate bowl, beat together the egg, milk, yogurt, melted butter,
    and orange zest until combined, using a hand whisk, then stir into the flour
    mixture. Fold in the chocolate, using a metal spoon. Divide the mixture evenly
    into the prepared pan.
3   Bake in the hot oven 20 to 25 minutes until the muffins rise and are golden
    brown. Remove from the oven and let cool in the pan 5 to 10 minutes, then
    remove from the pan and transfer to a wire rack to cool completely.

205 Double chocolate muffins

PREPARATION TIME 15 minutes   **COOKING TIME** 20 to 25 minutes   **MAKES** 12 muffins

1 stick plus 1 tbsp. butter, melted,
   plus extra for greasing
3 cups self-rising flour
3 tbsp. unsweetened cocoa powder
3/4 cup plus 1 tbsp. superfine sugar

2 eggs, lightly beaten
4 1/2 oz. bittersweet or milk
   chocolate chips
1 cup plus 2 tbsp. milk

1   Preheat the oven to 375°F. Grease a 12-hole muffin pan with butter.
2   In a large bowl, mix together all the ingredients until just combined, using a wooden spoon. Divide the mixture evenly into the prepared pan.
3   Bake in the hot oven 20 to 25 minutes until the muffins rise and are golden brown. Remove from the oven and let cool in the pan 5 to 10 minutes, then remove from the pan and transfer to a wire rack to cool completely.

206 White chocolate & strawberry muffins

PREPARATION TIME 15 minutes   **COOKING TIME** 18 to 20 minutes   **MAKES** 12 muffins

1 stick plus 1 tbsp. butter, melted,
   plus extra for greasing
1/3 cup plus 4 tsp. superfine sugar
1/2 cup milk
1 egg, lightly beaten

1 tsp. vanilla extract
2 cups self-rising flour
9oz. white chocolate chips
1/2 cup strawberry jam

1   Preheat the oven to 350°F. Grease a 12-hole muffin pan with butter.
2   In a large bowl, mix together all the ingredients except for the jam until
    blended. Spoon the mixture evenly into the prepared pan, to fill about halfway,
    then top with a spoonful of the strawberry jam. Cover the jam with the
    remaining muffin mixture.
3   Bake in the hot oven 18 to 20 minutes until the muffins rise and are golden
    brown. Remove from the oven and let cool in the pan 5 to 10 minutes, then
    remove from the pan and transfer to a wire rack to cool completely.

207 Flourless chocolate muffins

PREPARATION TIME 15 minutes   **COOKING TIME** 20 to 25 minutes   **MAKES** 12 muffins

1 stick plus 3 tbsp. butter,
   plus extra for greasing
7oz. bittersweet chocolate,
   broken into pieces

5 eggs, separated
1/2 cup plus 1 tsp. superfine sugar
1 1/2 cups ground almonds

1   Preheat the oven to 325°F. Grease a 12-hole muffin pan with butter.
2   In a small saucepan, heat the butter and chocolate together over low heat
    until just melted, then remove from the heat and set aside to cool slightly.
    When cool, add the egg yolks and 5 tbsp. of the sugar, and combine well,
    using a wooden spoon.
3   In a clean bowl, whisk the egg whites to soft peaks, using an electric hand
    mixer, then gradually add the remaining sugar and continue beating until
    thick, but not dry. Fold the chocolate mixture and the ground almonds into
    the whisked egg whites, using a metal spoon. Divide the mixture evenly
    into the prepared pan.
4   Bake in the hot oven 20 to 25 minutes until the muffins rise and are golden
    brown. Remove from the oven and let cool in the pan 5 to 10 minutes, then
    remove from the pan and transfer to a wire rack to cool completely.

208 Chocolate mud pastries

PREPARATION TIME 20 minutes   **COOKING TIME** 20 to 25 minutes   **MAKES** 12 pastries

13oz. packet ready-rolled
  puff pastry
2³/₄oz. bittersweet chocolate,
  broken into pieces
2 tbsp. butter, chopped

5 tbsp. superfine sugar
1 egg, lightly beaten
1 tsp. vanilla extract
1 tbsp. all-purpose flour
powdered sugar, sifted, for dusting

1 Preheat the oven to 400°F.

2 Cut the pastry into 12 squares of about 4in., which will roughly fit the holes
of a 12-hole muffin pan with about ¹/₂in. extra. Gently ease each pastry square
into a muffin hole without stretching it. Refrigerate while preparing the filling.

3 In a small saucepan, heat the chocolate and butter over low heat and stir until
just melted. Remove from the heat and set aside to cool 10 minutes, then stir
in the sugar, egg, vanilla extract, and flour. Spoon 1 to 2 tbsp. of the chocolate
mixture into the middle of each pastry cup, taking care not to overfill.

4 Bake in the hot oven 15 to 20 minutes, or until the pastry is golden and the
filling has puffed up. Remove from the oven and leave the pastries in the pans
5 minutes, then transfer to a wire rack to cool completely. Dust the pastries
with powdered sugar.

209 Chocolate caramel tarts

PREPARATION TIME 35 minutes, plus setting   **COOKING TIME** 15 minutes
MAKES 4 x 4in. tarts

1³/₄ cups sugar
1 stick plus 1 tbsp. butter, chopped,
  plus extra for greasing
¹/₂ cup heavy cream

4 x 4in. Chocolate Shortcrust
  Pastry shells, baked (see page 13)
1 recipe quantity Dark Chocolate
  Ganache (see page 209)

1 In a medium-sized saucepan, mix ¹/₂ cup water and the sugar together over low
heat and stir with a metal spoon from time to time until the sugar dissolves
completely. Turn up the heat and boil vigorously 10 to 12 minutes until the
mixture forms a dark caramel, swirling the pan from time to time. Remove from
the heat, add the butter and cream (be careful: the mixture will hiss and spit),
and stir well until combined, using a wooden spoon. Set the caramel mixture
aside to cool 15 minutes, then divide it equally between the baked pastry shells
and allow to set 15 to 20 minutes.

2 Top each tart with dark chocolate ganache, spreading it evenly over the tarts
with a palette knife. Allow the tarts to set at room temperature 1 to 2 hours.

210 Mincemeat & chocolate tart

PREPARATION TIME 30 minutes   **COOKING TIME** 15 to 20 minutes   **MAKES** 1 x 9in. tart

1 x 9in. Chocolate Shortcrust
  Pastry shell, baked (see page 13)
1 tbsp. brandy
1¹/₂ cups mincemeat
1³/₄oz. bittersweet chocolate, melted
  and left to cool

FOR THE TOPPING:
3 tbsp. all-purpose flour
2 tbsp. packed light brown sugar
¹/₂ stick butter, chopped
¹/₂ tsp. cinnamon

1   Preheat the oven to 350°F. Place the baked pastry shell on a baking sheet.
2   In a large bowl, combine the brandy and mincemeat, using a wooden spoon, and spread evenly over the bottom of the tart shell. Place the topping ingredients in the bowl of a food processor and pulse until smooth, then sprinkle the topping mixture evenly over the mincemeat.
3   Bake in the hot oven 15 to 20 minutes until the tart is golden brown, then remove from the oven and let the tart cool on the baking sheet 15 minutes. Place the melted chocolate in a piping bag with a fine nozzle and drizzle randomly over the top of the tart. Serve warm or cold.

211 Chocolate pear tart

PREPARATION TIME 30 minutes   **COOKING TIME** 30 to 35 minutes   **MAKES** 1 x 9in. tart

1 x 9in. Chocolate Shortcrust
  Pastry shell, baked (see page 13)
7oz. bittersweet chocolate, melted
  and left to cool
1 egg, lightly beaten

1 cup plus 2 tbsp. heavy cream
1 tsp. vanilla extract
3 large ripe pears, peeled, cored,
  and halved

1   Preheat the oven to 350°F. Place the baked pastry shell on a baking sheet.
2   In a large bowl, beat the chocolate, egg, cream, and vanilla extract together, using an electric hand mixer, to make a chocolate custard. Place the pears on the bottom of the pastry shell and pour the chocolate custard mixture over the top, taking care not to overfill.
3   Bake in the hot oven 30 to 35 minutes, or until the custard has set, then remove from the oven and let the tart cool on the baking sheet 30 minutes before transferring to a serving plate.

212 Chocolate & raspberry tart

PREPARATION TIME 20 minutes **COOKING TIME** 35 to 40 minutes **MAKES** 1 x 9in. tart

1 x 9in. Sweet Shortcrust Pastry
  shell, baked (see page 13)
5¹/₂oz. bittersweet chocolate,
  broken into pieces
¹/₃ cup heavy cream
6 tbsp. butter, chopped
2 eggs

3 tbsp. plus 3 tsp. superfine sugar
1 tbsp. light corn syrup
1 cup raspberries, plus extra
  for serving (optional)
powdered sugar, for dusting
1 recipe quantity Chocolate Marsala
  Cream (see page 352)

1 Preheat the oven to 300°F. Place the baked pastry shell on a baking sheet.
2 In a small saucepan, melt the chocolate, cream, and butter together over low
   heat, then remove the pan from the heat and set aside to cool. In a large bowl,
   beat the eggs, sugar, and light corn syrup together for a few minutes until
   pale and light, using an electric hand mixer. Stir in the chocolate mixture, using
   a wooden spoon. Scatter the raspberries over the bottom of the tart and pour
   the chocolate filling on top, taking care not to overfill.
3 Bake in the warm oven 35 to 40 minutes, or until the middle of the tart is just
   set. Remove from the oven and let cool completely on the baking sheet.
4 Dust the tart with powdered sugar just before serving and serve with extra
   raspberries, if desired, and the chocolate Marsala cream.

213 Chocolate tart with cardamom

PREPARATION TIME 30 minutes   **COOKING TIME** 20 to 25 minutes   **MAKES** 1 x 9in. tart

1 x 9in. Sweet Shortcrust Pastry
  shell, baked (see page 13)
¹/₂ stick butter
9oz. bittersweet chocolate, broken
  into pieces

3 eggs, separated
5 tbsp. superfine sugar
¹/₂ cup heavy cream
1 tsp. ground cardamom

1   Preheat the oven to 400°F. Place the baked pastry shell on a baking sheet.
2   In a small saucepan, melt the butter and chocolate together over low heat,
    then remove the pan from the heat and and set aside to cool. In a separate
    bowl, whisk the egg whites to soft peaks, using an electric hand mixer, then
    gradually add the sugar and whisk until stiff. Beat the yolks into the chocolate
    mixture, then fold in the cream, cardamom, and whisked egg whites, using
    a metal spoon until just combined. Pour the mixture into the baked pastry shell,
    taking care not to overfill.
3   Bake in the hot oven 20 to 25 minutes, or until the tart is just firm around the
    edges but the middle is still soft. Remove the tart from the oven and serve warm.

214 Chocolate-crusted lemon tart

PREPARATION TIME 35 minutes   **COOKING TIME** 30 to 35 minutes   **MAKES** 1 x 9in. tart

1 recipe quantity Chocolate
  Crumb Crust (see page 13)
juice and finely grated zest of
  3 lemons

²/₃ cup plus 1¹/₂ tsp. superfine sugar
²/₃ cup heavy cream
4 eggs, lightly beaten
powdered sugar, sifted, for dusting

1   Preheat the oven to 300°F. Press the chocolate crumb crust into the bottom
    and sides of a fluted, loose-bottomed 9in. flan pan, 1¹/₂in. deep.
2   In a large bowl, beat together the lemon juice and zest and the sugar until
    the sugar dissolves, using an electric hand mixer. Whisk in the cream and
    eggs, then pour the lemon filling into the prepared crumb crust, taking care
    not to overfill.
3   Bake in the warm oven 30 to 35 minutes, or until the tart is just set but
    the middle is still slightly wobbly. Remove from the oven and let the tart
    cool completely in the pan, then remove the tart from the pan and dust
    with powdered sugar.

215 Chocolate custard tart

PREPARATION TIME 25 minutes   **COOKING TIME** 35 to 40 minutes   **MAKES** 1 x 9in. tart

1 x 9in. Sweet Shortcrust Pastry
  shell, baked (see page 13)
2 eggs plus 2 egg yolks
3 tbsp. plus 1 tsp. superfine sugar

2 cups plus 1 tbsp. milk
3¹/₂oz. bittersweet chocolate,
  broken into pieces
1 tsp. vanilla extract

1   Preheat the oven to 300°F. Place the baked pastry shell on a baking sheet.
2   In a large bowl, beat together the eggs, egg yolks, and sugar, using an electric
    hand mixer. In a small saucepan, heat the milk and chocolate together over
    low heat until the chocolate is just melted. Whisk the warm chocolate milk into
    the egg mixture and stir in the vanilla extract, then pour the resulting custard
    mixture into the pastry shell, taking care not to overfill.
3   Bake in the warm oven 35 to 40 minutes, or until the custard is set but still
    wobbly. Remove from the oven and let cool completely on the baking sheet.

216 White chocolate & berry tarts

PREPARATION TIME 30 minutes   **COOKING TIME** 8 to 10 minutes   **MAKES** 12 tarts

1 stick plus 1 tbsp. butter, melted,
  plus extra for greasing
8 sheets filo pastry
5 tbsp. superfine sugar
²/₃ cup heavy cream, whipped
  to soft peaks

4¹/₂oz. white chocolate, melted
  and left to cool
1¹/₂ cups mixed raspberries
  and blackberries

1   Preheat the oven to 350°F. Grease a 12-hole muffin pan with butter.
2   Lay a sheet of filo pastry on the work surface and brush with melted butter.
    Sprinkle over some of the sugar. Place a second layer of pastry on top of the
    first layer, lightly butter, then sprinkle with sugar. Repeat until all of the layers
    have been used, finishing with a butter and sugar layer. Cut the pastry stack into
    12 squares and ease a square into each hole of the muffin pan.
3   Bake in the hot oven 8 to 10 minutes, or until the pastry is golden brown.
    Remove from the oven and let the filo cases cool in the pan.
4   For the filling, gently fold the cream and melted chocolate together in a bowl,
    using a metal spoon. Remove the tart cases from the pan and, just before
    serving, divide the filling mixture evenly between them and spoon the mixed
    berries over.

217 Double chocolate tart

PREPARATION TIME 25 minutes **COOKING TIME** 25 to 30 minutes **MAKES** 1 x 9in. tart

1 x 9in. Sweet Shortcrust Pastry
shell, baked (see page 13)
7oz. bittersweet chocolate,
broken into pieces
6oz. milk chocolate, broken
into pieces

1½ sticks butter, chopped,
4 eggs, lightly beaten
5 tbsp. superfine sugar
powdered sugar, for dusting

1 Preheat the oven to 350°F. Place the baked pastry shell on a baking sheet.
2 In a small saucepan, heat both chocolates and the butter over low heat until just melted. Remove the pan from the heat and set aside to cool slightly. In a large bowl, beat the eggs and sugar together until thick and pale, using an electric hand mixer, then fold in the cooled chocolate mixture, using a metal spoon. Pour the mixture into the pastry shell, taking care not to overfill.
3 Bake in the hot oven 25 to 30 minutes, or until the tart is just firm. Remove from the oven and let the tart cool on the baking sheet completely, then dust with powdered sugar.

218 Italian-style chocolate tart

PREPARATION TIME 25 minutes **COOKING TIME** 30 to 35 minutes
MAKES 1 x 14 x 4½in. rectangular tart

1 recipe quantity Chocolate
Shortcrust Pastry (see page 13),
baked in a 14 x 4½in. rectangular
pan, 1½in. deep
1 cup plus 2 tbsp. milk
3½oz. bittersweet chocolate,
broken into pieces

1 tsp. vanilla extract
¼ cup superfine sugar
2 eggs
1½ tbsp. all-purpose flour
1 tbsp. Marsala wine
powdered sugar, sifted, for dusting

1 Preheat the oven to 325°F. Place the baked pastry shell on a baking sheet.
2 In a medium-sized saucepan, heat the milk, chocolate, and vanilla extract over low heat until the chocolate is just melted. In a large bowl, beat the sugar, eggs, and flour together, using an electric hand mixer, then beat in the warm chocolate mixture. Return the mixture to the saucepan and heat until the mixture has thickened, stirring constantly with a wooden spoon. Remove from the heat, stir in the Marsala wine, then pour the mixture into the pastry shell, taking care not to overfill.
3 Bake in the hot oven 25 to 30 minutes, or until the custard is firm around the edges but still wobbly in the middle. Remove from the oven and let the tart cool completely on the baking sheet, then dust with powdered sugar.

219 Tangy lemon & chocolate tarts

PREPARATION TIME 35 minutes   **COOKING TIME** 17 to 20 minutes   **MAKES** 4 x 4in. tarts

4 x 4in. Sweet Shortcrust Pastry
   shells, baked (see page 13)
juice and finely grated zest of
   3 lemons
$^2/_3$ cup plus 1$^1/_2$ tsp. superfine sugar
5 eggs, lightly beaten

1 stick plus 3 tbsp. butter, chopped
3$^1/_2$oz. bittersweet chocolate, melted,
   plus shards to decorate
unsweetened cocoa powder, sifted,
   for dusting

1 Preheat the oven to 350°F. Place the baked pastry shells on a baking sheet.
2 Place the lemon juice and zest, the sugar, eggs, and butter in the top
   of a double boiler and heat, stirring constantly with a wooden spoon, about
   15 minutes until the mixture thickens and coats the back of the spoon.
   Remove from the heat and stir in the melted chocolate. Pour the mixture into
   the baked pastry shells, filling them about two-thirds full.
3 Bake in the hot oven 12 to 15 minutes, or until the custard is just firm,
   then remove from the oven and let the tarts cool completely on the sheet.
   Place a shard of chocolate on each tart and dust with cocoa just before serving.

220 Chocolate Bakewell tart

PREPARATION TIME 35 minutes   **COOKING TIME** 30 to 35 minutes   **MAKES** 1 x 9in. tart

1 x 9in. Chocolate Shortcrust Pastry
  shell, baked (see page 13)
²/₃ cup raspberry or
  strawberry jam
6 tbsp. butter, softened
5 tbsp. superfine sugar

1 egg, lightly beaten
2 tbsp. ground almonds
¹/₂ cup plus 2 tbsp. self-rising flour
2 tbsp. unsweetened cocoa powder
3 tbsp. milk

1   Preheat the oven to 375°F. Place the baked pastry shell on a baking sheet
and spread the jam over the base.

2   In a large bowl, beat the butter and sugar together until light and creamy, using
an electric hand mixer, then beat in the egg. Fold in the almonds, flour, cocoa,
and milk, using a metal spoon, and spread the filling mixture over the jam in the
pastry shell, taking care not to overfill.

3   Bake in the hot oven 15 minutes, then lower the oven temperature to 325°F
and bake a further 15 minutes, or until the top of the tart is firm. Remove from
the oven and serve warm or cold.

221 Chocolate-glazed peanut butter tart

PREPARATION TIME 20 minutes, plus chilling   **COOKING TIME** 5 minutes
MAKES 1 x 14 x 4½in. rectangular tart

3 egg yolks
¹/₃ cup plus 1 tbsp. packed light
  brown sugar
2 tsp. all-purpose flour
1¹/₄ cups plus 1 tbsp. milk
¹/₂ cup smooth peanut butter
1 tsp. vanilla extract

1 recipe quantity Sweet Shortcrust
  Pastry (see page 13), baked in
  a 14 x 4¹/₂in. rectangular pan,
  1¹/₂in. deep
3¹/₂oz. bittersweet chocolate, melted
  and left to cool

1   In a medium-sized bowl, beat together the egg yolks, brown sugar, and flour
until well combined, using a wooden spoon. In a medium-sized saucepan, heat
the milk until it just comes to a boil and then whisk the hot milk into the egg
yolk mixture, stirring well. Return the mixture to the pan and place over low
heat. Bring the mixture to a boil and boil until it thickens, stirring constantly
with a wooden spoon. Allow to boil gently 1 further minute, then remove from
the heat. Whisk in the peanut butter and vanilla extract. Set the filling mixture
aside to cool 10 minutes.

2   Pour the filling mixture into the baked pastry shell on a serving plate. While the
mixture is still warm, pour the melted chocolate over the top. Let the tart cool
completely, then refrigerate 30 minutes before serving.

222 Chocolate mascarpone tart

PREPARATION TIME 35 minutes, plus chilling **COOKING TIME** 5 minutes
MAKES 1 x 9in. tart

12oz. bittersweet chocolate, broken
  into pieces
1 cup plus 2 tbsp. milk
½ stick butter, chopped
2 tsp. vanilla extract
1 Chocolate Crumb Crust, baked
  (see page 13)

9oz. mascarpone cheese, softened
1 cup plus 2 tbsp. heavy cream
2 tbsp. superfine sugar
unsweetened cocoa powder, sifted,
  for dusting

1 Place the chocolate, milk, butter, and half the vanilla extract in a saucepan
and stir constantly over low heat until the chocolate is just melted, using
a wooden spoon. Remove from the heat and set aside until cool. Do not allow
it to set. Pour the chocolate mixture into the baked crumb crust and chill 1 hour.

2 In a large bowl, beat the mascarpone, cream, sugar, and remaining vanilla
extract together until light, using an electric hand mixer. Spoon over the top
of the chocolate mixture. Refrigerate the tart for another hour, or until firm.
Dust with cocoa just before serving.

223 Chocolate pecan tart

PREPARATION TIME 15 minutes **COOKING TIME** 40 to 45 minutes **MAKES** 1 x 9in. tart

1 x 9in. Chocolate Shortcrust Pastry
  shell, baked (see page 13)
¾ cup plus 2 tbsp. superfine sugar
3 tbsp. unsweetened cocoa powder
2 eggs
1 tsp. vanilla extract

⅔ cup plus 1 tbsp. heavy cream
½ stick butter, melted and left
  to cool
⅔ cup plus 1 tsp. pecans,
  roughly chopped

1 Preheat the oven to 350°F. Place the baked pastry shell on a baking sheet.

2 In a large bowl, whisk the sugar, cocoa, eggs, vanilla extract, cream, and butter
together until smooth, using an electric hand mixer. Sprinkle the pecans into
the bottom of the pastry shell and pour the filling mixture over, taking care
not to overfill.

3 Bake in the hot oven 40 to 45 minutes, or until the tart is just firm. Remove from
the oven, transfer to a wire rack, and let cool completely.

CHAPTER 3

Desserts

In this chapter you will find a range of hot and cold

desserts that make the perfect ending for any occasion.

I have included a versatile collection of crêpe recipes—from

the basic Chocolate Crêpes to a more exotic version filled

with orange, white chocolate, and ricotta. And for custard

lovers, the assortment of crème brûlée and crème caramel

recipes will really hit the spot. The Chocolate, Panettone

& Raisin Puddings and the Fig & Chocolate Bread Pudding

provide delicious variations on a traditional comfort-food

favorite. There are also a few indulgent puddings—the

Chocolate Puddings with Rum Sauce are a real favorite

of mine. They are served with a very adult sauce, which

can be substituted with cream for younger gourmets!

If you are trying to tone down the chocolate just a little,

you will also find some fruity chocolate recipes such as Baked

Bananas with Chocolate Rum Sauce or Fruit Kabobs with

Chocolate Fruit & Nut Sauce, any of which make a delicious

and healthy finale to a meal. Whatever kind of dessert you're

looking for, there is a recipe in this chapter just for you.

224   Chocolate pancakes

PREPARATION TIME 10 minutes   **COOKING TIME** 15 minutes
MAKES about 12 pancakes

2 cups self-rising flour
1 tbsp. unsweetened cocoa powder
1/3 cup plus 4 tsp. sugar
1 cup plus 2 tbsp. milk

1 egg, lightly beaten
butter, melted, for cooking pancakes
powdered sugar, sifted, for dusting

1   Sift the flour and cocoa into a large bowl, mix in the sugar, and make a well
in the middle of the mixture. In a small bowl, whisk the milk and egg together,
using a hand whisk, and pour into the well. Stir with a wooden spoon to form
a smooth batter.

2   Heat a nonstick skillet over medium heat and brush with melted butter.
Pour in the batter to make 3½in. rounds. Cook 1 to 2 minutes, or until the top
of each pancake begins to show small bubbles, then turn over with a spatula
and cook on the second side 30 seconds more. Remove from the pan and repeat
until all the pancake batter has been used.

3   Transfer the pancakes to plates, dust with powdered sugar, and serve warm.

225   Banana pancakes with chocolate sauce

PREPARATION TIME 5 minutes   **COOKING TIME** 15 minutes

1 recipe quantity Chocolate Pancake
   batter (see recipe 224)
2 bananas, mashed
butter, melted, for cooking pancakes

powdered sugar, sifted, for dusting
1 recipe quantity Rich Chocolate
   Sauce (see page 204)

1   In a large bowl, mix the prepared pancake batter with the bananas until well
combined, using a wooden spoon.

2   Heat a nonstick skillet over medium heat and brush with melted butter.
Pour in the batter to make 3½in. rounds. Cook 1 to 2 minutes, or until the top
of each pancake begins to show small bubbles, then turn over with a spatula and
cook on the second side 30 seconds more. Remove from the pan and repeat
until all the pancake batter has been used.

3   Transfer the pancakes to plates, dust with powdered sugar, and serve warm
with the rich chocolate sauce.

226   Chocolate & blueberry pancakes

PREPARATION TIME 5 minutes   **COOKING TIME** 15 minutes

1 recipe quantity Chocolate Pancake
   batter (see recipe 224)
1 cup blueberries

1¾oz. bittersweet chocolate,
   broken into very small pieces
butter, melted, for cooking pancakes
powdered sugar, sifted, for dusting

1   In a large bowl, mix the prepared pancake batter with the blueberries and
chocolate until well combined, using a wooden spoon.

2   Heat a nonstick skillet over medium heat and brush with melted butter.
Pour in the batter to make 3½in. rounds. Cook 1 to 2 minutes, or until the top
of each pancake begins to show small bubbles, then turn over with a spatula
and cook on the second side 30 seconds more. Remove from the pan and repeat
until all the pancake batter has been used.

3   Transfer the pancakes to plates, dust with powdered sugar, and serve warm.

227 Chocolate crêpes

PREPARATION TIME 20 minutes plus 30 minutes' standing **COOKING TIME** 20 minutes
MAKES about 12 crêpes

1 cup plus 3 tbsp. all-purpose flour
2 tbsp. unsweetened cocoa powder,
  sifted
2 tsp. sugar
1 egg, lightly beaten

1¼ cups plus 1 tbsp. milk
2 tbsp. butter, melted, plus extra
  for cooking crêpes
powdered sugar, sifted, for dusting

1   In a large bowl, combine the flour, cocoa, and sugar, stirring with a wooden
    spoon. In a clean bowl, beat together the egg, milk, and melted butter, using
    a hand whisk. Make a well in the middle of the flour mixture and pour in half
    the liquid mixture. Mix well with a wooden spoon, adding the remaining liquid
    as required so that the batter resembles thin cream. Allow the batter to stand
    30 minutes before using and add a little extra milk if required.
2   Place a crêpe pan or nonstick skillet over low heat and brush with a little
    melted butter. Pour in just enough batter to coat the base of the pan, then swirl
    it around and pour off any excess. Leave the batter to cook until the edges of the
    crêpe dry and begin to lift (about 50 to 55 seconds), then turn the crêpe over
    using a spatula. Cook 30 seconds more, then remove from the pan and repeat
    until all the crêpe batter has been used.
3   Transfer the crêpes to plates, dust with powdered sugar, and serve warm.

228 Chocolate crêpes with chestnut cream

PREPARATION TIME 20 minutes

7oz. canned, unsweetened
  chestnut purée
1 cup plus 2 tbsp. heavy cream
1 tsp. cinnamon
2 tbsp. sugar

1 recipe quantity Chocolate Crêpes,
  freshly cooked (see recipe 227)
1 recipe quantity Double Chocolate
  Sauce (see page 204)

1   In a large bowl, beat the chestnut purée until smooth, using an electric hand
    mixer. Stir in the cream, cinnamon, and sugar, then spread each warm crêpe
    with the chestnut cream and fold into quarters.
2   Place 3 chocolate crêpes on each plate, top with the double chocolate sauce,
    and serve immediately.

229 Chocolate crêpe gâteau

PREPARATION TIME 20 minutes, plus chilling **SERVES** 4 to 6

1 recipe quantity Chocolate Crêpes,
  cooked (see recipe 227)
1 recipe quantity Creamy Thick
  Chocolate Custard (see page 12)

3½ bittersweet or milk chocolate,
  grated
1 recipe quantity Rich Chocolate
  Sauce (see page 204) or Espresso
  Chocolate Sauce (see page 205)

1   Layer the crêpes, creamy thick chocolate custard, and grated chocolate on
    a serving plate, beginning and ending with a crêpe layer. Refrigerate 1 hour.
2   Using a large, sharp knife, cut the crêpe gateau into wedges and serve with
    the rich chocolate sauce or espresso chocolate sauce.

230 Chocolate & strawberry liqueur crêpes

PREPARATION TIME 20 minutes   **COOKING TIME** 15 to 20 minutes

2 tbsp. butter, plus extra
   for greasing
1 recipe quantity Chocolate Pastry
   Cream (see page 12)
1 tbsp. heavy cream

1 recipe quantity Chocolate Crêpes,
   cooked (see page 145)
3 tbsp. powdered sugar
2 cups strawberries, hulled and
   cut in half
2 tbsp. strawberry liqueur

1   Preheat the oven to 350°F. Grease a baking dish (large enough to hold the overlapping crêpes) with butter.
2   In a large bowl, mix the chocolate pastry cream with the cream. Lay out the crêpes on the work surface and divide the cream filling mixture equally among them. Fold each crêpe in half, and then in half again, to form a neat triangle. Arrange in the prepared dish.
3   In a nonstick saucepan, melt the butter with the powdered sugar over medium heat. Add the strawberries and the liqueur and heat just until the strawberries are coated with the syrup but are still firm to the touch. Spoon this mixture over the prepared crêpes.
4   Cover the dish with foil and bake the crêpes in the hot oven 10 to 15 minutes, or until heated through. Remove from the oven and serve immediately.

231 Chocolate crêpes with orange, white chocolate & ricotta

PREPARATION TIME 15 minutes   **COOKING TIME** 10 to 15 minutes

butter, for greasing
3/4 cup golden raisins
13oz. ricotta cheese
1/4 cup powdered sugar
1 tbsp. orange liqueur
zest of 1 orange, grated

1 3/4oz. white chocolate,
   melted and left to cool
1 recipe quantity Chocolate Crêpes,
   cooked (see page 145)
1 recipe quantity Double Chocolate
   Sauce (see page 204)

1   Preheat the oven to 350°F. Grease a baking dish (large enough to hold the overlapping crêpes) with butter.
2   To make the filling, place the golden raisins in a small bowl, cover with boiling water, and let stand 10 minutes. Drain and set aside to cool. In a large bowl, mix the ricotta, golden raisins, powdered sugar, liqueur, orange zest, and melted chocolate together until combined, using a wooden spoon.
3   Lay out the crêpes on the work surface and divide the filling mixture equally among them, spreading it to cover half of each crêpe. Fold each crêpe in half, and then in half again, to form a neat triangle. Place in the prepared dish. Repeat until all the crêpes and filling have been used.
4   Cover the dish with foil and bake the crêpes in the hot oven 10 to 15 minutes, or until heated through. Remove from the oven and serve with the double chocolate sauce.

232 Chocolate cherry crêpes

PREPARATION TIME 35 minutes   **COOKING TIME** 10 to 15 minutes

butter, for greasing
1 cup pitted cherries (canned),
  drained
1 recipe quantity Chocolate Pastry
  Cream (see page 12)

1 tbsp. cherry liqueur
1 recipe quantity Chocolate Crêpes,
  cooked (see page 145)
3¹/₂oz. bittersweet chocolate, grated
light cream, for serving (optional)

1   Preheat the oven to 350°F. Grease a baking dish (large enough to hold the
    overlapping crêpes) with butter.
2   To make the filling, cut the cherries in half with a sharp knife, place them
    in a large bowl with the chocolate pastry cream and liqueur, and mix well, using
    a wooden spoon.
3   Lay out the crêpes on the work surface and divide the cherry filling mixture
    equally among them, spreading it to cover half of each crêpe. Fold each crêpe
    in half, and then in half again, to form a neat triangle. Place in the prepared
    dish. Repeat until all the crêpes and filling have been used.
4   Sprinkle with the grated chocolate and bake the crêpes in the hot oven
    10 to 15 minutes, or until heated through. Remove the crêpes from the oven
    and serve warm with cream, if desired.

233 Chocolate soufflé crêpes

PREPARATION TIME 25 minutes   **COOKING TIME** 13 to 15 minutes

butter, for greasing
1 cup plus 2 tbsp. milk
2³/₄oz. bittersweet chocolate,
  broken into pieces
3 eggs, separated

6 tbsp. sugar
¹/₄ cup all-purpose flour
1 recipe quantity Chocolate Crêpes,
  cooked (see page 145)
powdered sugar, sifted, for dusting

1   Preheat the oven to 425°F. Grease 2 large baking dishes with butter.
2   In a small saucepan, heat the milk and chocolate together over low heat until
    the chocolate is just melted. In a large bowl, mix the egg yolks, ¹/₄ cup of the
    sugar, and the flour together, using a wooden spoon, then whisk in the warm
    chocolate milk, using an electric hand mixer. Return this custard mixture to the
    pan and continue cooking, stirring constantly, until thickened. Cook 1 minute
    more, then remove from the heat and set aside to cool completely.
3   In a clean bowl, whisk the eggs whites until soft peaks form, using clean
    attachments for the electric hand mixer, then add the remaining sugar and
    whisk to stiff peaks. Gently fold the whisked whites into the cooled custard,
    using a metal spoon.
4   Lay out the crêpes on the work surface and spoon 2 tbsp. of the filling mixture
    into the middle of each one. Spread it over each crêpe gently, then fold the
    crêpe in half. Using a spatula to help you, arrange 6 crêpes in a layer in each
    of the prepared baking dishes.
5   Bake the crêpes in the hot oven 8 to 10 minutes, or until the filling puffs
    up. Remove from the oven, dust the crêpes with powdered sugar, and
    serve immediately.

234 Chocolate orange creams

PREPARATION TIME 15 minutes, plus chilling **MAKES** 4 creams

4 eggs, separated
4½oz. bittersweet chocolate,
  melted and left to cool

2 tbsp. heavy cream
zest of 1 orange, finely grated

1 In a large bowl, beat the yolks into the melted chocolate, using an electric hand mixer, then stir in the cream and orange zest. In a clean bowl, whisk the egg whites to soft peaks, using clean attachments for the electric hand mixer, then fold into the chocolate mixture, using a metal spoon.

2 Divide the mixture between 4 dishes, then refrigerate 2 to 3 hours before serving.

235 Fig & chocolate bread pudding

PREPARATION TIME 20 minutes plus 30 minutes' standing **COOKING TIME** 35 to 40 minutes

2 tbsp. butter, softened, plus extra
  for greasing
1 small brioche loaf, cut into 8 slices
½ cup soft dried figs, sliced
3½oz. bittersweet chocolate, grated
4 eggs

½ cup plus 2 tsp. sugar
1 cup plus 2 tbsp. milk
1 cup plus 2 tbsp. heavy cream
1 tsp. vanilla extract

1 Preheat the oven to 300°F. Grease a 1½-quart baking dish with butter.

2 Butter the brioche slices on one side and cut in half diagonally. Arrange half the slices in the bottom of the prepared dish. Scatter the figs and chocolate over, then top with the remaining brioche slices. Beat the remaining ingredients together, using a hand whisk, and pour the resulting batter through a sieve over the top of the brioche slices. Let stand 30 minutes.

3 Place the ovenproof dish in a bain marie (see page 10) and bake in the warm oven 35 to 40 minutes, or until the pudding is just firm around the edges but still slightly wobbly in the middle. Remove from the oven and serve immediately.

236 Pear clafoutis with chocolate

PREPARATION TIME 25 minutes **COOKING TIME** 20 to 25 minutes

6 tbsp. butter, softened, plus
  extra for greasing
⅓ cup plus 4 tsp. sugar
2 eggs, lightly beaten
1 cup self-rising flour
¾ cup ground almonds

½ cup milk
3½oz. bittersweet chocolate, melted
  and left to cool
3 pears, ripe but not soft, peeled,
  quartered, and cored
light cream, to serve (optional)

1 Preheat the oven to 350°F. Grease a 1½-quart baking dish with butter.

2 In a large bowl, cream the butter and sugar together, using an electric hand mixer, then beat in the eggs, a little at a time. Combine the flour and ground almonds and fold into the butter mixture with the milk and melted chocolate to make a batter. Scatter the pears in the bottom of the baking dish and pour the batter mixture over.

3 Bake in the hot oven 20 to 25 minutes; the middle should still be soft. Remove from the oven and let the clafoutis cool slightly, before serving with cream, if desired.

237 Mocha creams with ricotta & coffee liqueur

PREPARATION TIME 25 minutes, plus chilling   **COOKING TIME** 5 minutes

1 cup plus 3 tbsp. heavy cream
1³/₄oz. bittersweet chocolate,
    broken into pieces
12oz. ricotta cheese

³/₄ cup plus 4 tsp. powdered sugar
2 tbsp. coffee liqueur
1 tbsp. coffee beans, freshly ground

1   In a small saucepan, heat ½ cup plus 2 tbsp. of the cream over low heat until just simmering, then remove from the heat and add the chocolate. Stir until smooth, using a metal spoon, and pour into a clean bowl to cool.
2   Place the ricotta, powdered sugar, liqueur, and coffee beans in the bowl of a food processor and process until smooth. Add the remaining cream and process briefly until all the ingredients are just combined.
3   Divide the ricotta mixture evenly between 4 glasses. Spoon 1 tbsp. of the chocolate mixture on top of the ricotta mixture in each glass and refrigerate 30 to 40 minutes until just firm.

238 Chocolate apple pudding

PREPARATION TIME 25 minutes   **COOKING TIME** 55 to 60 minutes

butter, for greasing
6 cooking apples, peeled, cored,
   and sliced
3/4 cup sugar
1 cinnamon stick

4 eggs, separated
4 1/2oz. bittersweet chocolate,
   melted and left to cool
1 1/4 cups double cream, whipped
   to soft peaks

1   Preheat the oven to 350°F. Grease a 1 1/2-quart ceramic baking dish with butter.
2   Place the prepared apples in a medium-sized saucepan with 1/3 cup plus 4 tsp.
    of the sugar and the cinnamon stick and pour in just enough water to come
    one-third of the way up the apples. Bring to a boil, then lower the heat and
    simmer 20 minutes, or until soft. Drain off any excess liquid, discard the
    cinnamon stick, and pour the apples into the prepared dish.
3   In a large bowl, stir the egg yolks into the melted chocolate, then fold in the
    cream with a metal spoon. Whisk the egg whites to soft peaks, using an electric
    hand mixer, then gradually whisk in the extra sugar until thick and glossy.
    Gently fold into the chocolate cream, then spread the mixture over the apple
    layer in the prepared dish.
4   Bake in the hot oven 35 to 40 minutes, or until slightly puffed and dark brown.
    Remove from the oven and serve immediately.

239 Chocolate panettone & raisin puddings

PREPARATION TIME 40 minutes plus 30 minutes' standing   **COOKING TIME** 30 to 35 minutes

butter, for greasing
3/4 cup golden raisins
1 tbsp. dark rum
4 medium slices panettone or
   4 slices brioche
3 eggs

1/3 cup plus 4 tsp. sugar
1 tsp. vanilla extract
3 1/2oz. bittersweet chocolate,
   melted and left to cool
1/2 cup milk
3/4 cup plus 2 tbsp. heavy cream

1   Preheat the oven to 300°F. Grease 4 x 1-cup ramekins with butter.
2   Place the golden raisins and rum in a small bowl and heat in the microwave
    1 minute. Set aside 10 minutes. Cut the panettone or brioche slices into small
    cubes, using a sharp knife, and divide evenly between the 4 dishes. Sprinkle
    over the golden raisins. In a large bowl, beat together the eggs, sugar, vanilla
    extract, melted chocolate, milk, and cream, using a hand whisk, and pour
    evenly over the dishes. Let stand 30 minutes.
3   Bake the puddings in a bain marie (see page 10) in the warm oven 30 to 35
    minutes until set but still a little wobbly in the middle. Remove from the oven
    and set aside to cool 10 minutes before turning out of the dishes to serve.

240 Chocolate croissant bread pudding

PREPARATION TIME 15 minutes **COOKING TIME** 40 to 45 minutes

6 mini or 3 large chocolate
   croissants
5 eggs
1 tsp. vanilla extract

$\frac{1}{3}$ cup plus 4 tsp. sugar
6$\frac{1}{2}$ cups milk
light cream, for serving (optional)

1   Preheat the oven to 300°F. Cut the chocolate croissants into slices about
    $\frac{1}{4}$in. thick and place them in the bottom of a 2-quart baking dish about 9in.
    in diameter.
2   In a large bowl, beat together the eggs, vanilla extract, and sugar, using a hand
    whisk. Then whisk in the milk.
3   Place the dish in a bain marie (see page 10) and bake in the warm oven
    40 to 45 minutes, or until the sides are firm but the middle is still slightly wobbly.
4   Remove the dish from the oven and let cool 5 minutes before serving with
    cream, if desired.

241 Chocolate crèmes caramels

PREPARATION TIME 15 minutes, plus chilling **COOKING TIME** 35 to 42 minutes

3/4 cup plus 2 tbsp. sugar
13/4 cups milk
3 eggs, lightly beaten

31/2oz. bittersweet chocolate,
melted and left to cool

1 Preheat the oven to 300°F. Place 4 x 1-cup ramekins in the oven to warm.
2 Place half of the sugar with 1/2 cup water in a saucepan over low heat, swirling until the sugar dissolves. Turn up the heat and boil until the mixture begins to brown around the edges. Swirl again and continue cooking until the sugar becomes an even caramel color. Divide the sugar mixture evenly between the warm ramekins and set aside.
3 In a large bowl, beat the remaining sugar together with the milk, eggs, and melted chocolate, using a hand whisk, and pour the mixture through a sieve into the ramekins.
4 Place the ramekins in a bain marie (see page 10) and bake in the warm oven 25 to 30 minutes, or until the sides are firm but the middles are still wobbly. Remove the ramekins from the water using tongs and set aside to cool 30 minutes.
5 Refrigerate the caramels 30 minutes, then remove from the refrigerator. Run a sharp knife around the edges of the caramels to loosen them from the ramekins, then turn out onto plates.

242 White chocolate crèmes brûlées

PREPARATION TIME 15 minutes, plus chilling **COOKING TIME** 40 to 45 minutes

5 egg yolks
1/2 cup plus 1 tbsp. sugar
2 cups plus 2 tbsp. heavy cream

41/2oz. white chocolate, broken
into pieces
1/2 tsp. vanilla extract

1 Preheat the oven to 250°F.
2 In a large bowl, beat the egg yolks and 1/3 cup plus 4 tsp. of the sugar together, using a hand whisk. In a small saucepan, heat the cream and chocolate together over low heat until the chocolate is just melted. Remove the chocolate mixture from the heat and whisk until smooth, then whisk it into the egg yolk mixture with the vanilla extract until well combined.
3 Divide the mixture evenly between 4 x 5oz. ramekins. Place the ramekins in a bain marie (see page 10) and bake in the warm oven 35 to 40 minutes, or until the custards are just set.
4 Remove the dish from the oven and take the ramekins out of the dish using tongs, then let cool 30 minutes before refrigerating overnight.
5 Remove from the refrigerator. Sprinkle the remaining sugar over the tops of the custards and place under a very hot broiler until the sugar melts and caramelizes (or use a domestic blowtorch). Serve immediately.

243 Chocolate crèmes brûlées

PREPARATION TIME 15 minutes, plus chilling   **COOKING TIME** 40 to 45 minutes

2½ cups plus 2 tbsp. heavy cream
2¾oz. bittersweet chocolate,
   broken into pieces
1 tsp. vanilla extract

6 egg yolks
3 tbsp. sugar
⅓ cup packed light brown sugar

1   Preheat the oven to 250°F.
2   In a small saucepan, heat the cream and chocolate together over low heat until the chocolate is just melted. In a large bowl, beat the vanilla extract, egg yolks, and sugar together, using a hand whisk, then whisk in the heated cream mixture, combining well.
3   Divide the mixture evenly between 4 x 5oz ramekins or other baking dishes. Place the ramekins in a bain marie (see page 10) and bake in the warm oven 35 to 40 minutes, or until the custards are just set.
4   Remove the dish from the oven and take the ramekins out of the dish using tongs, then let cool 30 minutes before refrigerating overnight.
5   Remove from the refrigerator. Sprinkle the brown sugar over the tops of the custards and place under a very hot broiler until the sugar melts and caramelizes (or use a domestic blowtorch). Serve immediately.

244 Baked chocolate custard

PREPARATION TIME 10 minutes **COOKING TIME** 45 to 50 minutes

3³/₄ cups milk
3¹/₂oz. bittersweet chocolate,
  broken into pieces
4 eggs

²/₃ cup plus 1 tsp. sugar
1 tbsp. unsweetened cocoa powder
1 tsp. vanilla extract

1 Preheat the oven to 300°F.
2 In a large saucepan, heat the milk and chocolate together over low heat until
   the chocolate starts to melt. Remove from the heat and whisk until smooth.
   In a large bowl, beat the eggs, sugar, cocoa, and vanilla extract together, using
   a hand whisk, then whisk in the chocolate mixture. Pour through a sieve into
   a 1-quart ceramic baking dish.
3 Place the dish in a bain marie (see page 10) and bake in the warm oven
   40 to 45 minutes, or until the custard edges are just firm but the middle stays
   wobbly. Remove from the oven and let cool 10 minutes before serving.

245 Chocolate sticky pudding & caramel sauce

PREPARATION TIME 20 minutes **COOKING TIME** 20 to 25 minutes

6 tbsp. butter, softened,
  plus extra for greasing
³/₄ cup plus 2 tbsp. packed
  light brown sugar
2 eggs, lightly beaten
2³/₄oz. bittersweet chocolate,
  melted and left to cool

1 cup plus 3 tbsp. self-rising flour
1 recipe quantity Chocolate
  Caramel Sauce (see page 204)

1 Preheat the oven to 325°F. Grease a 1-quart baking dish with butter.
2 In a large bowl, cream the butter and sugar together with a wooden spoon.
   Add the eggs a little at a time, beating well between additions. Stir in the melted
   chocolate and flour and pour the mixture into the prepared dish.
3 Bake in the hot oven 20 to 25 minutes, or until the pudding has risen and is just set
   in the middle. Remove from the oven and serve with chocolate caramel sauce.

246 Mocha pudding cakes

PREPARATION TIME 25 minutes **COOKING TIME** 20 to 30 minutes

7 tbsp. butter, softened,
  plus extra for greasing
¹/₂ cup plus 2 tsp. sugar
2 eggs, separated
3 tbsp. unsweetened cocoa powder

¹/₂ cup plus 2 tbsp. all-purpose flour
2 tsp. instant coffee powder
1 tsp. vanilla extract
¹/₂ cup milk

1 Preheat the oven to 350°F. Grease 4 x 6oz. ramekins with butter.
2 In a large bowl, beat the butter and ¹/₃ cup plus 4 tsp. of the sugar together,
   using an electric hand mixer, then add the egg yolks. Add the cocoa, flour,
   coffee, vanilla extract, and milk, stirring with a wooden spoon until just
   combined. In a clean bowl, whisk the egg whites to soft peaks, using clean
   attachments for the electric hand mixer, then gradually whisk in the remaining
   sugar. Fold the resulting meringue gently into the chocolate mixture and pour
   evenly between the ramekins.
3 Place the pudding cakes in a bain marie (see page 10) and bake in the hot oven
   20 to 30 minutes, or until they are slightly puffed and look dry. Remove from
   the oven and let the cakes cool before serving.

247 Chocolate self-saucing pudding

PREPARATION TIME 15 minutes   **COOKING TIME** 20 to 25 minutes

6 tbsp. butter, plus extra
   for greasing
1 cup plus 3 tbsp. self-rising flour
2 tbsp. unsweetened cocoa powder
1/3 cup plus 4 tsp. sugar
1/2 cup milk
1 tsp. vanilla extract
1 egg, lightly beaten

FOR THE TOPPING
1/2 cup packed light brown sugar
2 tbsp. unsweetened cocoa powder

1   Preheat the oven to 350°F. Grease a 1 1/2-quart baking dish with butter.
2   In a medium-sized bowl, combine the flour, cocoa, and sugar. In a small
   saucepan, heat the butter, milk, and vanilla extract over low heat until the
   butter has just melted, then set aside to cool 5 minutes. Whisk in the egg, using
   a hand whisk, then stir all of the liquid ingredients into the dry ingredients to
   combine. Pour the mixture into the prepared ovenproof dish.
3   For the topping, combine the brown sugar with the cocoa in a bowl, then sprinkle
   over the chocolate mixture in the dish. Pour over 1 1/4 cups boiling water. Bake in
   the hot oven 15 to 20 minutes, or until the pudding is firm but still slightly soft
   in the middle.
4   Remove from the oven and let cool 5 minutes before serving.

248 Chocolate rice pudding

PREPARATION TIME 10 minutes   **COOKING TIME** 30 to 35 minutes

2/3 cup short-grain rice
2 tbsp. sugar
1 tsp. vanilla extract
2 cups plus 1 tbsp. milk

3/4 cup plus 1 tbsp. heavy cream
2 3/4oz. bittersweet chocolate,
   broken into pieces

1   Rinse the rice well under cold water and place in a medium-sized saucepan
   with the remaining ingredients. Bring to a boil, stirring well, then reduce to
   a low simmer 25 to 30 minutes, or until most of the liquid is absorbed and the
   rice is tender, stirring often to prevent it from sticking.
2   Serve warm or at room temperature.

249 White chocolate rice pudding

PREPARATION TIME 15 minutes   **COOKING TIME** 30 to 35 minutes

2 cups plus 1 tbsp. milk
3/4 cup plus 1 tbsp. heavy cream
1 tsp. nutmeg
zest of 1 large orange, finely grated

2/3 cup short-grain rice
1 tbsp. sugar
3 1/2oz. white chocolate, broken into
   small pieces

1   Place the milk, cream, nutmeg, and orange zest in a large saucepan over
   low heat and bring to a boil.
2   Rinse the rice well under cold water and add to the milk mixture along with the
   sugar. Return to a boil, stirring well, then reduce to a low simmer 25 to 30 minutes,
   or until the rice is tender, stirring often to prevent it from sticking.
3   Stir in the chocolate until it melts. Serve warm or at room temperature.

250 White chocolate & coconut rice pudding

PREPARATION TIME 10 minutes **COOKING TIME** 30 to 35 minutes

½ cup short-grain rice
1½ cups coconut milk
3 tbsp. plus 1 tsp. sugar

1 tsp. vanilla extract
3½oz. white chocolate, melted
1 tsp. nutmeg

1 Rinse the rice well under cold water. Place the rice, coconut milk, and 1 cup water in a medium-sized saucepan and bring to a boil. Reduce to a low simmer 25 to 30 minutes, or until most of the liquid is absorbed and the rice is tender, stirring often to prevent it from sticking.
2 Remove from the heat and stir in the sugar, vanilla extract, melted chocolate, and nutmeg. Serve warm or at room temperature.

251 Simple chilled chocolate puddings

PREPARATION TIME 15 minutes, plus chilling **COOKING TIME** 5 minutes

1¾ cups heavy cream
7oz. bittersweet chocolate,
  broken into pieces
6 tbsp. butter, chopped
2 tbsp. sugar

1 tsp. vanilla extract
whipped cream, for serving
chocolate milk powder, for dusting

1 Heat the cream, chocolate, butter, and sugar in a medium-sized saucepan until just boiling, then remove from the heat and stir until smooth. Add the vanilla extract. Divide evenly between 4 x 7oz. ramekins.
2 Leave until cool then refrigerate 2 hours or overnight. Top with the whipped cream and dust with the chocolate milk powder just before serving.

252 Steamed banana pudding with chocolate

PREPARATION TIME 20 minutes **COOKING TIME** 1¾ hours **SERVES** 4 to 6

1 stick plus 1 tbsp. butter, softened,
  plus extra for greasing
⅓ cup plus 4 tsp. sugar
2 eggs, lightly beaten
2⅓ cups plus 1 tbsp. self-rising flour

2 tbsp. unsweetened cocoa powder
3 tbsp. milk
1 tsp. vanilla extract
1 banana, thinly sliced
3½oz. white chocolate chips

1 Grease a 1½-quart pudding basin or heatproof round bowl with butter. In a large bowl, beat the butter and sugar together until light and creamy, using an electric hand mixer. Beat in the eggs a little at a time until well combined. Fold in the flour, cocoa, milk, vanilla extract, banana, and chocolate chips.
2 Spoon into the prepared basin and cover with a double layer of foil secured with string. Place the basin in a large saucepan and fill with water to come halfway up the side of the basin. Bring the water to a boil, turn down to a simmer, and steam the pudding 1¾ hours, adding extra boiling water as required.
3 Remove the basin from the saucepan and let cool 10 minutes then turn the pudding out onto a serving plate.

253 Steamed chocolate pudding

PREPARATION TIME 20 minutes **COOKING TIME** 1¾ hours **SERVES** 4 to 6

7 tbsp. butter, softened, plus extra
 for greasing
⅓ cup plus 4 tsp. sugar
2 eggs, lightly beaten
¾ cup plus 1 tbsp. self-rising flour
2 tbsp. unsweetened cocoa powder

3½oz. bittersweet chocolate, melted
2 tbsp. milk
1 recipe quantity Rich Chocolate
 Sauce (see page 204) or Espresso
 Chocolate Sauce (see page 205)

1　Grease a 1½-quart pudding basin or heatproof round bowl with butter. In a
 large bowl, beat the butter and sugar together until light and creamy, using an
 electric hand mixer, then add the eggs a little at a time until smooth. Sift the
 flour and cocoa together and fold into the mixture with the chocolate and milk.
2　Spoon into the prepared basin and cover with a double layer of foil secured with
 string. Place the basin in a large saucepan and fill with water to come halfway
 up the side of the basin. Bring the water to a boil, turn down to a simmer, and
 steam the pudding 1¾ hours, adding extra boiling water as required.
3　Remove the basin from the saucepan and let cool 10 minutes, then turn the
 pudding out onto a serving plate. Serve with one of the chocolate sauces.

254 Lemon & white chocolate pudding

PREPARATION TIME 25 minutes   **COOKING TIME** 18 to 20 minutes

7 tbsp. butter, softened,
  plus extra for greasing
³/₄ cup sugar
2¹/₄oz. white chocolate,
  finely chopped

juice and finely grated zest
  of 2 lemons
4 eggs, separated
¹/₄ cup all-purpose flour
²/₃ cup milk
powdered sugar, sifted, for dusting

1 Preheat the oven to 350°F. Grease an 8 x 12in. baking dish with butter.
2 In a large bowl, mix the butter and sugar until light and creamy, using an electric hand mixer. Stir in the white chocolate, lemon zest, and egg yolks and mix well. Gently mix in the flour and milk, then stir in the lemon juice. (The juice may cause the mixture to curdle slightly, but do not worry.) In a clean bowl, whisk the egg whites to soft peaks, using clean attachments for the electric hand mixer, and fold into the pudding mixture, using a metal spoon. Pour the mixture into the prepared ovenproof dish.
3 Bake in the hot oven 18 to 20 minutes, or until lightly browned. Remove from the oven and let cool 5 minutes, then dust with powdered sugar and serve.

255 Chocolate puddings with rum sauce

PREPARATION TIME 75 minutes plus resting   **COOKING TIME** 35 to 40 minutes

5 tbsp. butter, softened, plus extra
  for greasing
¹/₄ cup sugar
¹/₄ cup all-purpose flour
2³/₄oz. bittersweet chocolate, broken
  into pieces
¹/₂ cup milk
3 eggs, separated

RUM SAUCE
3 tbsp. plus 1 tsp. sugar
¹/₄ cup rum
1 egg yolk
¹/₂ cup heavy cream,
  whipped to soft peaks

1 Preheat the oven to 375°F. Grease 4 x 1¹/₂-cup pudding molds or heatproof bowls with butter. Start to prepare the rum sauce. In a small bowl, combine the sugar and rum and stir well. Let stand 30 minutes.
2 To make the puddings, cream the butter and sugar together with a wooden spoon, in a large bowl, then stir in the flour. In a small saucepan, heat the chocolate with the milk over low heat until just melted. Pour the warm chocolate milk over the butter mixture, stirring well, then pour the mixture into the saucepan, return to the heat, and cook until the mixture begins to thicken. Remove the pan from the heat and add the egg yolks, stirring constantly, using a wooden spoon.
3 In a large bowl, whisk the egg whites until stiff, but not dry, using an electric hand mixer, and gently fold into the chocolate mixture. Pour the mixture evenly into the prepared molds. Place the molds in a bain marie (see page 10) and bake in the hot oven 30 to 35 minutes, or until just firm.
4 While the puddings are baking, finish making the sauce. In a clean bowl, beat the egg yolk until creamy, add the rum mixture, and let rest a further 30 minutes. Fold in the whipped cream and refrigerate 5 to 10 minutes.
5 Remove the puddings from the oven and let cool 5 minutes before turning them out onto plates. Serve topped with the chilled sauce.

256 Chocolate amaretti pears

PREPARATION TIME 25 minutes   **COOKING TIME** 15 to 20 minutes

6 tbsp. butter, melted, plus extra
　for greasing
5¹/₂oz. amaretto cookies
2³/₄oz. bittersweet chocolate,
　melted and left to cool

1 egg yolk
4 ripe pears
1 recipe quantity Chocolate &
　Amaretto Sauce (see page 204)

1　Preheat the oven to 400°F. Grease a baking dish (large enough to hold the
　pears) with butter.
2　Crush the cookies in a food processor and mix with the melted butter, melted
　chocolate, and egg yolk. Cut the pears in half lengthwise and scoop out the
　seeds using a sharp knife. Spoon the prepared cookie filling into each pear
　cavity, press down firmly, then spread enough filling over the surface of
　each pear to cover it completely.
3　Place the pears in the prepared dish and bake in the hot oven 15 to 20 minutes,
　until the pears are soft and the filling is dark brown. Remove from the oven and
　serve immediately with the chocolate and amaretto sauce.

257 Chocolate & banana fritters

PREPARATION TIME 20 minutes   **COOKING TIME** 20 to 28 minutes

1¹/₂ cups plus 2 tbsp. self-rising flour
2 tbsp. unsweetened cocoa powder
3 tbsp. plus 1 tsp. sugar, plus extra
　for sprinkling
1 egg
1 cup plus 2 tbsp. milk

vegetable oil. for deep-frying
4 ripe, firm bananas, peeled and
　cut into thirds
1 recipe quantity Rich Chocolate
　Sauce (see page 204)

1　In a large bowl, sift the flour and cocoa together, then add the sugar. In a clean
　bowl, whisk the egg and milk together, using a hand whisk, then add to the flour
　mixture, stirring well with a wooden spoon to form a smooth batter.
2　Heat the oil in a wide skillet until a cube of bread turns brown within 30 seconds
　of being placed in it. Dip the bananas into the batter, then deep-fry in batches
　of 3 pieces 5 to 7 minutes until golden brown. Remove the bananas from the
　pan, drain on paper towel, and sprinkle with a little extra sugar.
3　Serve the banana fritters immediately with the rich chocolate sauce.

258 Fruit kabobs with chocolate fruit & nut sauce

PREPARATION TIME 15 minutes

1 small pineapple, peeled and
  cut into chunks
2 cups strawberries, hulled
1 ripe mango, cut into chunks

1 cup seedless grapes
1 recipe quantity Chocolate
  Fruit & Nut Sauce (see page 206)

1 Thread the fruit alternately onto 8 wooden skewers, dividing the pieces evenly between the skewers.
2 Serve with the chocolate fruit and nut sauce.

259 Baked bananas with chocolate rum sauce

PREPARATION TIME 10 minutes   **COOKING TIME** 17 to 20 minutes

butter, for greasing
4 ripe, firm bananas, peeled and
  halved lengthwise
³/₄ cup plus 2 tbsp. heavy cream

¹/₄ cup packed light brown sugar
2 tbsp. unsweetened cocoa powder
1 recipe quantity Chocolate Rum
  Sauce (see page 206)

1 Preheat the oven to 350°F. Grease an ovenproof ceramic dish (large enough to hold the bananas) with butter.
2 Arrange the bananas in the prepared dish. In a small saucepan, whisk the cream, sugar, and cocoa together over low heat until hot, then pour over the bananas.
3 Bake in the hot oven 12 to 15 minutes, or until the bananas are soft. Remove from the oven and serve the bananas warm, with the chocolate rum sauce.

260 Berries with white chocolate sauce

PREPARATION TIME 10 minutes   **COOKING TIME** 5 minutes

¹/₂ stick butter, chopped
¹/₄ cup sugar
1 tbsp. strawberry liqueur

3 cups mixed berries
1 recipe quantity White Chocolate
  Sauce (see page 206)

1 In a nonstick skillet, melt the butter with the sugar over medium heat, then add the liqueur. Turn the heat to low and stir in the berries with a wooden spoon. Cook 3 to 4 minutes, or until the berries are just beginning to soften.
2 Divide the berries between 4 dishes and top with the white chocolate sauce.

261 Roast figs with chocolate sauce

PREPARATION TIME 10 minutes **COOKING TIME** 15 to 20 minutes

6 tbsp. butter, plus extra
  for greasing
8 large figs
2 tbsp. sugar

1 cup plus 2 tbsp. heavy cream,
  whipped to soft peaks
1 recipe quantity Rich Chocolate
  Sauce (see page 204)

1 Preheat the oven to 350°F. Grease a baking dish (large enough to hold
  the figs) with butter.
2 Cut a cross in the top of each fig, taking care to keep the fig in one piece.
  Divide the butter into 8 pieces and place one piece inside each fig.
  Place the figs in the prepared dish and sprinkle with the sugar.
3 Bake in the hot oven 15 to 20 minutes, or until the figs are soft but still hold
  their shape. Remove from the oven and set the baked figs aside in the dish
  to cool 10 minutes.
4 Divide the figs between 4 plates and top with a spoonful of cream and the rich
  chocolate sauce.

CHAPTER 4

Ices

I have never tasted anything so wonderful as freshly churned ice cream. If you have ever thought about making your own, then now is the time, because chocolate and ice cream are the perfect combination. You will need an ice-cream maker, which come in a range of models from hand-churned to battery-operated and electric. If you really want to splash out, a fully automatic, electric ice-cream maker is simple to use, and, while it is an investment, I guarantee it will not remain idle on your counter for long. Homemade ice cream is refreshingly free of preservatives and colorings, so it has a shorter shelf life (about 7 to 10 days) than the commercial variety, but, in my experience, it never lasts that long anyway! The natural qualities of homemade ice cream also mean that it tends to freeze to a harder consistency than commercial varieties and therefore needs to be removed from the freezer and placed in the refrigerator about 30 minutes before you want to serve it. However, the very best way to eat fresh ice cream, if not always the most practical, is straight from the churn. Scoop it into a chilled bowl and enjoy!

262 Rich chocolate ice cream

PREPARATION TIME 20 minutes, plus chilling and churning **COOKING TIME** 5 minutes
MAKES 4⅓ cups

1¼ cups plus 1 tbsp. milk
1¼ cups plus 1 tbsp. heavy cream
12oz. bittersweet or milk chocolate,
   broken into pieces

4 egg yolks
⅓ cup plus 4 tsp. sugar

1 In a small saucepan, heat the milk, cream, and chocolate together over low
heat until the chocolate is just melted. Remove the pan from the heat and
stir with a wooden spoon until smooth.

2 In a large bowl, beat the egg yolks and sugar together, using a hand whisk, then
pour in the hot chocolate mixture, whisking constantly. Return the mixture to
the saucepan and heat, stirring constantly with a wooden spoon, until the
mixture just begins to thicken and lightly coats the back of the spoon. Do not
allow the mixture to boil or it will curdle.

3 Remove from the heat, pour into a clean bowl, and let cool completely.
Refrigerate 3 hours or overnight, then churn in an ice-cream maker according
to the manufacturer's instructions.

263 Chocolate & banana ice cream

PREPARATION TIME 15 minutes, plus chilling and churning **MAKES** 4⅓ cups

3 ripe bananas
⅓ cup plus 4 tsp. sugar
1¼ cups plus 1 tbsp. milk
2 cups plus 2 tbsp. heavy cream

1 egg, lightly beaten
7oz. bittersweet chocolate,
   melted and cooled

1 Pulse the bananas with the sugar in the bowl of a food processor, then add
the milk, cream, egg, and melted chocolate. Process until just combined.

2 Refrigerate 3 hours or overnight, then churn in an ice-cream maker according
to the manufacturer's instructions.

264 Chocolate orange ice cream

PREPARATION TIME 20 minutes, plus chilling and churning **COOKING TIME** 5 minutes
MAKES 4⅓ cups

1¼ cups plus 1 tbsp. milk
2 cups plus 2 tbsp. heavy cream
7oz. bittersweet chocolate, broken
   into pieces
⅓ cup plus 4 tsp. sugar

4 egg yolks
1 tbsp. cornstarch
¾ cup orange-flavoured
   chocolate, chopped
1 tbsp. rosewater (optional)

1 In a medium-sized saucepan, heat the milk, cream, and chocolate together over
low heat until the chocolate is just melted.

2 In a large bowl, beat the sugar and egg yolks together, using a hand whisk, then
pour in the chocolate mixture, whisking constantly. Return the mixture to the pan
and heat, stirring constantly with a wooden spoon, until the mixture just begins
to thicken and just coats the back of the spoon. Do not let it boil or it will curdle.

3 Remove from the heat, pour into a clean bowl, and let cool completely.
Refrigerate 3 hours or overnight. Stir in the chopped orange chocolate and
rosewater, if using, then churn in an ice-cream maker according to the
manufacturer's instructions.

265 Chocolate, raisin & amaretto ice cream

PREPARATION TIME 25 minutes, plus chilling and churning **COOKING TIME** 5 minutes
MAKES 4$\frac{1}{3}$ cups

60g/2$\frac{1}{4}$oz./$\frac{1}{2}$ cup raisins
1$\frac{1}{2}$ tsp. amaretto liqueur
$\frac{1}{3}$ cup plus 4 tsp. sugar
1 cup plus 2 tbsp. milk
1$\frac{3}{4}$ cups heavy cream

2 tsp. vanilla extract
3$\frac{1}{2}$oz. bittersweet chocolate, grated

1 Place the raisins and liqueur in a small bowl and microwave 30 seconds. Set aside to cool completely.
2 In a medium-sized saucepan, heat the sugar and milk together over low heat, stirring, until the sugar dissolves. Remove from the heat and add the cream. Pour into a clean bowl and let cool completely. Refrigerate 3 hours or overnight.
3 When cold, stir in the marinated raisins, vanilla extract, and chocolate, then churn in an ice-cream maker according to the manufacturer's instructions.

266 White chocolate ice cream

PREPARATION TIME 20 minutes, plus chilling and churning **COOKING TIME** 5 minutes
MAKES 4$\frac{1}{3}$ cups

1 cup plus 2 tbsp. heavy cream
$\frac{1}{2}$ cup milk
6oz. white chocolate, broken
    into pieces

1 tsp. vanilla extract
2 eggs
$\frac{1}{3}$ cup plus 4 tsp. sugar

1 In a medium-sized saucepan, heat the cream, milk, chocolate, and vanilla extract over low heat until the chocolate is just melted.
2 In a large bowl, beat the eggs and sugar together, using a hand whisk, then pour in the hot chocolate mixture, whisking constantly. Return the mixture to the saucepan and heat, stirring constantly with a wooden spoon, until the mixture just begins to thicken and lightly coats the back of the spoon. Do not allow the mixture to boil or it will curdle.
3 Remove from the heat, pour into a clean bowl, and let cool completely. Refrigerate 3 hours or overnight, then churn in an ice-cream maker according to the manufacturer's instructions.

267 Strawberry & white chocolate cheesecake ice cream

PREPARATION TIME 15 minutes, plus chilling and churning **MAKES** 4$\frac{1}{3}$ cups

7oz. cream cheese, softened
heaped $\frac{2}{3}$ cup sugar
1 cup plus 2 tbsp. heavy cream
1 cup plus 2 tbsp. sour cream

1 cup strawberries, chopped
4$\frac{1}{2}$oz. white chocolate, melted
    and left to cool

1 In a large bowl, beat the cream cheese and sugar together until soft, using an electric hand mixer. Whisk in the cream and sour cream, then stir in the strawberries and melted chocolate until just combined.
2 Refrigerate 3 hours or overnight, then churn in an ice-cream maker according to the manufacturer's instructions.

268 Caramel & chocolate ice cream

PREPARATION TIME 20 minutes, plus chilling and churning   **COOKING TIME** 5 minutes
MAKES 4^1/$_3$ cups

1^3/$_4$ cups milk
1^1/$_4$ cups plus 1 tbsp. heavy cream
7oz. bittersweet chocolate, broken
   into pieces
^{1}/$_3$ cup plus 4 tsp. sugar

3 egg yolks
1 tbsp. cornstarch
2 tbsp. dulce de leche or
   similar caramel paste

1 In a medium-sized saucepan, heat the milk, cream, and chocolate over low
heat until the chocolate is just melted.
2 In a large bowl, beat the sugar, egg yolks, and cornstarch together, using
a hand whisk, then pour in the hot chocolate mixture, whisking constantly.
Return the mixture to the saucepan and heat, stirring constantly with a wooden
spoon, until the mixture just begins to thicken and lightly coats the back of the
spoon. Do not allow the mixture to boil or it will curdle.
3 Remove from the heat and stir in the dulce de leche until smooth, then pour into
a clean bowl, and let cool completely. Refrigerate 3 hours or overnight, then
churn in an ice-cream maker according to the manufacturer's instructions.

269 Mocha ice cream

PREPARATION TIME 25 minutes, plus chilling and churning   **COOKING TIME** 5 minutes
MAKES 4^1/$_3$ cups

1 cup plus 2 tbsp. milk
1 cup plus 2 tbsp. heavy cream
3 tsp. instant coffee powder
6 egg yolks

^{1}/$_2$ cup packed light brown sugar
7oz. bittersweet chocolate, melted
   and left to cool

1 In a small pan, heat the milk, cream, and coffee over low heat until just warm.
2 In a large bowl, beat the egg yolks and sugar together, using a hand whisk, then
pour in the hot coffee mixture, whisking constantly. Return the mixture to the
pan and heat, stirring constantly with a wooden spoon, until it begins to thicken
and coats the back of the spoon. Do not allow the mixture to boil or it will curdle.
3 Remove from the heat, pour into a clean bowl, and let cool slightly before whisking
in the melted chocolate, then let cool completely. Refrigerate 3 hours or overnight,
then churn in an ice-cream maker according to the manufacturer's instructions.

270 Roasted macadamia & chocolate ice cream

PREPARATION TIME 30 minutes, plus chilling and churning   **COOKING TIME** 5 minutes
MAKES 4^1/$_3$ cups

^{1}/$_2$ stick butter
heaped ^{1}/$_2$ cup macadamia nuts,
   chopped
2 tbsp. packed light brown sugar
1^1/$_2$ cups plus 2 tbsp. milk

1^1/$_2$ cups plus 2 tbsp. heavy cream
2 tbsp. maple syrup
4^1/$_2$oz. bittersweet chocolate,
   melted and left to cool

1 In a nonstick frying pan, heat the butter until melted, then stir in the chopped
macadamia nuts. Sprinkle the sugar over, then cook over medium heat
3 to 4 minutes, or until the nuts brown lightly.
2 In a large bowl, beat together the milk, cream, maple syrup, and melted
chocolate, then stir in the sugared nuts. Refrigerate 3 hours or overnight, then
churn in an ice-cream maker according to the manufacturer's instructions.

271 Ginger & chocolate ice cream

PREPARATION TIME 25 minutes, plus chilling and churning   **COOKING TIME** 5 minutes
MAKES 4¹/₃ cups

1 cup plus 2 tbsp. milk
3¹/₂oz. bittersweet chocolate,
 broken into pieces
3 egg yolks

¹/₃ cup plus 4 tsp. sugar
2 cups plus 2 tbsp. heavy cream
3¹/₂oz. candied ginger, chopped
1 tbsp. light corn syrup

1   In a small saucepan, heat the milk and chocolate together over low heat until
just melted.
2   In a large bowl, beat the egg yolks and sugar together, using a hand whisk, then
pour in the hot chocolate mixture, whisking constantly. Return the mixture to
the saucepan and heat, stirring constantly with a wooden spoon, until the mixture
just begins to thicken and lightly coats the back of the spoon. Do not allow the
mixture to boil or it will curdle.
3   Remove from the heat, pour into a clean bowl, and let cool completely, then stir
in the cream, ginger, and corn syrup. Refrigerate 3 hours or overnight, then
churn in an ice-cream maker according to the manufacturer's instructions.

272 Chocolate ice-cream & ginger cookie sandwiches

PREPARATION TIME 40 minutes, plus chilling   **COOKING TIME** 12 to 15 minutes

7 tbsp. butter, softened, plus extra
   for greasing
³/₄ cup plus 1 tbsp. powdered sugar
2 egg yolks
1 cup plus 4 tsp. all-purpose flour
4 tsp. ground ginger

2 tbsp. unsweetened cocoa powder
1 recipe quantity Rich Chocolate
   Ice Cream (see page 164)
powdered sugar, sifted, for dusting
   (optional)

1 Preheat the oven to 350°F. Grease a baking sheet with butter.
2 In a large bowl, beat the butter and sugar together until pale and light, using
   an electric hand mixer, then beat in the egg yolks. In a clean bowl, mix the
   flour, ginger, and cocoa together and gently stir into the butter mixture to
   form a dough. Wrap the dough in plastic wrap, flatten slightly, and refrigerate
   45 minutes, or until the dough is firm but not hard.
3 Roll the dough out on a lightly floured surface to about ¼in. thick and cut out
   8 cookie rounds using a large cookie cutter. Place the rounds on the prepared
   baking sheet, prick them with a fork, and bake in the hot oven 12 to 15 minutes,
   or until the cookies are firm and lightly golden.
4 Remove from the oven and let the cookies cool completely on the baking sheet.
   Sandwich pairs of cookies together with the chocolate ice cream. Dust with
   powdered sugar, if desired.

273 Honeycomb & chocolate ice cream

PREPARATION TIME 20 minutes, plus chilling and churning   **COOKING TIME** 5 minutes
MAKES 4¹/₃ cups

1¹/₄ cups plus 1 tbsp. milk
2 cups plus 2 tbsp. heavy cream
7oz. bittersweet chocolate,
   broken into pieces
5 tbsp. sugar
4 egg yolks
1 tbsp. cornstarch

2 tbsp. honey
3¹/₂oz. chocolate-coated honeycomb
   pieces, finely chopped
1 tsp. vanilla extract
1 recipe quantity Chocolate Caramel
   Sauce (see page 204)

1 In a medium-sized saucepan, heat the milk, cream, and chocolate together over
   low heat until the chocolate is just melted.
2 In a large bowl, beat the sugar, egg yolks, and cornstarch together, using
   a hand whisk, then pour in the hot chocolate mixture, whisking constantly.
   Return the mixture to the saucepan and heat, stirring constantly with a wooden
   spoon, until the mixture just begins to thicken and lightly coats the back of the
   spoon. Do not allow the mixture to boil or it will curdle.
3 Remove from the heat and and whisk in the honey, then pour into a clean bowl
   and let cool completely. Refrigerate 3 hours or overnight. Remove from the
   refrigerator and stir in the chopped honeycomb and vanilla extract just before
   churning in an ice-cream maker according to the manufacturer's instructions.
   Serve with chocolate caramel sauce.

274 Chocolate nougat ice cream

PREPARATION TIME 20 minutes, plus chilling and churning **COOKING TIME** 5 minutes
MAKES 4¹/₃ cups

1¹/₄ cups plus 1 tbsp. milk
7oz. bittersweet chocolate,
 broken into pieces
4 egg yolks
¹/₃ cup plus 4 tsp. sugar

1¹/₄ cups plus 1 tbsp. heavy cream
3¹/₂oz. soft torrone-style nougat,
 finely chopped
1 tsp. vanilla extract

1 In a small saucepan, heat the milk and chocolate together over low heat
until the chocolate is just melted.
2 In a large bowl, beat the egg yolks and sugar together, using a hand whisk,
then whisk in the warm chocolate milk. Return the mixture to the pan and
heat, stirring constantly with a wooden spoon, until the mixture just begins
to thicken and lightly coats the back of the spoon. Do not allow the mixture
to boil or it will curdle.
3 Remove from the heat, pour into a clean bowl, and let cool completely.
Refrigerate 3 hours or overnight. Remove from the refrigerator and stir
in the cream, nougat, and vanilla extract, then churn in an ice-cream maker
according to the manufacturer's instructions.

275 Chocolate ice cream with Irish Cream

PREPARATION TIME 20 minutes, plus chilling and churning **COOKING TIME** 5 minutes
MAKES 4¹/₃ cups

1¹/₄ cups plus 1 tbsp. milk
2 cups plus 2 tbsp. heavy cream
5¹/₂oz. bittersweet chocolate,
 broken into pieces
¹/₃ cup plus 4 tsp. sugar
4 egg yolks

1 tbsp. cornstarch
4 meringue shells, roughly crushed
8 tbsp. Irish Cream liqueur
1 recipe quantity Espresso Chocolate
 Sauce (see page 205)

1 In a medium-sized saucepan, heat the milk, cream, and chocolate together over
low heat until the chocolate is just melted.
2 In a large bowl, beat the sugar, egg yolks, and cornstarch together, using
a hand whisk, then whisk in the warm chocolate milk. Return the mixture
to the pan and heat, stirring constantly with a wooden spoon, until it just begins
to thicken and lightly coats the back of the spoon. Do not allow the mixture
to boil or it will curdle.
3 Remove from the heat, pour into a clean bowl, and let cool completely, then
refrigerate 3 hours or overnight. Remove from the refrigerator and stir in the
crushed meringue shells and half the liqueur, then churn in an ice-cream
maker according to the manufacturer's instructions. Serve the ice cream with
the remaining liqueur and the espresso chocolate sauce poured over the top.

276 Mint chocolate-chip ice cream

PREPARATION TIME 20 minutes, plus chilling and churning   **COOKING TIME** 5 minutes
MAKES 4¹/₃ cups

1¹/₂ cups plus 2 tbsp. milk
¹/₂ cup plus 2 tsp. sugar
1¹/₂ cups plus 2 tbsp. heavy cream
6oz. bittersweet chocolate, grated

2 tsp. peppermint extract
2 to 3 drops green coloring (optional)

1   In a medium-sized saucepan, heat the milk and sugar together over medium heat until the sugar dissolves. Pour into a clean bowl and add the cream. Leave the mixture to cool completely before stirring in the chocolate, peppermint extract, and green coloring, if using.
2   Refrigerate 3 hours or overnight, then churn in an ice-cream maker according to the manufacturer's instructions.

277 Chocolate mint sorbet

PREPARATION TIME 15 minutes, plus chilling and churning   **COOKING TIME** 5 minutes
MAKES 4¹/₃ cups

²/₃ cup plus 1 tsp. sugar
1 tbsp. unsweetened cocoa powder

4¹/₂oz. bittersweet chocolate,
   broken into pieces
3 drops peppermint extract

1   In a large saucepan, heat 3¹/₄ cups water and the sugar together over medium heat until the sugar dissolves, stirring frequently. In a large bowl, combine the cocoa and chocolate and pour over the hot sugar mixture. Let stand 2 minutes, then whisk until smooth, using a hand whisk. Stir in the peppermint extract and set aside to cool completely.
2   Refrigerate 2 hours or overnight, then churn in an ice-cream maker according to the manufacturer's instructions.

278 Chocolate semifreddo with Marsala

PREPARATION TIME 25 minutes, plus freezing   **SERVES** 4 to 6

3¹/₄ cups heavy cream
1¹/₂ cups plus 1 tsp. sugar
6 egg yolks
1 tsp. vanilla extract
2 tbsp. Marsala wine

7oz. bittersweet chocolate, melted,
   plus 5 tbsp. grated
1 recipe quantity Rich Chocolate
   Sauce (see page 204)

1   Line a 9 x 4½in. loaf pan (ideally silicone) with plastic wrap so that it hangs over the edges of the pan.
2   In a large bowl, whisk the cream and half the sugar together until the cream forms soft peaks, using an electric hand mixer. In a clean bowl, beat the egg yolks, vanilla extract, Marsala wine, and the remaining sugar together until the mixture is thick and pale, using the electric hand mixer, then stir in the melted chocolate. Fold the cream and the chocolate mixtures together, using a metal spoon, then stir in the grated chocolate.
3   Pour the mixture into the prepared loaf pan, covering the top with the plastic wrap to make a well-enclosed bundle, and freeze 8 hours or overnight.
4   Take the semifreddo out of the freezer, turn out from the pan onto a serving plate, and remove the plastic wrap. Serve with the rich chocolate sauce.

279 Chocolate sorbet

PREPARATION TIME 30 minutes, plus chilling and churning   **COOKING TIME** 25 minutes
MAKES 4¹/₃ cups

1 cup plus 4 tsp. sugar
1 cup plus 3 tbsp. unsweetened
  cocoa powder, sifted

2 tsp. vanilla extract

1   In a large saucepan, mix together the sugar and 3³/₄ cups water over medium heat, stirring well until the sugar dissolves. Whisk in the cocoa, using a hand whisk. Bring to a boil, then reduce the heat and simmer 20 minutes over low heat, stirring occasionally. Remove from the heat, pour into a clean bowl, and add the vanilla extract, then let cool completely.

2   Refrigerate 2 hours or overnight, then churn in an ice-cream maker according to the manufacturer's instructions.

280 Chocolate & nougat semifreddo

PREPARATION TIME 25 minutes, plus freezing   **SERVES** 4 to 6

3¹/₄ cups heavy cream
1¹/₄ cups plus 3 tbsp. sugar
6 egg yolks
1 tbsp. amaretto liqueur
1 cup raspberries, lightly crushed,
    plus extra, whole, for serving
    (optional)

3¹/₂oz. soft torrone-style nougat,
    chopped
²/₃ cup almonds, roasted
    and chopped
4¹/₂oz. bittersweet chocolate, grated
1 recipe quantity Traditional Hot
    Fudge Sauce (see page 206)

1   Line a 9 x 4¹/₂in. loaf pan (ideally silicone) with plastic wrap so that it hangs over
    the edges of the pan.
2   In a large bowl, whisk together the cream and half the sugar until soft peaks
    form, using an electric hand mixer. In a clean bowl, whisk the yolks, liqueur,
    and remaining sugar until the mixture is thick and pale. Fold the yolk mixture
    into the whipped cream, then fold in the raspberries, nougat, almonds, and
    grated chocolate.
3   Pour the mixture into the prepared loaf pan, covering the top with the
    overhanging plastic wrap to make a well-enclosed bundle. Freeze 8 hours
    or overnight.
4   Take the semifreddo out of the freezer, turn out from the pan onto a serving
    plate, and remove the plastic wrap. Serve with the extra raspberries, if desired,
    and the traditional hot fudge sauce.

281 Chocolate semifreddo

PREPARATION TIME 25 minutes, plus freezing   **SERVES** 4 to 6

2 eggs, separated
¹/₃ cup plus 4 tsp. sugar
4¹/₂oz. bittersweet chocolate,
    melted and left to cool
1 tbsp. frangelico liqueur
pinch salt

1¹/₂ cups plus 2 tbsp. double cream,
    whipped to soft peaks
1 recipe quantity Espresso Chocolate
    Sauce (see page 205)

1   Line a 9 x 4¹/₂in. loaf pan (ideally silicone) with plastic wrap so that it hangs over
    the edges of the pan.
2   In a large bowl, beat the egg yolks and sugar together until thick and pale,
    using an electric hand mixer, then stir in the chocolate and liqueur. In a clean
    bowl, whisk the egg whites with the salt until stiff.
3   Fold the cream and the egg whites into the chocolate mixture, using a metal
    spoon, and pour into the prepared pan, covering the top with the overhanging
    plastic wrap to make a well-enclosed bundle. Freeze 8 hours or overnight.
4   Take the semifreddo out of the freezer, turn out from the pan onto a serving
    plate, and remove the plastic wrap.

282 Frozen espresso mousse with chocolate sauce

PREPARATION TIME 30 minutes, plus freezing

4 egg yolks
$^1/_3$ cup plus 4 tsp. sugar
$^1/_2$ cup strong, hot, black coffee
2 tbsp. coffee liqueur

1 cup plus 2 tbsp. heavy cream,
    whipped to soft peaks
1 recipe quantity Rich Chocolate
    Sauce (see page 204)

1   In a large bowl, beat the egg yolks and sugar together until pale, using an electric hand mixer. Slowly pour the hot coffee into the yolk mixture, whisking constantly, and continue whisking until the mixture is very thick. Using a metal spoon, fold in the liqueur and cream until just combined.
2   Divide the mixture evenly between 4 freezerproof $^3/_4$-cup ceramic dishes and freeze 3 hours or overnight.
3   Take the dishes out of the freezer, dip them briefly in warm water, run a knife around the edges, and turn the mousses out onto plates. Serve with the rich chocolate sauce poured over the top.

283 Coffee parfait with chocolate sauce

PREPARATION TIME 15 minutes, plus freezing   **SERVES** 4 to 6

$^1/_2$ cup strong, hot, black coffee
$^1/_4$ cup sugar
16oz. can sweetened condensed milk

1 cup plus 2 tbsp. heavy cream,
    whipped to soft peaks
1 recipe quantity Traditional Hot
    Fudge Sauce (see page 206)

1   In a small bowl, mix the hot coffee and the sugar together until the sugar dissolves, stirring with a metal spoon. Set aside to cool completely. In a large bowl, beat together the sweetened condensed milk and the cooled coffee mixture, using an electric hand mixer.
2   Fold the whipped cream into the coffee milk. Divide the mixture evenly between 4 to 6 freezerproof ceramic dishes and freeze 3 hours or overnight.
3   Take the parfaits out of the freezer and serve with the traditional hot fudge sauce.

284 White chocolate & raspberry parfait

PREPARATION TIME 25 minutes, plus freezing **COOKING TIME** 5 minutes

½ cup heavy cream
4½oz. white chocolate, broken
   into pieces
2 egg whites
⅓ cup plus 4 tsp. sugar

1 cup raspberries, lightly crushed,
   plus extra, whole, for serving
1 tbsp. strawberry or raspberry
   liqueur

1   In a small saucepan, heat the cream and chocolate together over low heat until just melted, then set aside to cool. In a large bowl, whisk the egg whites until soft peaks form, using an electric hand mixer, then gradually add the sugar until the mixture is thick and shiny. Fold in the chocolate cream, raspberries, and liqueur and divide evenly between 4 freezerproof ¾-cup molds. Freeze the parfaits 3 hours or overnight.

2   Remove the parfaits from the freezer, turn out onto individual plates, and serve with the extra raspberries.

285 Chocolate affogatto
PREPARATION TIME 5 minutes

8 scoops Rich Chocolate Ice Cream
  (see page 164) or good-quality
  store-bought ice cream

¹/₄ cup hot espresso coffee
¹/₄ cup Frangelico liqueur

1   Place 2 scoops of ice cream in each of 4 glasses.
2   Pour 1 tbsp. of the hot espresso and 1 tbsp. of the liqueur over each helping
    and serve immediately.

286 Quick honeycomb & chocolate ice cream
PREPARATION TIME 10 minutes   **MAKES** 4¹/₃ cups

3¹/₄ cups homemade or good-quality
  store-bought vanilla ice cream,
  slightly softened
5¹/₂oz. chocolate-coated honeycomb
  pieces, chopped
5¹/₂oz. bittersweet chocolate, grated

1 recipe quantity Rich Chocolate
  Sauce (see page 204)

1   In a large bowl, mix together the softened ice cream, chopped honeycomb
    pieces, and grated chocolate, using a wooden spoon.
2   Serve with the rich chocolate sauce.

287 Crushed candied ice cream
PREPARATION TIME 10 minutes   **MAKES** 4¹/₃ cups

1 cup multi-colored candy-coated
  chocolates
3 tbsp. chocolate sauce

1 recipe quantity Rich Chocolate Ice
  Cream (see page 164) or same
  quantity good-quality store-bought
  ice cream, softened

1   Place the candy-coated chocolates in the bowl of a food processor and process
    until they are broken into small pieces. In a large bowl, fold the chocolate
    sauce and candy pieces into the softened ice cream (leaving it streaky), using
    a wooden spoon.
2   Serve immediately.

288 Chocolate marshmallow ice cream
PREPARATION TIME 20 minutes, plus chilling and churning   **COOKING TIME** 5 minutes
MAKES 4¹/₃ cups

2 cups plus 2 tbsp. milk
3¹/₂oz. bittersweet chocolate,
  broken into pieces

40 marshmallows
1 tsp. vanilla extract
1 cup plus 2 tbsp. heavy cream

1   In a large saucepan, heat the milk, chocolate, and marshmallows together
    over low heat, stirring with a wooden spoon until the chocolate is just melted.
    Stir in the vanilla extract, add the cream, and transfer the mixture to a clean
    bowl. Set aside to cool completely, then refrigerate 3 hours or overnight.
2   Churn in an ice-cream maker according to the manufacturer's instructions.

289 Frozen Mississippi mud pie

PREPARATION TIME 35 minutes, plus chilling and churning   **COOKING TIME** 5 minutes
MAKES 1 x 9in. pie

1 recipe quantity Chocolate
   Crumb Crust (see page 13)
2$^1/_2$ cups plus 2 tbsp. Rich Chocolate
Ice Cream (see page 164) or
   good-quality store-bought ice
   cream, slightly softened
2$^1/_2$ cups plus 2 tbsp. good-quality
   store-bought coffee ice cream,
   slightly softened

6oz. bittersweet chocolate,
   broken into pieces
2 tbsp. heavy cream
1 tbsp. light corn syrup
1 tsp. vanilla extract
chocolate curls, for decorating

1   Press the chocolate crumb crust into the bottom and sides of a fluted,
    loose-bottomed 9in. tart pan, 1$^1/_2$in. deep, then freeze 30 minutes.
2   Spoon the chocolate ice cream over the crumb crust, spreading it evenly,
    then layer with the coffee ice cream. Return to the freezer 1 hour.
3   In a medium-sized saucepan, heat the chocolate, cream, light corn syrup,
    and vanilla extract together over low heat until the chocolate is just melted.
    Remove from the heat and stir until smooth, using a wooden spoon. Set aside
    to cool 15 minutes, then pour over the ice-cream mixture. Return to the freezer
    a further 30 minutes or until firm.
4   Decorate the pie with chocolate curls before serving.

290 Frozen zabaglione with chocolate sauce

PREPARATION TIME 25 minutes, plus freezing   **COOKING TIME** 15 minutes

4 egg yolks
$^1/_3$ cup plus 4 tsp. sugar
1 cup plus 2 tbsp. heavy cream
$^1/_4$ cup Marsala wine

1 recipe quantity Rich Chocolate
   Sauce (see page 204)
2 tbsp. slivered almonds, toasted

1   Place the egg yolks and sugar in a medium-sized bowl set over a pan of just
    simmering water (taking care not to let the bowl touch the water or the yolks
    will curdle) and beat together until thick. Remove from the heat and whisk
    a few more minutes as the mixture cools. Pour into a clean bowl.
2   In a second clean bowl, whisk the cream and Marsala wine together until
    soft peaks form, using an electric hand mixer, then fold into the egg mixture,
    using a metal spoon. Divide the mixture evenly between 4 freezerproof
    $^2/_3$-cup dishes and freeze 3 hours or overnight.
3   When ready to serve, remove from the freezer, dip each dish briefly into hot
    water, then turn out onto individual plates. Pour over the rich chocolate sauce
    and sprinkle with slivered almonds.

291 Tiramisu ice-cream cake

PREPARATION TIME 40 minutes, plus chilling   **COOKING TIME** 5 minutes
MAKES 1 x 9in. cake

3/4 cup plus 2 tbsp. sugar
1 1/2 cups plus 2 tbsp. strong coffee
2 tbsp. Marsala wine
1 x 9in. sponge cake
6 tbsp. chocolate, grated

2 cups plus 2 tbsp. good-quality
store-bought coffee ice cream,
slightly softened
2 cups plus 2 tbsp Rich Chocolate Ice
Cream (see page 164) or good-
quality store-bought ice cream,
slightly softened

1   In a small saucepan, heat the sugar and 2/3 cup water over medium heat until
the sugar dissolves, stirring frequently with a metal spoon. Remove from the
heat, pour into a clean bowl, and add the coffee and Marsala wine. Set aside
to cool completely.
2   Line a 9in. springform cake pan with baking paper. Cut the sponge cake
horizontally to create two layers and place the bottom layer in the prepared pan.
Using a pastry brush, spread half of the cooled coffee syrup over the bottom
layer of the sponge cake and sprinkle over half the grated chocolate.
3   In a large bowl, whisk the coffee ice cream until it is spreadable, using an
electric hand mixer, then spread it over the bottom layer of sponge, using
a palette knife. Sprinkle over the remaining grated chocolate and place the
remaining sponge cake layer on top. Using a pastry brush, brush the top sponge
cake layer with the rest of the coffee syrup. In a large bowl, whisk the chocolate
ice cream until it is spreadable, then use a palette knife to spread over the top
sponge cake layer.
4   Place the ice-cream cake in the freezer 30 minutes, or until firm. Remove from
the freezer and serve immediately.

292 Chocolate baked Alaska

PREPARATION TIME 10 minutes   **COOKING TIME** 4 to 5 minutes   **SERVES** 6

1 recipe quantity Chocolate Fudge
Brownies, baked in an 8in. round
or square pan (see page 98)
3 egg whites
1/2 cup plus 2 tsp. sugar
pinch cream of tartar

2 cups plus 2 tbsp. good-quality
store-bought vanilla ice cream,
slightly softened
2 cups plus 2 tbsp. Rich Chocolate
Ice Cream (see page 164) or
good-quality store-bought ice
cream, slightly softened

1   Place the brownie (uncut) on a foil-lined baking sheet. Preheat the oven
to 455°F.
2   In a large bowl, whisk the egg whites to stiff peaks, using an electric hand
mixer, then whisk in the sugar and cream of tartar until the meringue is thick
and shiny. Scoop the vanilla and chocolate ice creams onto the top of the baked
brownie, alternating the flavors. Spread the meringue over the sides and top of
the ice-cream cake, so that the ice cream is completely covered, and bake in the
very hot oven 4 to 5 minutes until the meringue is lightly browned.
3   Remove the baked Alaska from the oven and serve immediately.

293 Chocolate pear sundae with roasted almonds

PREPARATION TIME 20 minutes   **COOKING TIME** 5 minutes

⅓ cup plus 4 tsp. sugar
4 ripe pears
8 scoops Ginger & Chocolate
 Ice Cream (see page 167),
 slightly softened

1 recipe quantity Double Chocolate
 Sauce (see page 204)
1½ cups slivered almonds, roasted

1   In a small saucepan, heat the sugar and a scant ½ cup water together over
    medium heat until the sugar dissolves, stirring frequently with a metal spoon.
2   Peel the pears and cut in half vertically, keeping the stalks intact if possible.
    Remove the seeds and core, using a melon baller to create a neat shape.
    Toss the halved pears in the sugar syrup until lightly coated.
3   Divide the pears between 4 serving dishes. Place 2 scoops of ice cream on each
    dish and spoon over the double chocolate sauce. Sprinkle with slivered almonds.

294 Broiled pineapple, macadamia & chocolate sundaes

PREPARATION TIME 15 minutes   **COOKING TIME** 5 minutes

1 small, ripe pineapple, peeled
⅓ cup plus 2 tsp. packed light
 brown sugar
2 tbsp. dark rum
8 scoops Rich Chocolate Ice Cream
 (see page 164) or good-quality
 store-bought ice cream,
 slightly softened

1 recipe quantity Chocolate Rum
 Sauce (see page 206)
½ cup macadamia nuts, roasted
 and chopped
4 ice-cream wafers (optional)

1   Cut the pineapple into quarters and remove the core, then slice into ½in. slices.
    Place the slices in a large bowl with the brown sugar and dark rum and toss
    until well combined.
2   Place the pineapple slices on a broiler pan under a hot broiler and broil a few
    minutes until the pineapple has warmed slightly and has a light glaze.
3   Divide the broiled pineapple slices between 4 plates and top each one with
    2 scoops of chocolate ice cream and the chocolate rum sauce. Sprinkle with
    chopped macadamia nuts and serve with ice-cream wafers, if using.

295 Peach & amaretto sundae with chocolate

PREPARATION TIME 30 minutes, plus cooling **COOKING TIME** 15 to 17 minutes

²/₃ cup sugar
4 ripe, firm, yellow peaches
8 scoops Rich Chocolate Ice Cream
 (see page 164) or good-quality
 bought ice cream, slightly softened

1 recipe quantity Rich Chocolate
 Sauce (see page 204)
¹/₂ cup crushed amaretto cookies

1 In a small saucepan, heat the sugar and 1 cup water together over medium heat until the sugar dissolves, stirring frequently with a metal spoon. Bring to a simmer, then add the peaches and cook 8 to 10 minutes until just tender. Remove the peaches from the syrup using a slotted spoon and set aside in a bowl to cool completely, then peel, cut in half horizontally, and remove the pits.

2 Return the syrup to the heat and bring to a boil, then reduce the heat and simmer until the syrup is reduced by half. Pour into a bowl and let cool.

3 Divide the peach halves equally between 4 dishes and spoon over some of the syrup. Place a scoop of chocolate ice cream on each peach half, top with some rich chocolate sauce, and sprinkle with the crushed amaretto cookies.

296 Chocolate sorbet with pineapple carpaccio

PREPARATION TIME 15 minutes, plus chilling

1 small, ripe pineapple, peeled
juice of 1 orange

8 scoops Chocolate Sorbet
   (see page 171) or good-quality
   store-bought sorbet
3 tbsp. mint leaves, finely chopped

1   Cut the pineapple in half lengthwise and remove the core. Using a very sharp knife, cut the pineapple into wafer-thin slices. Place the pineapple slices in a bowl and refrigerate 30 minutes.
2   Divide the pineapple evenly between 4 plates and drizzle over the orange juice. Top each plate with 2 scoops of chocolate sorbet and sprinkle with the mint.

297 Marsala strawberries layered with chocolate ice cream

PREPARATION TIME 40 minutes, plus marinating

2 cups strawberries,
   sliced
1/4 cup Marsala wine
2 tbsp. powdered sugar
4 scoops Rich Chocolate Ice Cream
   (see page 164) or good-quality
   store-bought ice cream

1 recipe quantity Chocolate Chantilly
   Cream (see page 208)
3oz. bittersweet chocolate,
   melted and left to cool

1   In a large bowl, mix together the strawberries, Marsala wine, and powdered sugar, stirring well to combine. Leave to marinate 30 minutes.
2   Place a scoop of the chocolate ice cream in each of 4 bowls and divide the strawberry mixture equally over the ice cream. Place a spoonful of chocolate chantilly cream on top of each scoop. Drizzle the ice cream with melted chocolate just before serving.

298 Mulled berries with chocolate ice cream

PREPARATION TIME 20 minutes   **COOKING TIME** 8 minutes

2 cups mixed berries
1 cup red wine
1/3 cup plus 4 tsp. sugar
zest and juice of 1 orange
1 cinnamon stick

2 cloves
8 scoops Rich Chocolate Ice Cream
   (see page 164) or good-quality
   store-bought ice cream

1   Place the berries in a bowl—slicing the strawberries and pitting the cherries, if using.
2   In a medium-sized saucepan, heat the red wine, sugar, orange zest and juice, cinnamon stick, and cloves until boiling. Lower the heat and simmer 5 minutes, then remove from the heat. Let cool 15 minutes, then pour the mulled wine mixture over the berries.
3   Place 2 scoops of ice cream in each of 4 tall glasses and pour the warm berries, along with some of the liquid over. Serve immediately.

299 Frozen chocolate yogurt

PREPARATION TIME 20 minutes, plus chilling and churning   **COOKING TIME** 5 minutes
MAKES 4⅓ cups

⅓ cup plus 4 tsp. sugar
1 tbsp. cornstarch
1½ cups plus 2 tbsp. milk
1 egg, lightly beaten
½ cup chocolate sauce

1 tbsp. honey
1½ cups plus 2 tbsp. plain
   or vanilla-flavored yogurt
1 tsp. vanilla extract

1   In a small bowl, mix the sugar and cornstarch to a paste, using a little of the milk. Place the remaining milk in a small saucepan over low heat and, using a hand whisk, whisk in the cornstarch mixture and the egg. Continue to heat, stirring constantly with a wooden spoon, until the mixture thickens and coats the back of the spoon. Pour the mixture into a clean bowl and stir in the chocolate syrup and honey. Set aside until cold, then refrigerate 3 hours.
2   Whisk in the yogurt and vanilla extract, using a hand whisk, then churn in an ice-cream maker according to the manufacturer's instructions.

CHAPTER 5

Chocolates & drinks

Handmade chocolates and treats make a very special way to enjoy chocolate at any time of day. An assortment of truffles passed around after dinner will make your friends and family feel truly indulged. Alternatively, a selection of truffles, fudge squares, and chocolate-dipped fruits presented in a decorative box makes a perfect gift.

Bear in mind that handmade chocolates are best kept in a cool, dry place if you are intending to keep them for a while. If the weather is warm, you might like to keep them in the refrigerator; however, the moisture may cause them to develop a "bloom." Although this doesn't look so nice, if you do find that your chocolates have developed a bloom, don't despair—it will do very little damage to the flavor and texture of the chocolates.

To round off this chapter I have included a number of chocolate drinks, from Spiced Hot Chocolate and White Hot Chocolate to warm up cold winter months, to a refreshingly chilled Divine Iced Mint Chocolate for hot summer days.

300 Cranberry & port chocolate truffles

PREPARATION TIME 25 minutes, plus chilling   **COOKING TIME** 5 minutes   **MAKES** 30 truffles

7oz. bittersweet chocolate,
  broken into pieces
¼ cup heavy cream
2 tbsp. port

¼ cup dried cranberries,
  chopped
9oz. white chocolate,
  melted and left to cool

1   In a small saucepan, combine the chocolate and cream over low heat until
    the chocolate is just melted, stirring frequently with a wooden spoon. Remove
    from the heat and stir until smooth, then add the port and dried cranberries.
    Pour into a clean bowl and let cool completely, then refrigerate about
    30 minutes until firm.
2   Roll teaspoonfuls of the mixture in the melted white chocolate to form balls,
    put on a baking sheet lined with wax paper and refrigerate 1 hour until firm.

301 Double chocolate truffles

PREPARATION TIME 25 minutes, plus chilling   **COOKING TIME** 5 minutes   **MAKES** 20 truffles

5½oz. bittersweet chocolate,
  broken into pieces
¼ cup heavy cream

2 tbsp. liqueur of your choice
  (e.g. Kahlua, Grand Marnier)
2 tbsp. unsweetened cocoa powder,
  sifted

1   In a small saucepan, combine the chocolate and cream over low heat until the
    chocolate is just melted, stirring frequently with a wooden spoon. Remove from
    the heat and add the liqueur. Pour the mixture into a clean bowl and let cool
    completely, then refrigerate about 30 minutes until firm.
2   Roll teaspoonfuls of the mixture into small balls and toss in the cocoa to coat.
    Place the cocoa-coated balls on a baking sheet lined with wax paper and
    refrigerate 1 hour until firm.

302 Peanut butter & milk chocolate truffles

PREPARATION TIME 30 minutes, plus chilling   **COOKING TIME** 5 minutes   **MAKES** 30 truffles

7oz. milk chocolate,
  broken into pieces
scant ½ cup heavy cream

3 tbsp. crunchy peanut butter
scant ⅔ cup roasted peanuts,
  crushed

1   In a small saucepan, combine the chocolate and cream over low heat until the
    chocolate is just melted, stirring frequently with a wooden spoon. Remove from
    the heat, add the peanut butter, and stir until smooth. Pour into a clean bowl
    and let cool completely, then refrigerate about 30 minutes until firm.
2   Roll rounded teaspoonfuls of the mixture in the crushed peanuts, then place
    on a baking sheet lined with wax paper and refrigerate 1 hour until firm.

303 Chocolate rum truffles

PREPARATION TIME 20 minutes, plus chilling   **COOKING TIME** 5 minutes   **MAKES** 18 truffles

5¹/₂oz. bittersweet chocolate,
  broken into pieces
¹/₄ cup heavy cream

3 tbsp. rum
1 cup chocolate sprinkles

1   In a small saucepan, combine the chocolate and cream over low heat until the chocolate is just melted, stirring frequently with a wooden spoon. Remove from the heat and add the rum. Pour into a clean bowl and let cool completely, then refrigerate about 30 minutes until firm.
2   Roll teaspoonfuls of the mixture into balls and toss in the chocolate sprinkles to coat. Place on a baking sheet lined with wax paper and refrigerate 1 hour until firm.

304 Chocolate & orange truffles

PREPARATION TIME 20 minutes, plus chilling   **COOKING TIME** 5 minutes   **MAKES** 18 truffles

5¹/₂oz. bittersweet chocolate,
  broken into pieces
¹/₄ cup heavy cream

3 tbsp. orange liqueur
zest of 1 orange, finely grated
powdered sugar, sifted, for coating

1   In a small saucepan, combine the chocolate and cream over low heat until the chocolate is just melted, stirring frequently with a wooden spoon. Remove from the heat and stir in the liqueur and orange zest, using a wooden spoon. Pour into a clean bowl and let cool completely, then refrigerate about 30 minutes until firm.
2   Roll teaspoonfuls of the mixture into balls and coat with powdered sugar. Place on a baking sheet lined with wax paper and refrigerate 1 hour until firm.

305 Candied citrus peel

PREPARATION TIME 30 minutes   **COOKING TIME** 20 minutes   **MAKES** 24 pieces

3 ripe lemons or oranges
5 tbsp. sugar

3¹/₂oz. bittersweet chocolate,
  melted and left to cool

1   Remove the peel from the fruit, using a wide-bladed vegetable peeler. Using a sharp knife, cut away any remaining white pith (this will be bitter) and cut the rind into strips about ¹/₂in. wide. Place the strips in a small saucepan, cover with water, then bring to a boil. Drain immediately in a colander, then rinse under cold water.
2   In a small saucepan, heat the sugar and ¹/₂ cup water over medium heat until the sugar dissolves, then add the blanched rind. Continue to cook over medium heat about 15 minutes until the liquid evaporates and the peel is brightly colored and shiny. Remove the peel from the water using a slotted spoon and spread on baking paper to cool.
3   Pour the melted chocolate into a bowl, dip each piece of candied citrus peel in the chocolate, and place on baking paper to set.

306 White chocolate, citrus & coconut truffles

PREPARATION TIME 25 minutes, plus chilling   **COOKING TIME** 5 minutes   **MAKES** 30 truffles

scant ½ cup coconut cream
12oz. white chocolate,
  broken into pieces
2 tsp. lemon zest, finely grated

2 tsp. lime zest, finely grated
2 tbsp. coconut rum liqueur
1 cup flaked coconut

1   In a small saucepan, combine the coconut cream and chocolate together
    over a low heat until just melted, stirring frequently with a wooden spoon.
    Remove from the heat and stir until smooth. Pour into a clean bowl and let
    cool, then stir in the lemon and lime zests and liqueur. Refrigerate about
    30 minutes until firm.
2   Roll teaspoonfuls of the mixture in the flaked coconut to form balls. Place
    on a baking sheet lined with wax paper and refrigerate 1 hour until firm.

307 Chocolate graham cracker truffles

PREPARATION TIME 20 minutes, plus chilling **MAKES** 36 truffles

10$\frac{1}{2}$oz. graham crackers,
 finely crushed
2 tbsp. unsweetened cocoa powder

generous 1 cup condensed milk
1 cup flaked coconut

1 In a large bowl, mix the crushed crackers, cocoa, and sweetened condensed milk together until well combined.
2 Roll teaspoonfuls of the mixture into balls and toss in the coconut to coat. Place on a baking sheet lined with wax paper and refrigerate 1 to 2 hours until firm.

308 Gingernut & chocolate truffles

PREPARATION TIME 25 minutes, plus chilling **MAKES** 30 truffles

10$\frac{1}{2}$oz. ginger snaps, finely crushed
3 tbsp. unsweetened cocoa powder
2 pieces preserved ginger, finely
 chopped

generous 1 cup sweetened
 condensed milk
1 cup flaked coconut

1 In a large bowl, mix together the ginger snaps, cocoa, ginger, and sweetened condensed milk until well combined.
2 Using slightly wet hands, roll rounded teaspoonfuls of the mixture into balls and roll in the coconut to coat. Place on a baking sheet lined with wax paper and refrigerate 1 hour until firm.

309 Roasted macadamia & ginger white chocolate drops

PREPARATION TIME 15 minutes, plus chilling **COOKING TIME** 5 minutes
MAKES 18 truffles

7oz. white chocolate, broken
 into pieces
1 cup whole macadamia nuts,
 roasted

3 pieces preserved ginger, finely
 chopped

1 In a small saucepan, melt the chocolate over low heat, stirring until smooth. Add the nuts and ginger, and stir to combine, using a wooden spoon.
2 Place teaspoonfuls of the mixture on a baking sheet lined with wax paper to create neat drops, then refrigerate about 30 minutes until firm.

310 Roasted almond drops

PREPARATION TIME 15 minutes, plus chilling   **COOKING TIME** 5 minutes   **MAKES** 18 drops

7oz. bittersweet or milk chocolate,
broken into pieces

2 cups slivered almonds, toasted

1   In a small saucepan, melt the chocolate over low heat, stirring until smooth.
    Remove from the heat and stir in the toasted almonds until well combined.
2   Let cool 5 minutes, then place teaspoonfuls of the mixture on a baking sheet
    lined with wax paper and refrigerate about 30 minutes until firm.

311 Cranberry & raisin chocolate drops

PREPARATION TIME 15 minutes, plus chilling   **COOKING TIME** 5 minutes
MAKES 14 drops

5½oz. white chocolate,
   broken into pieces

¾ cup dried cranberries
¼ cup raisins

1 In a small saucepan, melt the chocolate over low heat, stirring until smooth.
   Stir in the cranberries and raisins to combine, and let cool slightly.
2 Place teaspoonfuls of the mixture on a baking sheet lined with wax paper
   to create neat drops, then refrigerate about 30 minutes until firm.

312 Mint chocolate fudge

PREPARATION TIME 30 minutes, plus chilling   **COOKING TIME** 5 minutes   **MAKES** 16 squares

12oz. bittersweet chocolate,
   broken into pieces
1 x 14oz. can sweetened
   condensed milk

scant 1½ cups powdered sugar
2 tsp. vanilla extract
1 tbsp. peppermint extract

1 Line a shallow 9in. square cake pan with baking paper.
2 In a small saucepan, combine the chocolate and sweetened condensed milk
   over low heat until just melted. Remove from the heat and stir until smooth,
   using a wooden spoon, then stir in the sugar and both extracts.
3 Pour the fudge mixture into the prepared pan and let cool completely, then
   refrigerate about 30 minutes until firm. Turn out of the pan, using the paper
   to help you, before cutting the fudge into squares, using a sharp knife.

313 Chocolate marshmallow fudge

PREPARATION TIME 20 minutes, plus chilling   **COOKING TIME** 15 minutes   **MAKES** 16 squares

6 tbsp. butter
scant 1⅓ cups superfine sugar
scant ⅔ cup milk

6oz. bittersweet chocolate,
   broken into pieces
6oz. marshmallows
1 tsp. vanilla extract

1 Line a 9in. square, shallow-sided cake pan with baking paper.
2 In a small saucepan, heat the butter, sugar, and milk together, stirring
   occasionally with a wooden spoon, and bring to a boil. Lower the heat and
   simmer about 10 minutes, stirring constantly with a wooden spoon, until
   a small amount of the mixture dropped into a glass of cold water forms
   a soft ball. Stir in the chocolate until it melts, then add the marshmallows
   and vanilla extract.
3 Pour the fudge mixture into the prepared pan, smoothing the top with a palette
   knife. Let the fudge cool completely at room temperature. Turn out of the pan,
   using the paper to help you, before cutting into squares with a sharp knife.

314 Chocolate hazelnut fudge

PREPARATION TIME 30 minutes   **COOKING TIME** 10 minutes   **MAKES** 16 squares

²/₃ cup evaporated milk
1¹/₂ cups superfine sugar
heaped ¹/₃ cup hazelnuts,
   roasted and roughly chopped

12oz. milk chocolate,
   broken into pieces

1   Line a shallow 9in. square cake pan with baking paper.
2   In a saucepan, bring the milk and sugar to a boil, stirring occasionally with a wooden spoon. Lower the heat and simmer 5 minutes, stirring frequently. Remove the pan from the heat and add the hazelnuts and chocolate, stirring constantly until the chocolate melts.
3   Pour the fudge mixture into the prepared pan, smoothing the top with a palette knife. Leave in the pan until completely set, then turn out from the pan, using the paper to help you, and cut into 1in. squares, using a sharp knife.

315 Cappuccino slims

PREPARATION TIME 15 minutes, plus chilling   **COOKING TIME** 5 minutes   **MAKES** 16 squares

7oz. bittersweet chocolate,
   broken into pieces
1 tsp. instant coffee powder
1 tbsp. coffee liqueur

5¹/₂oz. white chocolate,
   broken into pieces
2 tsp. unsweetened cocoa powder,
   sifted

1   Line a shallow 9in. square cake pan with baking paper, letting the edges hang over the sides of the pan.
2   In a small saucepan, heat the bittersweet chocolate over low heat until just melted, then remove from the heat and stir until smooth, using a wooden spoon. Stir in the coffee and liqueur. Spread the mixture over the base of the prepared pan, using a palette knife, and refrigerate about 30 minutes until firm.
3   In a small saucepan, heat the white chocolate over low heat until melted, then spread it over the bittersweet chocolate mixture using a palette knife. Dust the top with cocoa.
4   Refrigerate 30 minutes, then remove from the refrigerator and turn out from the pan, using the paper to help you, before cutting into squares with a knife that has been dipped in hot water first to warm it.

316 Mint slims

PREPARATION TIME 10 minutes, plus chilling   **COOKING TIME** 5 minutes   **MAKES** 16 squares

7oz. bittersweet or milk chocolate,
   broken into pieces
2 tsp. peppermint extract

5¹/₂oz. mint-flavored chocolate,
   roughly chopped

1   Line a shallow 9in. square cake pan with baking paper, letting the edges hang over the sides of the pan.
2   In a small saucepan, heat the chocolate over low heat until just melted, remove the pan from the heat, and stir until smooth, using a wooden spoon. Stir in the peppermint extract and let cool 10 minutes.
3   Stir in the chopped mint-flavored chocolate. Pour the mixture into the prepared pan and refrigerate about 30 minutes until firm. Remove from the refrigerator and turn out from the pan, using the paper to help you, then cut into squares with a knife that has been dipped in hot water first to warm it.

317 Chocolate-dipped dried fruits

PREPARATION TIME 15 minutes, plus chilling   **COOKING TIME** 5 minutes
MAKES 24 chocolates

9oz. bittersweet chocolate,
  broken into pieces

24 pieces dried fruit, including
  apricots, pear, and pineapple

1 In a small saucepan, heat the chocolate over low heat until just melted,
   then remove from the heat and stir until smooth.
2 Wipe the dried fruit with paper towel and dip each piece in the melted chocolate
   to cover halfway. (If the chocolate runs off without making a nice coating, let it
   cool a few minutes, then try again.)
3 Place the dipped fruit on a baking sheet lined with wax paper and refrigerate
   about 30 minutes until the chocolate has set.

318 Marshmallow Lamingtons

PREPARATION TIME 30 minutes

7oz. white marshmallows
9oz. bittersweet chocolate, melted
  and left to cool

2 cups flaked coconut

1 Pierce a marshmallow with a long skewer and dip into the melted chocolate. Put the coconut in a large bowl and roll the marshmallow in it until well coated. Remove from the coconut and place on a baking sheet lined with wax paper to set.
2 Repeat until all the marshmallows are coated.

319 Chocolate popcorn

PREPARATION TIME 20 minutes   **COOKING TIME** 5 minutes   **MAKES** 1 large bowl

1 tbsp. vegetable oil
$^1/_4$ cup popcorn kernels

7oz. bittersweet chocolate, melted

1 In a large saucepan, heat the oil for a few moments, then add the popcorn kernels and place the lid on the pan. Leave 1 to 2 minutes until all the kernels have popped (shake the pan after the first minute) and then pour the popcorn into a large bowl to cool slightly.
2 Pour over the melted chocolate. Stir to coat well and then spread the chocolate-coated popcorn over a baking sheet lined with wax paper to set.

320 Chocolate hedgehog

PREPARATION TIME 25 minutes, plus chilling   **COOKING TIME** 5 minutes   **MAKES** 16 squares

2 sticks butter, chopped
1 cup plus 2 tbsp. superfine sugar
3 tbsp. unsweetened cocoa powder
1 egg, lightly beaten
$10^1/_2$oz. graham crackers,
  roughly crushed

1 cup walnuts, chopped
$5^1/_2$oz. milk chocolate,
  melted and left to cool
1 recipe quantity Dark Chocolate
  Ganache (see page 209)

1 Line an 8 x12in. cake pan with baking paper, leaving enough to come up the sides slightly.
2 In a small saucepan, melt the butter over low heat, remove from the heat, and let cool. When cool, add the sugar, cocoa, and egg and beat together, using a hand whisk.
3 In a large bowl, mix together the graham crackers and walnuts, then add the melted chocolate and butter mixture, stirring well with a wooden spoon to combine. Pour the mixture into the prepared pan and spread it evenly over the base. Cool, then refrigerate about 30 minutes until firm. Ice with the dark chocolate ganache and let set.
4 Remove from the pan, using the paper to help you, and and cut into squares with a sharp knife.

321 White chocolate & raspberry brittle

PREPARATION TIME 15 minutes   **COOKING TIME** 5 minutes   **MAKES** 16 squares

5¹/₂oz. white chocolate,
  broken into pieces

¹/₂ cup raspberries, puréed

1   Line a 9in. square shallow-sided cake pan with baking paper, leaving some overlapping the edges.
2   In a small saucepan, heat the chocolate over low heat until just melted. Remove from the heat and stir until smooth, using a wooden spoon, then spread the melted chocolate over the base of the prepared pan using a palette knife.
3   Drizzle the raspberry purée over the top of the chocolate mixture with a spoon, then swirl through the white chocolate with a skewer to create a marbled effect.
4   Leave the brittle in a cool place until firm. (Refrigerate only if it is a warm day.) Remove from the pan, using the paper to help you, before cutting into squares.

322 White chocolate & nut treats

PREPARATION TIME 15 minutes, plus chilling   **MAKES** 24 treats

7oz. white chocolate, melted
¹/₂ cup slivered almonds,
  lightly toasted

1³/₄ cups flaked coconut

1   In a medium-sized bowl, mix all the ingredients together, then place teaspoonfuls of the mixture on a baking sheet lined with wax paper.
2   Refrigerate about 30 minutes until firm.

323 White chocolate & pistachio log

PREPARATION TIME 15 minutes, plus chilling   **COOKING TIME** 5 minutes
MAKES 1 log

7oz. white chocolate,
  broken into pieces
6 tbsp. butter
¹/₃ cup pistachio nuts,
  roughly chopped

heaped ¹/₃ cup hazelnuts,
  roasted and roughly chopped
¹/₂ cup desiccated coconut,
  lightly toasted

1   In a small saucepan, melt the white chocolate and butter together over a very low heat. Remove from the heat and set aside until cool but still liquid.
2   In a bowl, mix together the nuts and coconut until well combined, using a wooden spoon, then add the cooled chocolate mixture and stir well.
3   Spoon the mixture into the middle of a piece of plastic wrap, roll over a flat surface to form a log shape, then twist the ends of the plastic wrap together. Refrigerate about 30 minutes until firm.
4   Remove from the refrigerator, take off the plastic wrap, and cut the log into slices.

324 Marzipan-stuffed chocolate prunes

PREPARATION TIME 25 minutes, plus setting   **MAKES** 20 chocolate prunes

2³/₄oz. marzipan
20 large pitted prunes

5¹/₂oz. bittersweet chocolate,
melted and left to cool

1 Knead the marzipan until soft, then take small balls of it and stuff them inside the prunes.
2 Dip each prune into the melted chocolate to coat half and place on a baking sheet lined with wax paper. Set aside at room temperature to set.

325 Chocolate panforte

PREPARATION TIME 25 minutes   **COOKING TIME** 15 minutes   **MAKES** 24 slices

butter, for greasing
1¹/₄ cups roasted hazelnuts, chopped
1 cup plus 2 tbsp. roasted almonds,
  chopped
1³/₄ cups roasted walnuts, chopped
1 cup dried figs, chopped
1 cup dried apricots, chopped
³/₄ cup dried prunes, chopped
2 tbsp. unsweetened cocoa powder,
  plus extra, sifted, for dusting

1 cup all-purpose flour
1 tsp. nutmeg, grated
¹/₂ tsp. ground cloves
¹/₂ tsp. cinnamon
²/₃ cup superfine sugar
scant ²/₃ cup honey

1 Preheat the oven to 350°F. Grease a 10in. springform cake pan with butter and line with baking paper.
2 In a large bowl, combine the nuts, dried fruits, cocoa, flour, and spices. In a small saucepan, heat the sugar and honey together over low heat until boiling, stirring constantly with a wooden spoon. Reduce the heat and simmer 1 minute, then pour the honey syrup over the fruit and nut mixture, stirring well to combine. (The mixture will be very thick.)
3 Spoon the mixture into the prepared pan and smooth the surface with slightly wet hands. Bake in the hot oven 15 minutes. While still warm, run a sharp knife around the edges of the panforte to release it from the pan.
4 Leave the panforte to cool completely in the pan, before cutting into thin slices, using a sharp knife. Dust with cocoa before serving.

326 Chocolate-coated coffee beans

PREPARATION TIME 10 minutes, plus chilling   **COOKING TIME** 5 minutes   **MAKES** 1¹/₄ cups

²/₃ cup large, good-quality coffee
  beans, roasted

2³/₄oz. bittersweet chocolate,
broken into pieces

1 Wipe the coffee beans with a paper towel and set aside.
2 In a small saucepan, heat the chocolate over low heat until just melted, then remove from the heat and stir until smooth. Let cool 5 minutes.
3 Toss the coffee beans in the melted chocolate and stir well to coat, then remove the beans with a fork, draining off any excess chocolate, and arrange the chocolate-coated beans on a baking sheet lined with wax paper. Refrigerate about 30 minutes until firm.

327 Chocolate florentines

PREPARATION TIME 35 minutes   **COOKING TIME** 6 to 8 minutes   **MAKES** 24 florentines

½ stick butter, plus extra for
   greasing
3 tbsp. plus 1 tsp. superfine sugar
2 tsp. honey
½ cup sliced almonds

¼ cup red candied cherries,
   chopped
heaped ⅓ cup golden raisins
5½oz. milk chocolate,
   melted and cooled

1   Preheat the oven to 350°F. Line 2 large baking sheets with baking paper.
2   In a small saucepan, melt the butter, sugar, and honey together over low
   heat until melted. Remove the pan from the heat. In a large bowl, mix
   together the almonds, candied cherries, and golden raisins, then pour
   the butter mixture into the bowl, stirring well with a wooden spoon to
   combine. Place tablespoonfuls of the mixture on the baking sheet, leaving
   2in. between them for room to spread, and press down lightly to flatten
   the mixture into rounds.
3   Bake in the hot oven 6 to 8 minutes, or until lightly golden. Remove the baking
   sheets from the oven, let the florentines cool 5 minutes, then transfer them to
   a wire rack to cool completely.
4   When cold, turn the florentines over (the backs will be smooth) and spread with
   melted chocolate. Once the chocolate has cooled slightly, make lines using a
   fork or wavy icing spreader. Leave on the baking sheets until the chocolate sets.

328 Chocolate ginger snap squares

PREPARATION TIME 25 minutes, plus chilling   **COOKING TIME** 5 minutes   **MAKES** 16 squares

14oz. bittersweet chocolate,
  broken into pieces
1 stick plus 1 tbsp. butter,
  chopped
1 x 14oz. can sweetened
  condensed milk

5 pieces preserved ginger,
  finely chopped
9oz. ginger snaps, crushed
3/4 cup flaked coconut, toasted,
  plus 3 tbsp. for sprinkling

1 Line a shallow 9in. square cake pan with kitchen foil, leaving enough at the
   edges to hang over the sides.
2 In a small saucepan, heat the chocolate and butter together until just melted,
   then remove from the heat and stir until smooth. Stir in the remaining
   ingredients and spoon into the prepared pan. Sprinkle with the extra coconut.
3 Refrigerate the chocolate ginger snap mixture until firm. Remove from the
   refrigerator and turn out of the pan, using the foil to help you, then cut into
   squares with a sharp knife.

329 Chocolate & almond truffle squares

PREPARATION TIME 35 minutes, plus chilling   **COOKING TIME** 5 minutes   **MAKES** 16 squares

1lb. bittersweet chocolate,
  broken into pieces
1/2 cup heavy cream

3 tbsp. amaretto liqueur
1/3 cup roasted almonds,
  roughly chopped

1 Line a shallow 8in. square cake pan with foil.
2 In a small saucepan, heat 12oz. of the chocolate with the cream over a low heat
   until just melted. Remove the pan from the heat and stir until smooth, using
   a wooden spoon. Stir in the amaretto, then set the mixture aside.
3 In a clean pan, melt the remaining chocolate separately over low heat. Spread
   half of the melted chocolate over the bottom of the prepared pan.
4 Refrigerate the pan until the chocolate is firm, then top with the truffle mixture
   and sprinkle with the chopped almonds. Drizzle the remaining melted chocolate
   over the truffle mixture in a decorative pattern. Refrigerate about 30 minutes
   until firm, then turn out using the foil to help you, before cutting into squares,
   using a sharp knife.

330 Chocolate raisin clusters

PREPARATION TIME 15 minutes, plus chilling   **MAKES** 14

5 1/2oz. milk, bittersweet, or white
  chocolate, melted and left to cool
heaped 3/4 cup raisins

1/3 cup roasted almonds,
  roughly chopped

1 In a large bowl, mix together the melted chocolate, raisins, and almonds,
   and let cool slightly.
2 Place rounded teaspoonfuls of the chocolate and raisin mixture on a baking
   sheet lined with wax paper. Refrigerate about 30 minutes until set.

331 Best-ever hot chocolate

PREPARATION TIME 15 minutes   **COOKING TIME** 5 minutes

1 cup plus 2 tbsp. milk
1 cup plus 2 tbsp. heavy cream
2 tbsp. superfine sugar

4¹/₂oz. bittersweet chocolate,
  broken into pieces
unsweetened cocoa powder,
  sifted for dusting (optional)

1   Heat the milk and half the cream in a saucepan until just boiling. Remove from the heat and beat in the sugar and chocolate, using an electric hand mixer.
2   Divide the chocolate milk equally between 4 small cups (the mixture is very rich). Whip the remaining cream until it forms soft peaks, using an electric hand mixer, then place a tablespoonful on each cup and dust with unsweetened cocoa powder, if using. Serve immediately.

332 Spiced hot chocolate

PREPARATION TIME 10 minutes, plus standing   **COOKING TIME** 5 minutes

1 quart plus 1/3 cup milk
1/4 cup packed light brown sugar
6 cardamom pods, crushed
6 cloves
1 cinnamon stick
1 star anise, lightly crushed

1/2 tsp. whole coriander seeds
1/2 tsp. ground nutmeg
1/4 tsp. red pepper flakes
3 tbsp. unsweetened cocoa powder
1/2 tsp. vanilla extract

1   In a medium-sized saucepan, combine the milk, sugar, cardamom, cloves, cinnamon, star anise, coriander seeds, nutmeg, and red pepper flakes over medium heat until hot. Remove the pan from the heat, whisk in the cocoa, using a hand whisk, then let stand 20 minutes.

2   Strain the spiced milk into a clean saucepan and reheat until just boiling. Stir in the vanilla extract, then divide the chocolate drink equally between 4 cups.

333 Cinnamon hot chocolate

PREPARATION TIME 10 minutes   **COOKING TIME** 5 minutes

1 quart plus 1/3 cup milk
1/4 cup superfine sugar
1/4 cup unsweetened cocoa powder
1/4 tsp. cinnamon
1/2 tsp. vanilla extract

2 tbsp. bittersweet chocolate chips
1/4 cup Chocolate Chantilly Cream
(see page 208)
2 tbsp. grated bittersweet chocolate

1   In a medium-sized saucepan, heat the milk until it just begins to simmer. Remove the pan from the heat and whisk in the sugar, cocoa, cinnamon, and vanilla extract, using a hand whisk.

2   Divide the chocolate chips between 4 tall heatproof glasses or mugs and top with the hot chocolate milk. Place a tablespoonful of the Chocolate Chantilly Cream on top of each glass, and decorate with the grated chocolate.

334 Bittersweet hot chocolate

PREPARATION TIME 5 minutes   **COOKING TIME** 5 minutes

generous 2 1/2 cups milk
4 tsp. unsweetened cocoa powder
1/4 cup bittersweet chocolate chips

4 tsp. brandy or rum
1/4 cup Chocolate Chantilly Cream
(see page 208)

1   In a medium-sized saucepan, heat the milk until it just begins to simmer. Remove the pan from the heat and whisk in the cocoa, chocolate chips, and brandy or rum.

2   Divide the chocolate milk equally between 4 small heatproof glasses or mugs and top each one with a tablespoonful of the chocolate chantilly cream.

335 White hot chocolate

PREPARATION TIME 5 minutes   **COOKING TIME** 5 minutes

7$\frac{1}{2}$ cups milk
6oz. white chocolate,
  broken into pieces
1 tsp. vanilla extract

$\frac{1}{2}$ cup heavy cream, whipped
  to soft peaks
cinnamon, for sprinkling

1   In a medium-sized saucepan, heat the milk and chocolate over low heat until the chocolate is just melted, stirring with a wooden spoon. Remove the pan from the heat and add the vanilla extract.
2   Divide the chocolate milk equally between 4 cups. Top each cup with a tablespoonful of whipped cream, then sprinkle over a little cinnamon.

336 Rich mint hot chocolate

PREPARATION TIME 5 minutes   **COOKING TIME** 5 minutes

1$\frac{1}{4}$ cups milk
scant 2 cups heavy cream
7oz. bittersweet chocolate, grated,
  plus 3 tbsp. for sprinkling

4 tsp. superfine sugar (optional)
5 tbsp. peppermint liqueur

1   In a medium-sized saucepan, heat the milk, 1$\frac{1}{4}$ cups of the cream, and the chocolate over low heat until hot, stirring with a wooden spoon. Remove the pan from the heat, add the sugar to taste, and stir in the liqueur.
2   Whip the remaining cream to soft peaks using an electric hand mixer.
3   Divide the drink equally between 4 heatproof glasses or mugs and top each one with a tablespoonful of whipped cream and a little grated chocolate.

337 Hot chocolate with orange

PREPARATION TIME 5 minutes   **COOKING TIME** 5 minutes

generous 2 cups milk
peel from 1 orange, cut into strips
7oz. bittersweet chocolate,
  broken into pieces

2 tsp. instant coffee powder
3 tbsp. orange liqueur

1   In a medium-sized saucepan, heat the milk and orange peel together until just boiling. Remove from the heat, strain the liquid through a sieve to remove the peel, then whisk in the chocolate and coffee, using an electric hand mixer.
2   Divide the liqueur between 4 tall heatproof glasses or mugs, then top with the chocolate mixture.

338 Nutty chocolate coffee

PREPARATION TIME 5 minutes   **COOKING TIME** 5 minutes

1 quart plus $\frac{1}{3}$ cup milk
4 tsp. unsweetened cocoa powder
4 tsp. instant coffee powder
$\frac{1}{4}$ cup superfine sugar

$\frac{1}{4}$ cup hazelnut liqueur
$\frac{1}{2}$ cup heavy cream, whipped
  to soft peaks
pinch cinnamon, to sprinkle

1   In a medium-sized saucepan, heat the milk until just boiling. Remove
from the heat and whisk in the cocoa, coffee, sugar, and liqueur.
2   Strain the mixture into a clean saucepan and divide equally between 4 cups.
Top each cup with a tablespoonful of the whipped cream, then sprinkle
over the cinnamon.

339 Chocolate Irish coffee

PREPARATION TIME 10 minutes

3 tbsp. unsweetened cocoa powder
$3\frac{3}{4}$ cups freshly brewed coffee
4 tsp. superfine sugar
2 tbsp. Irish whisky

$\frac{1}{4}$ cup Chocolate Chantilly Cream
  (see page 208)
3 tbsp. grated bittersweet chocolate

1   Place the cocoa in a bowl and blend to a paste with $\frac{1}{2}$ cup of the coffee. Whisk
in the remaining coffee, the sugar, and whisky, using a hand whisk.
2   Divide the coffee mixture evenly between 4 heatproof glasses or mugs. Top each
one with a tablespoonful of chocolate chantilly cream, then sprinkle with the
grated bittersweet chocolate.

340 Chocolate milkshakes

PREPARATION TIME 5 minutes

2 cups cold milk
1 tsp. vanilla extract
$\frac{1}{4}$ cup chocolate sauce

8 tbsp. Rich Chocolate Ice Cream
  (see page 164) or good-quality
  store-bought ice cream

1   Combine all of the ingredients in a blender and process until well combined.
2   Divide the milkshake mixture equally between 4 glasses.

341 Iced mocha shake

PREPARATION TIME 20 minutes, plus chilling

$3\frac{3}{4}$ cups hot, strong coffee
3 tbsp. unsweetened cocoa powder
2 tbsp. superfine sugar
4 scoops Rich Chocolate Ice Cream
  (see page 164) or good-quality
  store-bought ice cream

$\frac{1}{2}$ cup heavy cream, whipped
  to soft peaks
$\frac{1}{4}$ cup grated bittersweet chocolate

1   Pour the coffee into a large bowl. In a small bowl, mix the cocoa to a paste with
2 tablespoonfuls of the coffee. Whisk the paste back into the remaining coffee,
with the sugar, using a hand whisk, then stir well with a wooden spoon until the
sugar dissolves. Let cool completely, then refrigerate 30 minutes.
2   Place a scoop of chocolate ice cream in the bottom of each of 4 tall glasses.
Pour the coffee over, dividing it equally between the glasses. Spoon a generous
tablespoonful of the whipped cream over the top of each glass, then sprinkle
with grated chocolate. Serve immediately.

342 Divine iced mint chocolate

PREPARATION TIME 15 minutes

2³/₄oz. bittersweet or milk chocolate, melted and left to cool
1³/₄ cups cold milk
scant ²/₃ cup natural or vanilla-flavored yogurt

6 mint leaves, plus extra to decorate
4 scoops Rich Chocolate Ice Cream (see page 164) or good-quality store-bought ice cream

1 Place the chocolate, milk, yogurt, and mint in a blender; blend until smooth.
2 Divide the milk mixture equally between 4 tall glasses and top with a scoop of chocolate ice cream. Decorate with mint leaves and serve immediately.

CHAPTER 6

Sauces, Frostings & Icings

These recipes deserve a chapter devoted just to them

since you will use them time and time again. While a number

of the recipes throughout the book suggest a sauce, frosting,

or icing, feel free to mix and match them to your needs.

All of the recipes are very simple to make and will transform

a favorite recipe into a something special. This chapter

includes a deliciously indulgent Double Chocolate Sauce,

a Chocolate Caramel Sauce, and a wickedly mouthwatering

Chocolate & Amaretto Sauce, all of which can be used with

an assortment of the recipes or simply poured over a bowl

of fresh strawberries or vanilla ice cream. Try making two

or three sauces and surrounding them with a selection

of freshly cut fruit and letting your family and friends dip their

fruit into the sauce of their choice—a simple, but absolutely

delicious way to end a meal. Chocolate Fudge Frosting, White

Chocolate Frosting, or Chocolate Cream Cheese Frosting will

transform your favorite cake or bar cookie, so don't restrict

them just to the recipes in this book. Experiment and enjoy!

343 Rich chocolate sauce

PREPARATION TIME 10 minutes   **COOKING TIME** 5 minutes   **MAKES** 1½ cups

1 cup plus 2 tbsp. heavy cream
5½oz. bittersweet chocolate,
   broken into pieces

1 tbsp. chocolate liqueur (optional)
1 tbsp. powdered sugar
1 tsp. vanilla extract

1. In a small saucepan, combine the cream and chocolate over low heat, stirring with a wooden spoon until smooth. Remove the pan from the heat.
2. Stir in the liqueur, if using, sugar, and vanilla extract. Serve warm.

344 Double chocolate sauce

PREPARATION TIME 10 minutes   **COOKING TIME** 5 minutes   **MAKES** 1 cup

½ cup heavy cream
3½oz. bittersweet chocolate,
   broken into pieces

1oz. milk chocolate,
   broken into pieces

1. In a small saucepan, heat the cream until just boiling. Remove the pan from the heat.
2. Add both chocolates, stirring with a wooden spoon until they melt. Serve warm.

345 Chocolate caramel sauce

PREPARATION TIME 15 minutes   **COOKING TIME** 5 minutes   **MAKES** 1½ cups

7oz. bittersweet chocolate,
   broken into pieces
1 cup plus 2 tbsp. heavy cream

2 tbsp. dulce de leche or similar
   caramel paste
1 tsp. vanilla extract

1. In a small saucepan, combine the chocolate and cream over low heat until the chocolate melts. Remove the pan from the heat.
2. Add the dulce de leche and vanilla extract, stirring until smooth. Set aside to cool 10 minutes before serving.

346 Chocolate & amaretto sauce

PREPARATION TIME 10 minutes   **COOKING TIME** 5 minutes   **MAKES** 1½ cups

1 cup plus 2 tbsp. heavy cream
5½oz. dark or milk chocolate,
   broken into pieces

2 tbsp. amaretto liqueur
1 tsp. vanilla extract

1. In a small saucepan, combine the cream and chocolate over low heat until the chocolate melts, stirring with a wooden spoon until smooth. Remove the pan from the heat.
2. Stir in the amaretto and vanilla extract and set aside to cool 10 minutes before serving.

347 Espresso chocolate sauce

PREPARATION TIME 10 minutes   **COOKING TIME** 5 minutes   **MAKES** 1½ cups

1 cup plus 2 tbsp. heavy cream
5½oz. bittersweet chocolate,
   broken into pieces

¼ cup hot, strong espresso coffee
1 tbsp. coffee liqueur

1   In a small saucepan, combine the cream and chocolate over low heat until the
    chocolate melts. Remove the pan from the heat.
2   Add the coffee and liqueur and set aside to cool 10 minutes before serving.

348 Chocolate fruit & nut sauce

PREPARATION TIME 20 minutes   **COOKING TIME** 5 minutes   **MAKES** 1½ cups

3/4 cup plus 1 tbsp. raisins
3/4 cup plus 1 tbsp. dried cranberries
2 tbsp. orange liqueur
1 cup plus 2 tbsp. heavy cream
5½oz. milk or bittersweet chocolate,
   broken into pieces

2/3 cup roasted almonds,
   roughly chopped

1   Place the raisins and cranberries in a small, microwaveable bowl with the liqueur. Heat in the microwave 1 minute, then remove and let soak 10 minutes.
2   In a small saucepan, combine the cream and chocolate over low heat until the chocolate melts. Remove from the heat and stir with a wooden spoon until smooth.
3   Stir in the almonds and soaked fruits and serve immediately.

349 White chocolate sauce

PREPARATION TIME 10 minutes   **COOKING TIME** 5 minutes   **MAKES** 1½ cups

1 cup plus 2 tbsp. heavy cream
4½oz. white chocolate,
   broken into pieces

1 tsp. vanilla extract

1   In a small saucepan, combine the cream and chocolate over low heat until the chocolate melts. Add the vanilla extract and stir until smooth, using a wooden spoon.
2   Remove the pan from the heat and serve warm.

350 Traditional hot fudge sauce

PREPARATION TIME 10 minutes   **COOKING TIME** 5 minutes   **MAKES** 1½ cups

3½oz. dark or milk chocolate,
   broken into pieces
½ stick butter, chopped

3/4 cup plus 2 tsp. packed
   light brown sugar
1 tsp. vanilla extract
½ cup heavy cream

1   Place all of the ingredients in a saucepan over low heat, stirring well, until the mixture just comes to a boil—the chocolate should be melted and the sauce smooth.
2   Remove the pan from the heat and serve warm.

351 Chocolate rum sauce

PREPARATION TIME 10 minutes   **COOKING TIME** 5 minutes   **MAKES** 1¼ cups

1 cup plus 2 tbsp. heavy cream
2 tsp. sugar

3½oz. bittersweet chocolate,
   broken into pieces
2 tbsp. dark rum

1   In a small saucepan, heat the cream, sugar, and chocolate together over a low heat until the chocolate melts, stirring with a wooden spoon until smooth.
2   Remove the pan from the heat, stir in the rum, and serve warm.

352 Chocolate Marsala cream

PREPARATION TIME 10 minutes   **MAKES** 1 cup

1 cup plus 2 tbsp. heavy cream
1 tbsp. powdered sugar

1 tbsp. Marsala wine
unsweetened cocoa powder, sifted,
to dust

1   In a large bowl, combine the cream, powdered sugar, and Marsala wine and whip to soft peaks, using an electric hand mixer.
2   Dust the top of the cream with cocoa just before serving.

353 Chocolate chantilly cream

PREPARATION TIME 15 minutes   **MAKES** 1 cup

1 cup plus 2 tbsp. heavy cream
2 tbsp. powdered sugar

3^1/$_2$oz. dark or milk chocolate,
   melted and left to cool

1   In a large bowl, whip the cream and powdered sugar together to form
   soft peaks, using an electric hand mixer.
2   Gently fold in the melted chocolate until just combined, before using.

354 Chocolate mascarpone cream

PREPARATION TIME 10 minutes, plus chilling   **MAKES** 1 cup

4^1/$_2$oz. milk chocolate,
   melted and left to cool

1 tsp. vanilla extract
4oz. mascarpone cheese

1   In a large bowl, whisk all the ingredients together, using an electric hand mixer.
2   Refrigerate 30 minutes before using.

355 Chocolate buttercream

PREPARATION TIME 15 minutes, plus chilling   **MAKES** 1^1/$_2$ cups

1^1/$_2$ sticks butter
1 cup plus 1 tbsp. packed
   light brown sugar
1 egg yolk

1 tbsp. milk
1 tbsp. unsweetened cocoa powder
3^1/$_2$oz. bittersweet chocolate,
   melted and left to cool

1   In a large bowl, beat the butter and sugar together until light and fluffy, using
   an electric hand mixer. Add the remaining ingredients and continue beating
   until thick and light.
2   Refrigerate 30 minutes before using.

356 Mocha buttercream

PREPARATION TIME 45 minutes, plus cooling and chilling   **COOKING TIME** 5 minutes
MAKES 2 cups

^{3}/$_4$ cup milk
3^1/$_2$oz. bittersweet chocolate,
   broken into pieces
4 tsp. instant coffee granules

1 tsp. vanilla extract
3 egg yolks
7 tbsp. butter, softened
^{1}/$_2$ cup plus 2 tbsp. powdered sugar

1   In a large saucepan, combine the milk, chocolate, coffee, and vanilla extract
   over low heat until the chocolate melts, then remove the pan from the heat.
   Beat the yolks in a bowl and whisk in the chocolate mixture. Return the mixture
   to the pan and cook, stirring constantly with a wooden spoon, until the mixture
   begins to thicken and coats the back of the spoon. Do not allow to boil. Pour the
   mixture into a bowl and set aside to cool 30 minutes.
2   In a clean bowl, whisk the butter until light and creamy, using an electric hand
   mixer, then add the chocolate mixture with the powdered sugar. Continue to
   whisk until thick and glossy. Refrigerate 30 minutes before using.

357 Dark chocolate ganache

PREPARATION TIME 5 minutes, plus cooling **COOKING TIME** 5 minutes **MAKES** 1 cup

**6oz. bittersweet chocolate,
  broken into pieces**

2 tbsp. butter
½ cup heavy cream

1 In a small saucepan, combine all of the ingredients over low heat and stir until the chocolate and butter melt. Remove the pan from the heat.
2 Pour into a clean bowl and let cool about 20 minutes, or until the mixture begins to thicken. Use as a filling or topping for your chosen cake recipe or serve warm as a sauce.

358 White chocolate ganache

PREPARATION TIME 10 minutes, plus cooling   **COOKING TIME** 5 minutes
MAKES 1 cup

$^1/_2$ cup crème fraîche

$4^1/_2$oz. white chocolate,
broken into pieces

1   In a small saucepan, heat the crème fraîche over low heat. Remove the pan
from the heat and add the white chocolate. Stir gently until the chocolate melts,
using a wooden spoon, then continue stirring for a few more minutes until smooth.
2   Set aside to cool 30 minutes, or until the ganache has thickened slightly.

359 White chocolate frosting

PREPARATION TIME 10 minutes, plus cooling and chilling   **COOKING TIME** 5 minutes
MAKES $1^1/_2$ cups

$3^1/_2$oz. white chocolate,
broken into pieces

1 cup plus 2 tbsp. heavy cream
9oz. mascarpone cheese

1   In a small saucepan, combine the chocolate and a scant $^2/_3$ cup of the cream
over low heat until the chocolate melts. Remove the pan from the heat and
stir until smooth. Pour the mixture into a clean bowl and let cool 30 minutes,
stirring occasionally, then refrigerate about 1 hour.
2   In a large bowl, stir the mascarpone until smooth, using a wooden spoon.
Add the chocolate mixture and as much of the remaining cream as required
to make a spreadable consistency.

360 Chocolate sour cream frosting

PREPARATION TIME 15 minutes   **COOKING TIME** 5 minutes   **MAKES** $1^1/_2$ cups

$5^1/_2$oz. bittersweet chocolate,
broken into pieces
2 tbsp. butter

$^1/_2$ cup sour cream
1 tsp. vanilla extract
3 cups powdered sugar, sifted

1   In a small saucepan, combine the chocolate and butter over low heat until
just melted.
2   Remove the pan from the heat and let cool 10 minutes, then add the sour cream
and vanilla extract. Stir the powdered sugar into the chocolate mixture, using
a wooden spoon. Continue stirring until the mixture thickens. Add a little hot
water if the icing becomes too thick to spread.

361 Chocolate cream cheese frosting

PREPARATION TIME 10 minutes **MAKES** 1½ cups

9oz. cream cheese, softened
3½oz. bittersweet chocolate,
  melted and left to cool

1 tbsp. butter, softened
1 tsp. vanilla extract
2 cups powdered sugar, sifted

1 In a large bowl, beat the cream cheese until light, using an electric hand mixer.
2 Add the melted chocolate, butter, vanilla extract, and powdered sugar and
   continue beating until creamy and thickened.

362 Chocolate fudge frosting

PREPARATION TIME 15 minutes   **COOKING TIME** 5 minutes   **MAKES** 1½ cups

2¾oz. bittersweet chocolate,
  broken into pieces
6 tbsp. butter, chopped
2 cups powdered sugar

2 tbsp. unsweetened cocoa powder
5 tbsp. milk
1 tsp. vanilla extract

1   In a small saucepan, heat the chocolate and butter over low heat until just melted. In a medium-sized bowl, mix the powdered sugar and cocoa together and pour the melted chocolate over. Add the milk and vanilla extract and stir to combine well.
2   Put the bowl containing the mixture into a larger bowl containing a little iced water and beat the mixture with a wooden spoon until it is thick enough to spread and hold its shape.

363 Chocolate rum frosting

PREPARATION TIME 15 minutes   **COOKING TIME** 5 minutes   **MAKES** 1½ cups

3½oz. bittersweet chocolate,
  broken into pieces
2 tbsp. butter, chopped
2⅓ cups powdered sugar

scant ½ cup heavy cream
2 tbsp. dark or light rum
1 tsp. vanilla extract

1   In a small saucepan, combine the chocolate and butter together over low heat and stir until smooth.
2   Place the powdered sugar in a large bowl and, using a wooden spoon, mix in the chocolate mixture, cream, rum, and vanilla extract. Whisk until thick, using an electric hand mixer.

364 Creamy chocolate icing

PREPARATION TIME 10 minutes   **MAKES** 1 cup

scant 1⅔ cups powdered sugar
3 tbsp. unsweetened cocoa powder

2 tbsp. butter, melted
4 to 5 tbsp. milk

1   Sift the powdered sugar and cocoa into a bowl.
2   Stir in the butter and enough of the milk to make a creamy consistency.

365 Shiny chocolate icing

PREPARATION TIME 15 minutes   **MAKES** 1 cup

scant 3¼ cups powdered sugar
2 tbsp. unsweetened cocoa powder

1 tbsp. butter, softened

1 Place the powdered sugar and cocoa in a bowl and make a small well in the middle. Place the butter in the well and add 2½ tbsp. boiling water. Stir until the butter melts, then continue stirring until the icing reaches a spreadable consistency, adding about another 2½ tbsp. water as required.
2 Use immediately.

Index

Author's acknowledgements

My sincere thanks go to the entire team at Duncan Baird Publishers who helped in the creation of this book. My special thanks go to Grace Cheetham, my commissioning editor, and Alison Bolus, my food editor, for all of their patience, encouragement, and good humor. Thank you also to home economist Bridget Sargeson and photographer William Lingwood, who created the beautiful images throughout the book.